Medical Decision Making

Stefan Felder • Thomas Mayrhofer

Medical Decision Making

A Health Economic Primer

Second Edition

Stefan Felder
Department of Business and Economics
University of Basel
Basel, Switzerland

Thomas Mayrhofer
School of Business Studies
Stralsund University of Applied Sciences
Stralsund, Germany

ISBN 978-3-662-57137-8   ISBN 978-3-662-53432-8   (eBook)
DOI 10.1007/978-3-662-53432-8

Printed on acid-free paper

This Springer imprint is published by Springer Nature
The registered company is Springer-Verlag GmbH Germany
The registered company address is: Heidelberger Platz 3, 14197 Berlin, Germany

Preface to the Second Edition

The second edition of this textbook comes five years after its first publication. Teething troubles such as typos, arithmetic errors and misnomers have now (hopefully) been overcome; the authors thank colleagues, students and other readers for their indispensable comments.

There is more health economics in the second edition. While the analysis in the first edition captured beneficial and detrimental effects that tests and treatments can have on patients in utility terms, this edition monetizes these patient outcomes and includes the monetary costs of testing and treatment in the analysis of decision making. Furthermore, we added a section on imperfect agency, which assumes that physicians do not act as perfect agents for their patients and that they have a profit motive when practicing medicine.

A new chapter covers non-expected utility models which are commonly in vogue in medical journals, such as the dual theory of choice under risk. While these models are fruitful in explaining observed test and treatment decisions, they are not suitable for normative analyses aimed at providing guidance on medical decision making.

We would like to thank two people who have been very helpful in the preparation of this edition. Denis Bieri was (literally) the utility man, particularly helpful for checking the comparative static results. Hermione Miller-Moser did a great editorial job. Besides corrections of orthography and style, her comments often helped us to refine and improve lines of argument.

Basel, Switzerland   Stefan Felder
Stralsund, Germany   Thomas Mayrhofer
December 2016

Preface to the First Edition

The first author became acquainted with medical decision problems during his time as a faculty member of the Department of Medicine at the Otto-von-Guericke University of Magdeburg between 1997 and 2008. In his introductory lecture series on health economics, he sought to combine the economic approach to decision making under uncertainty with clinical epidemiology. These lectures were the starting point for this textbook. He thanks his colleague Bernt-Peter Robra for his companionship and advice during this journey into the world of medicine. Robra also contributed some of the chapters' introductory quotations.

The second author joined the project in 2008. He spent half the summer of 2009 preparing the first drafts of Chap. 4–6. He elaborated the final text for the first author in the summer and autumn of 2010, during a sabbatical semester. The material was also covered in a lecture series on medical decision making held by both authors at the Department of Economics and Business Administration of Duisburg-Essen University in 2009 and 2010. We are thankful to the many students who helped to improve the text with their questions and discussions.

In preparing this manuscript, we were supported by a team of students and research assistants at the University Duisburg-Essen. Linda Kerkemeyer helped with the literature and the identification of copyright, Daniel Hering assisted with the equations and exercises. Special thanks are due to Simon Decker, who adapted the text to the Springer style sheets with great diligence and attention to detail. We are grateful to all of them.

Springer provided professional support during the book's production process. We are thankful to Ms Feß for her advice and to Ms Kreisel for help with editing.

Cordial thanks go to Friedrich Breyer at the University of Konstanz, who provided valuable comments on Chap. 10.

Finally, we owe a special debt to Miriam Krieger, Scientific Assistant at the Chair of Health Economics. Not only did she greatly improve the English, but also provided numerous helpful suggestions for style and argument.

Basel, Switzerland   Stefan Felder
Essen, Germany   Thomas Mayrhofer
July 2011

Contents

List of Figures

List of Tables

List of Boxes

Chapter 1
Introduction

> Abzuwägen sind die Wahrscheinlichkeiten von Schaden
> und Nutzen im Verhältnis zur Größe der beiden.
> Eugen Bleuler[1]

In 1919 the famous Swiss psychiatrist Eugen Bleuler published the book 'Autistic undisciplined thinking in medicine and how to overcome it' in which he formulated the basic rule for medical decision making under uncertainty: 'The probabilities of harm and utility have to be weighed against each other in relation to their respective sizes' (p. 89). This precept provides physicians with a precise prescription for reaching optimal test and treatment decisions in the presence of diagnostic risk, i.e., not knowing whether a patient is actually sick, and therapeutic risk, i.e., not knowing whether a therapy works. It also prescribes the optimal choice of the positivity criterion for a test whose outcome is chosen by the decision maker.

Bleuler's systematic combination of utility, harm and their respective probabilities certainly appeals to economists. After all, economics is the science of behavior in situations in which scarcity governs such that people have to choose among less than perfect alternatives. To do one thing without giving up another is impossible at the frontier determined by the finiteness of time and money.

Over the last 150 years, economists have developed theories to explain individual decisions and about how individuals should make rational decisions. They distinguish between situations in which the consequences of an individual's actions are deterministic and situations in which they are stochastic. Economic theories of decisions under certainty and uncertainty are so general that they have many and broad areas of application. Medicine is one where economic decision theories can be put to particularly productive use.

A physician in private practice is well aware of the opportunity costs of his decisions. The time he invests in one patient reduces the time he has for treating

---

[1]Bleuler, E.—*Das autistisch-undisziplinierte Denken in der Medizin und seine Überwindung*—Springer, Berlin—1919.

© Springer-Verlag GmbH Germany 2017
S. Felder, T. Mayrhofer, *Medical Decision Making*,
DOI 10.1007/978-3-662-53432-8_1

another. Even in deciding what treatment to give a patient, he is confronted with the fact that no therapy is purely beneficial, and might cause potential harm. Indeed, the physician must often cause the patient discomfort or harm first—for instance in the case of an invasive treatment—before the success and benefits of therapy can unfold. The trade-off between the utility and cost of a treatment is complicated by the uncertainty surrounding medical decisions. Though the physician can make use of diagnostic technologies to detect the nature of an illness, this detection is often only partial. Moreover, diagnostic techniques frequently pose a risk to the patient's health.

In the course of their professional training, physicians learn how to deal with uncertainty in their test and treatment decisions. Epidemiology and in particular clinical epidemiology deals with decision making under uncertainty in a systematic way. The core curriculum here includes the knowledge of the Bayes' theorem, for instance, which allows physicians to update an a priori probability of illness with new information from a diagnostic test to obtain an a posteriori probability that a patient is sick. Physicians, however, are less well informed—despite Bleuler's insights almost 100 years ago—about how to evaluate the utility and harm of medical interventions and their monetary costs when making test and treatment decisions. There are few textbooks on medical decision making under uncertainty which explicitly address this topic.

The present publication aims to close this gap. Starting with von Neumann and Morgenstern's expected utility theory, we demonstrate how the parameters of Bayes' theorem can be combined with a value function of health states to arrive at informed test and treatment decisions. We distinguish between risk-neutral, risk-averse and prudent decision makers and demonstrate the effects of risk preferences on physicians' decisions.

1.1 Outline

The structure of this book is as follows. In Chap. 2, we introduce the basic methods in medical decision making, and explain the meaning and relevance of terms such as the 'prevalence rate', and the 'sensitivity' and 'specificity' of a test.

Chapter 3 presents the expected utility theory according to von Neumann and Morgenstern, which is the basic normative theory for decisions under uncertainty. This theory finds application in the concept of quality-adjusted life years (QALYs), which was introduced in medicine almost 50 years ago and is increasingly used as a measure for public funding of medical interventions. We also discuss the notion of risk aversion, which is rarely addressed explicitly in the medical literature. It implies that as health increases its marginal utility decreases. Health improvements are therefore valued more at low than at high levels of initial health. Risk aversion helps to explain why treatment decisions are categorized according the principle of acuteness, thus ensuring that a physician prioritizes patients whose health is particularly threatened. Prudence is a related concept which we introduce at the end of Chap. 3.

Chapter 4 deals with the treatment decision in situations where no diagnostic test is available. In this case, the physician faces the risk of a misdiagnosis: he may treat a patient who is healthy, or fail to treat one who is ill. We assume that the decision maker knows a sick person's utility gain from treatment and a healthy person's utility loss from treatment. This allows us to derive the so-called treatment threshold, which identifies that value of the a priori probability of illness at which the physician is indifferent between the options of treating or not treating the patient. We show that a risk-averse physician treats the patient at a lower a priori probability than a risk-neutral physician, since the former values the utility gain to the sick more and the utility loss to the healthy less than the latter. Furthermore, we introduce the cost of treatment and show that it renders the treatment option less attractive. In this chapter, we also analyze the therapeutic risk, i.e., the risk that treatment fails, and derive the success probability threshold above which the physician decides to treat the patient. In contrast to the diagnostic risk, the treatment threshold is higher here for a risk-averse physician than for a risk-neutral one. Moreover, considering the cost of treatment will increase the success probability threshold. Finally, we combine the diagnostic risk and the therapeutic risk and study the effects on the thresholds if both risks are simultaneously considered.

Chapter 5 extends the analysis of the treatment decision to include the diagnostic test. The test is a technology, which provides additional information on the probability that the patient is ill. Generally, since information is not perfect, the physician has to decide (again) under uncertainty whether to use the clinical test and treat patients presenting a positive test outcome or refrain from using the test and simply decide to either treat them or not treat them. The core descriptive concept guiding the physician's decision under these circumstances is the value ascribed to information that the test provides, which is the expected utility to be gained from using this information technology. For very low and very high a priori probabilities of illness, the value of information is not positive, and hence the test should not be applied. Between these upper and lower probability bounds, test and test-treatment thresholds can be identified. While the test threshold indicates that value of the a priori probability of illness at which the physician should start testing, the test-treatment threshold is that value of the a priori probability at which immediate treatment without prior testing is indicated. Obviously, these thresholds are influenced by the decision maker's risk preferences. For a risk-averse decision maker, the diagnostic test and the treatment serve as insurance devices, and he will use them more often than a risk-neutral decision maker. Finally, we analyze the effects that the risk of potential harm as well as the cost of testing and the cost of treatment have on the test and test-treatment thresholds.

Chapter 6 introduces the role of uncontrollable risk for the physician's decisions. Comorbidity risk can be regarded as uncontrollable, as it applies to the sick state only and is assumed to be exogenous: unlike diagnostic risk, it is not affected by the treatment decision. With this kind of risk underlying the test and treatment decisions, the notion of prudence becomes relevant. We demonstrate that prudent decision makers act even earlier than risk-averse ones.

Chapter 7 deals with the optimal test strategy if multiple diagnostic tests are available and can be employed simultaneously or sequentially. This complicates the task for the decision maker. He has to decide on a positivity criterion for the composite test, which can be conjunctive (positive if the results of all tests are positive, negative in all other cases) or disjunctive (negative if the results of all tests are negative, positive in all other cases) and on the order of the tests if he uses them sequentially. If testing is potentially harmful or involves monetary costs, it is easy to understand that sequential testing always dominates parallel testing.

Chapter 8 introduces a world where the number of available tests is infinite. This is the case if the test outcome has to be determined by the decision maker by setting a cutoff value. A good example is the prostate specific antigen (PSA) test for the detection of prostate cancer in men. The analysis of a blood sample results in a PSA value, which the physician judges as being positive or negative depending on his chosen cutoff value. We demonstrate how the optimal cutoff value depends on the a priori probability of the illness, as well as on the utility and potential harm from testing and treatment. This chapter also introduces a novel use of the receiver operating characteristic (ROC) curve which is well known in clinical epidemiology.

In Chaps. 9 and 10, we depart from the optimal test and treatment strategies for individual patients to deal with aggregate choices. Chapter 9 presents the concept of a test's total value of information, which is an aggregate value of the information that generates over the total a priori probability of illness range. To gain a dimensionless measure, we compare a given test with a perfect test. The resulting performance index lies between zero and one, where zero denotes a useless test and one a perfect one.

Chapter 10 extends the complexity of decision making in health economics by introducing consumption and a budget constraint to the decision makers' choice. A trade-off arises between enjoying health and consuming other goods, so that the extent of treatment and thus the potential improvement in the patient's health becomes endogenous. We distinguish between a health model and a health-survival model, where only the latter captures both quality and quantity aspects of medical investments. The health-survival model allows us to formalize the willingness to pay for health and life, which provides the basis for monetizing the outcome of medical interventions, which can subsequently be compared with the monetary cost. After characterizing individual choices within these models, we analyze the allocation chosen by a social planner who maximizes 'the greatest good of the greatest number'. We conclude the chapter by comparing the utilitarian solution to the allocation of medical investments based on the QALY model.

Chapter 11 takes a more realistic stance on medical decision making by assuming that physicians are only imperfect agents of their patients. Specifically, we assume that physicians internalize only a share of the patient's utility and follow a profit motive in their test and treatment decisions. We then analyze the effects of imperfect agency on the thresholds and discuss the role of liability rules and medical guidelines subject to imperfect agency. In this final chapter, non-expected utility models under risk and uncertainty (i.e., ambiguity) are also presented. While these models can explain observed test and treatment decisions, they are not suitable for normative analyses aimed at providing guidance on medical decision making.

Economists tend to write in a fairly abstract manner; this book is no exception. However, we have tried to make the content more accessible and concrete by providing graphs, examples from the medical literature and illustrative boxes. Exercises and further references at the end of each chapter give the reader the opportunity to delve further into the subject matter.

This text is written for students of both medicine and economics. In a medical curriculum the text could be used for courses on medical decision making and on health economics. In economics the book may be part of a course on applied microeconomics or a specialized health economics course at the undergraduate level.

1.2   Notes

Weinstein et al. (1980) is a well-known textbook on medical decision making. Another textbook with a strong focus on medical practice is Sox et al. (2007), first published in 1988. Eeckhoudt (2002) provides a rigorous economic treatise on medical decision making under uncertainty which also includes non-expected utility theories.

References

Eeckhoudt, L. (2002). *Risk and medical decision making*. Boston: Kluwer.

Sox, H. S., Blatt, M. A., Higgins, M. C., & Marton, K. I. (2007). *Medical Decision Making*. Butterworth-Heinemann, Boston: Philadelphia—American College of Physicians. Reprint, originally published: 1988.

Weinstein, M. C., Fineberg, H. V., Elstein, A. S., Frazier, H. S., Neuhauser, D., Neutra, R. R., et al. (1980). *Clinical decision analysis*. Philadelphia: W.B. Saunders.

Chapter 2
Basic Tools in Medical Decision Making

> Doctors have an almost irresistible
> tendency to find what they are looking for.
> Richard Dooling[1]

Before we turn to more complex issues of medical decision making, we start by explaining some basic terms and tools which will be used throughout the following chapters.

In the first section of this chapter, we explain the prevalence and incidence rates. We also discuss different usages of the term 'risk'. In the second section, we deal with the characteristics of a test and the difference between the a priori probability and the a posteriori probability of an illness using Bayes' theorem. The third section shows the connection between probabilities and odds and the use of likelihood ratios. In the last section, we consider tests with non-binary outcomes. In these cases, a cutoff value has to be chosen to determine a positive or negative outcome of the test. We discuss the trade-off between the test characteristics using the receiver operating characteristics curve.

2.1 Prevalence, Incidence and Risk

Many medical decisions start with rates:

$$\text{Rate} = \frac{\text{Number of cases}}{\text{Population subject to the risk}}.$$

Important examples are the mortality rate, the prevalence rate, and the incidence rate. While the mortality and the incidence rates represent flows, the prevalence rate

---

[1]Dooling, R.—*White Man's Grave*—Picador, New York—1995, p. 70.

© Springer-Verlag GmbH Germany 2017
S. Felder, T. Mayrhofer, *Medical Decision Making*,
DOI 10.1007/978-3-662-53432-8_2

is a stock variable. The latter indicates the number of ill individuals, for example, per 100,000 at any given date. The incidence rate counts the number of individuals, for example, per 100,000 who fall ill within a given time period.

The ratio of prevalence rate to incidence rate gives the average duration of an illness, provided circumstances remain constant:

$$\text{Average duration of an illness} = \frac{\text{Prevalence}}{\text{Incidence}}.$$

The stock is thus proportionally related to the flow via the average duration of the illness. As an illustration, consider the ratio between the water volume of a fountain and the size of the inflow per time unit. This ratio is equal to the average time that a water molecule remains in the fountain. In a fountain with a volume of 6000 liters and an inflow of 100 liters per minute, the water is renewed entirely once every hour.

For chronic illnesses that often last for years, the prevalence rate exceeds the incidence rate. By contrast, since acute illnesses are only temporary, the incidence rate for one year is often much higher than the prevalence rate measured at any one point in time of the year.

The prevalence rate is also called the a priori probability of an illness. It is the probability of the occurrence of an illness, inferred from either experience, from registries, or more generally from epidemiological literature. The a priori probability of an illness often refers to a specific situation, in which a physician considers the probability that a patient is ill. By contrast, the prevalence rate most often refers to the population at large.

The term risk is also used in the medical literature to indicate the probability of an illness. This is somewhat unfortunate, since common usage in economics relates risk to uncertainty. Uncertainty refers to the probability that possible outcomes may occur. The variance of the expected value of the outcomes is often used as a measure of risk. Consider the example of a 50-year-old patient who can expect to live for another 30 years, provided he survives a medical operation which has a success rate of 80 %. Assume that the remaining life expectancy falls to 10 years if the operation fails. The expected remaining life time of the patient is, then, 26 years[2] and its variance is 64 years.[3] The term risk usually does not refer to the expected value, and thus to the first moment, but to higher moments of the distribution.

2.2 Discriminatory Power and Predictive Values

A simple tool for presenting test-theoretic insights is a 2×2 contingency table with rows indicating possible test outcomes (positive, negative) and columns denoting the patient's possible health states (illness: yes, no) (see Table 2.1).

---

[2] $30 \cdot 0.8 + 10 \cdot 0.2 = 26$

[3] $(30 - 26)^2 \cdot 0.8 + (10 - 26)^2 \cdot 0.2 = 64$

Table 2.1 The 2 × 2 table

		Illness		
		yes	no	Sum
Test result	positive	a	b	$a+b$
	negative	c	d	$c+d$
	Sum	$a+c$	$b+d$	$n=a+b+c+d$

a Number of true positive cases (TP)
c Number of false negative cases (FN)
$(a+c)/n$ Prevalence of the illness (p)
$a/(a+c)$ Sensitivity (Se)
$a/(a+b)$ Positive predictive value (PPV)
a/n Detection rate

b Number of false positive cases (FP)
d Number of true negative cases (TN)
$(a+b)/n$ Share of positive test results
$d/(b+d)$ Specificity (Sp)
$d/(c+d)$ Negative predictive value (NPV)

The letters denote absolute frequencies or natural numbers. n patients are subject to the diagnostic test, of which $a+b$ patients receive a positive test result and $c+d$ patients a negative test result. We can characterize the following parameters:

The *prevalence rate* of an illness is usually known from external sources.

The *sensitivity* of a test is defined as the share of sick patients who receive a positive test result. It is a conditional probability, the condition being that the patients concerned are sick. The sensitivity thus characterizes the test's discriminatory power with respect to the detection of sick patients. A very sensitive diagnostic test will hardly miss any sick patients.

The *specificity* is the share of non-sick patients with a negative test result. This is also a conditional probability, the condition being that the patients concerned are healthy. The specificity therefore characterizes the test's discriminatory power with regard to the detection of healthy patients. A very specific test will diagnose only few healthy individuals as being sick.

The probability of being in the health state indicated by the test is called the *predictive value* of a test. We distinguish two forms of predictive values, positive and negative. The *positive predictive value* (*PPV*) is the probability of having a certain illness for a patient with a positive (i.e., striking) test result. The *negative predictive value* (*NPV*) is the probability of not having the illness when the test result is negative (i.e., unremarkable).

While the prevalence rate indicates the a priori probability of an illness before testing, the predictive value gives the a posteriori or post-test probability. The predictive value thus indicates the probability of the health state once the test result is known.

In the following 2 × 2 table, we replace absolute with relative frequencies, i.e., probabilities. Since the probabilities sum to unity (the sum of the probabilities of 'illness' and 'no illness' is 1), this table is also called the unity table (Table 2.2).

If we transform the definition of $PPV = a/(a+b)$ according to the unity table, we obtain Bayes' theorem:

Table 2.2 The 2 × 2 table as a unity table

		Illness		Sum
		yes	no	
Test result	positive	$p \cdot Se$	$(1-p) \cdot (1-Sp)$	$p \cdot Se + (1-p) \cdot (1-Sp)$
	negative	$p \cdot (1-Se)$	$(1-p) \cdot Sp$	$p \cdot (1-Se) + (1-p) \cdot Sp$
	Sum	p	$(1-p)$	1

p Prevalence rate
Se Sensitivity; also true positive rate (TPR)
$1 - Se$ Complement to sensitivity; also false negative rate (FNR)
Sp Specificity; also true negative rate (TNR)
$1 - Sp$ Complement to specificity; also false positive rate (FPR)

$$PPV = \frac{p \cdot Se}{p \cdot Se + (1-p) \cdot (1-Sp)}. \tag{2.1}$$

Accordingly, for the negative predictive value we have

$$NPV = \frac{(1-p)Sp}{p(1-Se) + (1-p)Sp}. \tag{2.2}$$

Bayes' theorem states the predictive value as a function of the prevalence rate, the sensitivity and the specificity of the test. The following relations apply:

- Since the predictive value is affected by the prevalence rate, it also depends on the target population subject to the diagnostic test. The higher the prevalence rate, the higher the positive predictive value and the lower the negative predictive value of the test's result will be.
- The more sensitive the design of a test, the better the negative predictive value will be (the surer the physician can be that a negative test result actually indicates the absence of the illness). Intuitively: the number of false negative cases c converges to zero as sensitivity increases, implying in turn that the *NPV* converges to 1.
- The more specific a test (and the smaller the complement of specificity), the higher the positive predictive value (the surer the physician can be that a positive test result confirms an existing illness). The explanation is that the number of false positive cases b converges to zero as specificity increases, implying that the *PPV* converges to 1.

Box 2.1: Bayes' Theorem and Physicians' Understanding of Conditional Probabilities
Bayes' theorem allows for the adjustment of the probability of a hypothesis to new information, for instance from a diagnostic test. It is difficult to interpret the gains from this new information—even for physicians, who deal with uncertainty in their professional life every day, as the following example shows (see Eddy 1982):

(continued)

Box 2.1 (continued)
- According to the literature, the probability that breast cancer is detected by a mammographic test (i.e., the sensitivity of mammography) is 80 %.
- The probability that a mammography falsely indicates breast cancer is 9.6 %; i.e., 1 − specificity is 9.6 %, thus specificity is 90.4 %.
- The probability that a woman at the age of 40 has breast cancer (i.e., the prevalence rate) is 1 %.

In a survey, physicians were asked the following question: 'If a woman at the age of 40 is tested positive, what is the probability that she has breast cancer?' 95 % of the physicians participating in the survey answered that the probability is between 70 % and 80 %.

In order to determine how high the probability really is, use of Bayes' theorem yields:

$$PPV = \frac{p \cdot Se}{p \cdot Se + (1-p) \cdot (1-Sp)} = \frac{0.01 \cdot 0.80}{0.01 \cdot 0.80 + 0.99 \cdot 0.096}.$$

The result is 0.078. The probability that a 40-year-old woman with a positive mammography has breast cancer is only 7.8 %. 95 % of the physicians overestimated the *PPV* for breast cancer by a factor of 10.

Gigerenzer and Hoffrage (1995) repeated the same experiment with absolute, instead of relative, frequencies, i.e. instead of giving the information in the format of Table 2.2, they used the format of Table 2.1. In a setting with natural numbers, almost half the physicians (46 %) gave the correct answer. Nevertheless, this study underlines the finding that physicians often fail to interpret test results correctly.

More information on this issue can be found online (see Kling 2010).

2.3 Probability, Odds and the Likelihood Ratio

A simpler concept equivalent to the probability of an illness is often used to interpret test results: the concept of odds, defined in the a priori form as

$$\text{Odds} = \frac{\text{probability of an event}}{\text{complement to probability of the event}}$$

or

$$\Omega = \frac{p}{1-p}. \tag{2.3}$$

The odds of a coin toss are thus not 0.5 (the probability), but 1 (since $0.5/0.5 = 1$). In general terms, the odds and the probability provide the same information.

Furthermore, the smaller the probability, the smaller is the difference between probability and odds. If the probability of an event is 0.99, then the odds are 99 (0.99/0.01). In this case, the difference between the two is very large. By contrast, if the probability is only 0.01, then odds are also roughly 0.01. The a posteriori odds of an illness are calculated accordingly, using the a posteriori probability, i.e., the predictive value. For the positive a posteriori odds, we derive

$$\Omega^+_{post} = \frac{p \cdot Se}{(1-p) \cdot (1-Sp)} = \Omega \cdot \frac{Se}{1-Sp}. \tag{2.4}$$

The a posteriori odds are larger than the a priori odds by a factor of $Se/(1-Sp)$. This ratio is called the positive (since it refers to a positive test result) likelihood ratio (LR):

$$LR^+ = \frac{Se}{1-Sp}. \tag{2.5}$$

The positive likelihood ratio indicates the relative discriminatory power of a positive test result in separating the sick from the healthy. LR^+ takes on values between zero (the test fails entirely to detect the sick, i.e., $Se=0$, $Sp<1$) and infinity (the test detects all healthy individuals, i.e., $Sp=1$, $Se>0$). The larger the value of the positive likelihood ratio, the better is the discriminatory power of the positive test results. It is the clinically most useful summary of sensitivity and specificity in one parameter. A test provides more information than a mere randomized classification of individuals as sick or healthy if its positive likelihood ratio is greater than one; specifically, one can infer $LR^+ > 1$ from the requirement that $Se + Sp > 1$.

For the a posteriori odds with a positive test result, we have

$$\Omega^+_{post} = \frac{PPV}{1-PPV} = \Omega \cdot LR^+. \tag{2.6}$$

Equation (2.6) corresponds to Bayes' theorem. We see that the a posteriori odds depend on the a priori odds as well as on the test's discriminatory power. The way the odds are expressed in Bayes' theorem reveals that prevalence and discriminatory power jointly determine the a posteriori odds. The joint effect is multiplicative; hence an increase in the odds Ω of an illness by a certain factor has the same effect on the a posteriori odds as an increase in the likelihood ratio by the same factor. The inequality $LR^+ > 1$ ensures that the a posteriori odds exceed the a priori odds.

For the complementary negative test, we have

$$\Omega^-_{post} = \frac{NPV}{1 - NPV} = \frac{1}{\Omega \cdot LR^-} \tag{2.7}$$

with

$$LR^- = \frac{1 - Se}{Sp}. \tag{2.8}$$

The negative likelihood ratio compares the relative probabilities of a negative test result for the sick versus one for the healthy. The smaller this ratio is, the better is the negative discriminatory power of the test. A test produces more information than a mere randomized classification of individuals as sick or healthy if its negative likelihood ratio is smaller than 1. This again leads to the requirement that $Se + Sp > 1$, and the inferred inequality $LR^- < 1$. The a posteriori odds ratio of a negative test result increases if either the a priori odds of an illness or the test likelihood ratio with respect to a negative outcome decreases.

It is also useful to express the predictive values as a function of the odds and the likelihood ratio. We find:

$$PPV = \frac{1}{1 + \frac{1}{\Omega \cdot LR^+}} \tag{2.9}$$

$$NPV = \frac{1}{1 + \Omega \cdot LR^-}. \tag{2.10}$$

Higher odds, thus, increase PPV, and decrease NPV. The predictive values benefit from an increase in the discriminatory power of a test: A higher positive likelihood ratio increases PPV, and a lower negative likelihood ratio increases NPV. If a test has no informational value, i.e., $LR^+ = LR^- = 1$, we have $PPV = p$ and $NPV = 1 - p$. It is thus not surprising that this test has no additional predictive power compared to the a priori situation.

The likelihood ratios do not depend on the prevalence of an illness since they refer to conditional probabilities. These probabilities are usually exogenous. That changes, however, if the decision maker can determine the outcome of a test. This is the case if he specifies the positivity criterion by choosing the cutoff value that separates positive from negative test results.

Box 2.2: Testing for Colorectal Polyps
In 2009, the New England Journal of Medicine published an article by Van Gossum et al. (2009) in which they compared capsule endoscopy with optical colonoscopy for the detection of colorectal polyps and cancer. The study included a total of 320 patients. Using capsule endoscopy as a diagnostic test, 93 patients received a positive test result (polyp larger than 6 mm), but only

---

(continued)

Box 2.2 (continued)

56 of these participants actually had a polyp of that size. Moreover, the test outcome was negative for 227 patients, of which 31, in fact, suffered from a polyp that fulfilled the criteria.

What is the 2 × 2 table in this example?

		Optical colonoscopy (reference test)		
		yes	no	Sum
Capsule endoscopy	positive	56	37	93
(colorectal polyp > 6 mm)	negative	31	196	227
	Sum	87	233	320

What is the prevalence rate in the diagnosed population?

$$p = \frac{87}{320} = 0.27.$$

How sensitive and specific is the employed test?

$$Se = \frac{56}{87} = 0.64; \quad Sp = \frac{196}{233} = 0.84.$$

What is the a posteriori probability of the test?

$$PPV = \frac{56}{93} = 0.60; \quad NPV = \frac{196}{227} = 0.86.$$

What are the odds of the illness, given a positive test result?

$$\Omega = \frac{0.27}{1 - 0.27} = 0.37; LR^{+} = \frac{Se}{(1 - Sp)} = \frac{0.64}{0.16} = 4; \Omega_{post}^{+} = \Omega \cdot LR^{+} = 1.48.$$

- Without knowing the entire clinical picture, one expects a prevalence rate of about 27 % for colorectal polyps (>6 mm).
- The likelihood ratio for colorectal polyps (>6 mm) is about 4 if clinical diagnostics produce a positive result.
- If the diagnostic test result is positive for colorectal polyps (>6 mm), then the a posteriori probability (PPV) of the patient actually suffering from colorectal polyps is 60 %.

2.4 Continuous Test Outcomes and Cutoff Values

The outcome of a diagnostic test is often not binary, but continuous. Examples are the measurement of blood pressure, biochemical tests of blood, saliva or amniotic fluid and scales in questionnaires. Such measurement values are called markers, as they are correlated with the presence of an illness. The distributions of markers for the sick and the healthy generally overlap. As a consequence, measured values cannot be translated one to one into binary variables, indicating who is sick and who is healthy. Rather, a cutoff value has to be chosen in order to decide on the diagnostic outcome.

Figure 2.1 illustrates this, showing the absolute frequencies of individuals tested with the corresponding value of marker x for the healthy ($h(x)$) and the sick ($s(x)$) for an exemplary test. If $\bar{x}$ is chosen as cutoff value, the correctly classified cases of the sick lie to the right. The sum of all true positive cases as a share of all sick cases corresponds to the sensitivity. False negative cases, i.e., individuals who are sick but remain undetected by the test, lie to the left of the cutoff value. In relative terms, they correspond to $1 - Se$, the probability complementary to sensitivity.

Among the healthy, true negative cases lie to the left of the cutoff value and false positive cases to the right. Here again, the share of the healthy on the left of the cutoff value out of all healthy individuals is the specificity, i.e., the probability that a healthy individual is correctly detected by the test. $1 - Sp$ is complementary to the specificity, the share of the healthy who are falsely classified as sick.

The choice of the cutoff value determines the sensitivity and the specificity of a test. In the situation illustrated in Fig. 2.1, increasing the cutoff value reduces sensitivity und increases specificity. This decreases the number of correctly detected sick, but increases the number of correctly identified healthy individuals. Shifting the cutoff value to the left increases sensitivity and decreases specificity. More sick individuals are detected as being sick, at the price of more healthy individuals being diagnosed as sick.

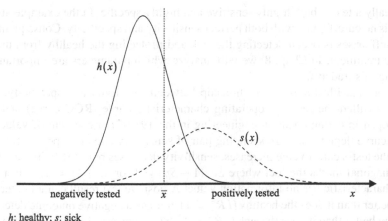

h: healthy; s: sick

Fig. 2.1 Absolute frequency of a measurement value for the sick and the healthy

Table 2.3 Trade-off between sensitivity and specificity

Blood sugar level (2 h after food intake) (mg/dl)	Sensitivity (%)	Specificity (%)
70	98.6	8.8
80	97.1	25.5
90	94.3	47.6
100	88.6	69.8
110	85.7	84.1
120	71.4	92.5
130	64.3	96.9
140	57.1	99.4
150	50.0	99.6
160	47.1	99.8
170	42.9	100.0
180	38.6	100.0
190	34.3	100.0
200	27.1	100.0

Source: Fletcher et al. (1996), p. 51

. Table 2.3 illustrates these relationships with a specific example. By labeling blood sugar values of 80 mg/dl as 'diabetic', one would overlook only few individuals with this illness (high sensitivity), but most healthy individuals would be wrongly considered to be diabetic (low specificity)—with the ensuing strain on health care resources.

If the cutoff were placed at 170 mg/dl, the test would show perfect specificity, but very low sensitivity. Individuals with a positive test result would then be known with certainty to have diabetes (since specificity is 100 %, there is no false positive case), but many diabetics would be overlooked by the test (since sensitivity is only 42.9 %).

Ideally a test is both highly sensitive and highly specific. In the example above, there is no cutoff value with both perfect sensitivity and specificity. Consequently, a trade-off arises between detecting the sick and protecting the healthy from unnecessary treatment. In Chap. 8, we will analyze which parameters are important for solving this tradeoff.

Figure 2.2 illustrates the relationship between sensitivity and specificity. This chart is called the receiver operating characteristic curve (ROC curve) and was developed in communication engineering in the 1950s. For each cutoff value, the ROC curve depicts the corresponding pair of sensitivity and $(1 - \text{specificity})$.

If the test's cutoff value increases, sensitivity decreases but specificity increases. The diagonal marks the loci where $Se/(1 - Sp) = 1$, or $Se + Sp = 1$. A test with this characteristic has no information value: A positive test result cannot detect the sick better than it does the healthy $(LR^+ = 1)$, nor can a negative outcome detect the healthy better than it does the sick $(LR^- = 1)$. The a posteriori odds are equal to the a priori odds and, equivalently, the a posteriori probability of an illness is equal to the a priori probability $(p = PPV)$.

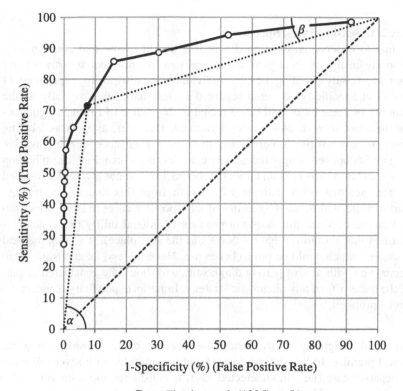

Data: Fletcher et al. (1996), p. 51.

Fig. 2.2 The ROC curve

The ROC curve for a useful test thus lies above the diagonal. Note that we can draw a line from any point of the ROC curve to the lower-left corner of the square, the slope of which—$\tan \alpha$—gives the test's LR^+ for that particular cutoff value—see Figure 2.2. Correspondingly, the slope of the line from a point on the ROC curve to the upper-right corner—$\tan \beta$—marks LR^-. As we move along the ROC curve from the lower-left corner towards the upper-right corner, the positive and the negative likelihood ratios both decrease. Correspondingly, the positive discriminatory power of the test decreases, while its negative discriminatory power increases.

The curvature of the ROC curve depends on the characteristics of the marker variable's distribution functions for the sick and the healthy. Contingent on the variance, skewness and overlap of the distributions, the same cutoff value leads to different values of sensitivity and specificity and thus to different shapes of the ROC curve.

If the cutoff value can be chosen, where is it optimal? If the decision maker weights sensitivity and specificity equally, he would, in our example, choose a cutoff value of about 110 mg/dl, which lies near the upper-left corner of the unity square. At this point, the total number of miss-specified individuals is minimized, as is the distance to the upper-left corner where the coordinates imply an error-free test.

Box 2.3: Sensitivity vs. Specificity

Failing to observe an existing illness is a liability issue that is taken very seriously in the medical profession (problem of imperfect sensitivity). By contrast, falsely labeling healthy individuals as test-positive (problem of imperfect specificity) is often regarded as less harmful, especially as the majority of these cases will be corrected in the course of further diagnostics and thus not receive unnecessary treatment. However, as soon as labeling someone test-positive involves health risks, for instance due to invasive diagnostics or even simply the anxiety experienced, a breach of the obligation to 'do no harm' arises as an ethical problem. This cannot always be justified by the fact that other patients will benefit from this diagnostic strategy. Furthermore, additional diagnostics of false positive cases must be organized and financed. Since this does not produce additional utility (a suspicion is clarified that should not have emerged in the first place), it wastes medical resources which could be put to better use. Nevertheless, false positives can occur even with almost perfect diagnostics and should be considered as part of the trade-offs of any diagnostic strategy. Imperfect specificity is thus not a trivial problem.

An equal weighting of true and false positive cases, however, is a rather untypical premise. In the clinical context and in particular with severe illnesses, a false negative case (i.e., an undetected case) is considered more important than a false positive case. The trade-off is solved at the cost of a decrease in specificity. In the extreme, the test characteristics would lie in the upper-right corner. The likelihood ratio there is close to one; hence, the test is not very useful, but hardly any sick individuals would be missed. Note that in the clinical context the a priori probability for an illness is often high.

If, however, the prevalence is small, as is the case, for example, with screening programs among the asymptomatic population, a compromise at the expense of specificity leads to many false positive cases. Many cases then need further examination and thereby raise resource use.

Choosing an optimal cutoff value thus requires trading off utility and cost for every test outcome and taking into account the prevalence of the population under examination. In the following chapter, we will analyze in depth how the utility of test results can be integrated into the use of diagnostic tests.

2.5   Notes

The material presented here is also covered in text books on clinical epidemiology, such as Sackett et al. (1991) and Fletcher et al. (1996), as well as in textbooks on medical decision making, such as Weinstein et al. (1980), Hunink et al. (2004) and Sox et al. (2007).

Exercises

1. There is a diagnostic test for prostate cancer which measures the concentration
   of PSA (prostate-specific antigens) in the blood. If the concentration exceeds a
   certain threshold, the physician applies advanced diagnostics and performs a
   biopsy. A positive outcome of the biopsy leads to a radical prostatectomy. If the
   PSA concentration is unremarkable, the physician will take another blood test
   one year later.
   To determine the quality of the PSA test, Hoffman et al. (2002) conducted the
   test as well as a biopsy on 2620 men of age 40 or older in the U.S. state of New
   Mexico. The biopsies revealed prostate cancer in 930 men. With a cutoff value
   of 4 ng/ml, the PSA test detected 800 true cases of sick men and 558 true cases of
   healthy men.

   (a) Calculate sensitivity and specificity for a critical serum concentration of
       4 ng/ml.
   (b) Fill out the 2 × 2 table for four age groups if the following 10-year preva-
       lence rates apply for Germany:

Age group	Prevalence rate (in percent)
<60	0.1
60–69	2.3
70–79	4.9
>80	5.5
All	0.8

       Source: Robert Koch Institut (2010), p. 102

   (c) Use the positive likelihood ratio to calculate the odds of a true positive case
       for each age group. Explain the relationship between the a priori and the a
       posteriori odds of identifying a true positive patient.
   (d) Regarding the calculated a posteriori odds for the four age groups, how
       useful is the test result given a cutoff value of 4 ng/ml? Which parameters
       would improve the test?
   (e) Calculate a prevalence rate at which 90 out of 100 men who were tested
       positive will in fact be sick (at a cutoff value of 4 ng/ml). Compared to the
       pertinent prevalence rate in Germany, what conclusions can be drawn from
       this case about the usefulness of the PSA test as a screening method?
   (f) Early AWMF[4] (2002) guidelines advised a critical value of 4 ng/ml for all
       age groups. Argue why this is not tenable, given the different prevalence
       rates in the age groups.

---

[4]AWMF = 'Arbeitsgemeinschaft der Wissenschaftlichen Medizinischen Fachgesellschaften',
Association of the Scientific Medical Societies in Germany

(g) According to these guidelines, family background (genetics) and fat intake are further risk factors for prostate cancer. Is it justified to offer the PSA test to targeted subgroups of the population?

2. The following table lists the sensitivity and specificity for PSA cutoff values between 1 and 20 ng/ml (see Hoffman et al. 2002) for men of age 40 and older.

PSA	Sensitivity	Specificity
1	98	9
2	95	20
3	91	26
4	86	33
5	75	44
6	63	57
7	56	66
8	49	74
9	42	80
10	38	84
15	23	93
20	17	97

(a) Draw the ROC curve.
(b) Calculate the positive likelihood ratio for each PSA cutoff value. How do sensitivity and specificity change along the ROC curve?
(c) Which consequences would arise from reducing the cutoff value from 4 to 2 ng/ml?
(d) In 2003, the German parliament called for coverage of PSA tests under the Social Health Insurance for all men older than 45. State the pros and cons of such a policy.

3. Prove that a test's likelihood ratio improves if either sensitivity or specificity increases.
4. Describe the distribution of the diagnostic measurement values for the sick and the healthy in Fig. 2.1 for a perfect test (sensitivity and specificity equal to unity). Where is the optimal cutoff value for testing?

References

AWMF (Arbeitsgemeinschaft der Wissenschaftlichen Medizinischen Fachgesellschaften). (2002). *PSA-Bestimmung in der Prostatakarzinomdiagnostik*. Leitlinie-Nr. 043/036.

Eddy, D. M. (1982). Probabilistic reasoning in clinical medicine: Problems and opportunities. In D. Kahneman, P. Slovic, & A. Tversky (Eds.), *Judgment under uncertainty: Heuristics and biases* (pp. 249–267). Cambridge: Cambridge University Press.

Fletcher, R. H., Fletcher, S. W., & Wagner, E. H. (1996). *Clinical epidemiology: The essentials*. Baltimore, MD: Williams & Wilkins.

Gigerenzer, G., & Hoffrage, U. (1995). How to improve Bayesian reasoning without instruction: Frequency formats. *Psychological Review, 102*(4), 684–704.

Hoffman, R. M., Gilliland, F. D., Adams-Cameron, M., Hunt, W. C., & Key, C. R. (2002). Prostate-specific antigen testing accuracy in community practice. *BMC Family Practice, 3* (19), 1–8.

Hunink, M., Glasziou, P., Siegel, J., Weeks, J., Pliskin, J., Elstein, A., et al. (2004). *Decision making in health and medicine*. Cambridge: Cambridge University Press.

Kling, A. (2010). *I thought you might be interested in Doctors' Statistical Ignorance*. EconLog. Library of Economics and Liberty. http://econlog.econlib.org/archives/2007/10/doctors_stat ist.html. Accessed 31 August 2010

Robert Koch Institut. (2010). *Verbreitung von Krebserkrankungen in Deutschland. Entwicklung der Prävalenzen zwischen 1990 und 2010. Beiträge zur Gesundheitsberichterstattung des Bundes*. Berlin: RKI.

Sackett, D. L., Guyatt, G. H., Haynes, R. B., & Tugwell, P. (1991). *Clinical epidemiology: A basic science for clinical medicine*. Philadelphia: Lippincott Williams & Wilkins.

Sox, H. S., Blatt, M. A., Higgins, M. C., & Marton, K. I. (2007). *Medical decision making*. Philadelphia: American College of Physicians, Butterworth-Heinemann (Reprint, originally published: 1988).

Van Gossum, A., Munoz-Navas, M., Fernandez-Urien, I., et al. (2009). Capsule endoscopy versus colonoscopy for the detection of polyps and cancer. *The New England Journal of Medicine, 361*(3), 264–270.

Weinstein, M. C., Fineberg, H. V., Elstein, A. S., Frazier, H. S., Neuhauser, D., Neutra, R. R., et al. (1980). *Clinical decision analysis*. Philadelphia: W.B. Saunders.

Chapter 3
Preferences, Expected Utility, Risk Aversion and Prudence

> More precisely we expect him, for any two alternative events which are put before him as possibilities, to be able to tell which of the two he prefers. It is a very natural extension of this picture to permit such an individual to compare not only events, but even combinations of events with stated probabilities.
>
> John von Neumann and Oskar Morgenstern[1]

A typical feature of medical decisions is that their consequences are not known with certainty in advance. They rather shift the probability that an individual will experience one or another health state. In this chapter we introduce the expected utility rule of von Neumann and Morgenstern which is the basic normative theory of behavior in a risky world.

We start by presenting the concept of an individual's preferences regarding possible health states under certainty. It is a choice theory that is based on the two fundamental assumptions of completeness and transitivity of preferences. Then, we clarify the relationship between preference ordering and utility functions.

The starting point for the presentation of choices under uncertainty is an individual's choice of action which leads to consequences. The relationship between actions and consequences is not deterministic: nature plays a decisive role in causing one particular state out of several options to arise. An individual's utility function is based not directly on his actions, but on their consequences. We assume here that these actions and the course of nature only affect the individual's health state. For the sake of our considerations, his utility function also relates only to his state of health. We also assume that the physician as decision maker acts entirely in the interest of the patient (i.e., as a perfect agent), not differentiating between the patient's and his own utility.

---

[1]Von Neumann, J. & Morgenstern, O.—*Theory of Games and Economic Behavior*, 2nd Edition—Princeton University Press, Princeton—1947, p. 17.

© Springer-Verlag GmbH Germany 2017
S. Felder, T. Mayrhofer, *Medical Decision Making*,
DOI 10.1007/978-3-662-53432-8_3

The structure of this chapter is as follows. In the next section, we focus on preferences and utility functions. In Sects. 3.2–3.4, we present the building blocks that lead to the expected utility rule as formulated by von Neumann and Morgenstern. Section 3.5 introduces the concept of quality-adjusted life years (QALYs), which is an application of expected utility theory. Sections 3.6 and 3.7 deal with decision makers' attitudes towards risk, as captured by the notions of risk aversion and prudence. Section 3.8 shortly addresses non-expected utility theories.

3.1 Preferences and Utility

Consider a physician who is treating a patient for rheumatoid arthritis. Using drugs, he can affect the patient's amount of joint pain and fine motoric skills. Depending on the dose of the administered medical treatment, the patient will suffer from side effects such as fatigue and nausea. This gives us four attributes connected to the treatment of the disease. The question then arises how the patient and his physician evaluate the trade-offs involved in the treatment decision.

Let us call the objects of patient choice health states. This is a complete list of health attributes that a patient with a certain disease might experience before, during and after treatment. For simplicity, assume that joint pain and fine motoric skills are the only two relevant attributes. Suppose that given any two health states involving the two attributes, (x_1, x_2) and (y_1, y_2), the patient can rank them according to their desirability. That is, the patient can determine that one of the health states is strictly better than the other, or decide that he is indifferent between the two states.

We use the symbol $\succ$ to mean that one state is strictly preferred to another, so that $(x_1, x_2) \succ (y_1, y_2)$ implies that the patient strictly prefers (x_1, x_2) to (y_1, y_2). This preference relation is meant to be an operational notion. If the patient prefers one health state to another, it means that he would choose one over the other, given the opportunity. Thus, the idea of preferences is based on the patient's behavior. If the patient is indifferent between two health states, we use the symbol $\sim$ and write $(x_1, x_2) \sim (y_1, y_2)$. Indifference means that the patient would be just as satisfied, according to his own preferences, experiencing health state (x_1, x_2) as he would be with health state (y_1, y_2). If the patient prefers or is indifferent between the two states, he weakly prefers (x_1, x_2) to (y_1, y_2) and we write $(x_1, x_2) \succsim (y_1, y_2)$.

Our basic theory assumes that the patient has a preference ordering, and that his preference ordering fulfills the following axioms:

Axiom of completeness. We assume that any two health states can be compared: That is, given any x-state and any y-state, we assume that $(x_1, x_2) \succsim (y_1, y_2)$, $(y_1, y_2) \succsim (x_1, x_2)$, or both, in which case the patient is indifferent between the two states.

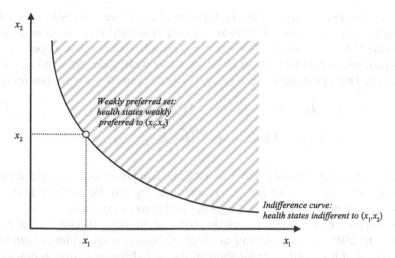

Fig. 3.1 Indifference curve and weakly preferred set

Axiom of transitivity. If $(x_1, x_2) \succsim (y_1, y_2)$ and $(y_1, y_2) \succsim (z_1, z_2)$, then $(x_1, x_2) \succsim (z_1, z_2)$.[2]

The theory of patient choice can be formulated in terms of preferences that satisfy these two axioms, plus a few more technical assumptions.

We can describe preferences graphically by using so-called indifference curves. Consider Fig. 3.1, which illustrates two axes representing a patient's levels of health attributes 1 and 2. The shaded area represents all health states that are weakly preferred to health state (x_1, x_2). This is called the weakly preferred set. The health states on the boundary of this set—the health states for which the consumer is just indifferent to (x_1, x_2) —form the indifference curve.

An indifference curve can be drawn through any health state. The indifference curve through a health state consists of all health states that leave the patient indifferent to the given state.

Well behaved indifference curves are downward sloping and convex as illustrated in Fig. 3.1. The negative slope follows from the assumption that preferences are monotonic. Monotonicity means that more is better. Thus, we are talking about goods, not bads. However, negative health attributes can also be considered as optional choices when using indifference curves. Joint pain, which is obviously a negative health attribute, can be revaluated and transformed into a positive health state attribute, by reversing its direction: i.e., the lesser the pain, the better.

More precisely, if (x_1, x_2) is a health state and (y_1, y_2) is a health state with at least the same levels of attributes and a higher level in one of the attributes, then $(y_1, y_2) \succ (x_1, x_2)$. The fact that the indifference curve is downward sloping under this assumption can be explained as follows: If we start at a health state (x_1, x_2) and

---

[2]We ought, also, for formal completeness, to assume explicitly that any state is at least as good as itself: $(x_1, x_2) \succsim (x_1, x_2)$ (axiom of reflexivity).

move NE, we must be moving to a preferred position. If we move SW, we must be moving to a worse position. So if we are moving to an indifferent position, we must be moving NW or SE: the indifference curve must have a negative slope.

Second, we assume that the set of health states weakly preferred to (x_1, x_2) is a convex set. Thus, we assume that if $(x_1, x_2) \sim (y_1, y_2)$ and $0 \leq \lambda \leq 1$, then for any λ

$$(\lambda x_1 + (1 - \lambda)y_1, \lambda x_2 + (1 - \lambda)y_2) \succsim (x_1, x_2)$$

$$(\lambda x_1 + (1 - \lambda)y_1, \lambda x_2 + (1 - \lambda)y_2) \succsim (y_1, y_2).$$

A convex set has the property that if we take any two points in the set and draw the line segment connecting the two points, that line segment lies entirely in the set. Convex preferences mean that averages are preferred to extremes.

The slope of the indifference curve is known as the marginal rate of substitution (MRS). The MRS measures the rate at which the patient is just willing to substitute one attribute of his health state for another. As the indifference curve is downward sloping, the MRS always involves reducing the level of one attribute in order to increase the level of the other for monotonic preferences. For a strictly convex indifference curve, the MRS decreases (in absolute terms) as we increase x_1. Thus, the indifference curves exhibit a diminishing marginal rate of substitution. This means that the rate at which a patient is just willing to substitute attribute 2 for attribute 1 decreases, as we increase the level of x_1. Convexity of the indifference curve appears to be very natural: it means that the higher a patient's level in one attribute, the more willing he is to give some of it up in exchange for achieving a higher level in another attribute.

A *utility function* is a way of assigning a number to every possible health state such that the more-preferred states are assigned larger numbers than less-preferred states. That is, a state (x_1, x_2) is preferred to a state (y_1, y_2) if, and only if, the utility of (x_1, x_2) is larger than the utility of (y_1, y_2): in symbols, $(x_1, x_2) \succ (y_1, y_2)$ if, and only if, $u(x_1, x_2) > u(y_1, y_2)$.

The only important property of a utility assignment is how it orders the states of health. The magnitude of the utility function only matters insofar as it ranks the different health states; the size of the utility differences between any two states, however, is not relevant. Because of this emphasis on ordering health states, this kind of utility is referred to as ordinal utility.

Let us assume a patient with health state (x_1, x_2). How does his utility change as we give him a little more or less of one of the health attributes? This rate of change is called the marginal utility with respect to the respective attribute. It measures the rate of change in utility associated with a small increase in the level of one attribute, holding the level of the other fixed. Formally, we partially differentiate the utility function with respect to attribute 1 or 2, respectively:

$$MU_1 = \frac{\partial u(x_1, x_2)}{\partial x_1}, \quad MU_2 = \frac{\partial u(x_1, x_2)}{\partial x_2}.$$

Marginal utility itself has no behavioral content. Choice behavior only reveals information about how a patient ranks different health states. However, there is a relationship between the marginal rate of substitution and the ratio of marginal utilities. Consider a change in the level of each attribute (dx_1, dx_2) that leaves utility constant; that is, a change in the health state that moves us along the indifference curve. Then, we must have

$$MU_1 dx_1 + MU_2 dx_2 = dU = 0.$$

Solving for the slope of the indifference curve, we have

$$MRS = \frac{dx_2}{dx_1} = -\frac{MU_1}{MU_2}. \tag{3.1}$$

Note that the utility function, and therefore the marginal utility function, is not uniquely determined. Any monotonic transformation of a utility function gives another equally valid utility function. The ratio of marginal utilities is independent of any transformation of the utility function, and so is the MRS.

In observing the behavior of patients, we can infer their MRS, as we will see in the chapters that follow. Thus, the MRS tells us how patients evaluate the utilities of attributes 1 and 2 at the margin.

3.2 Decisions Under Uncertainty: Menu of Actions, States of Nature and Consequences

The analysis so far concerned a patient's preferences under conditions of certainty. However, most choices made by patients take place under uncertainty. In the following sections, we explore how the theory can be modified to describe such behavior.

A patient and his physician have to choose among alternative courses of action. In order to detect an illness, the physician can undertake diagnostic tests, the results of which will determine whether treatment is indicated or not. Alternatively, he may treat the patient without prior testing, or neither test, nor treat. There is uncertainty regarding the patient's state of health, i.e., whether he is sick or not, which may be said to be determined by nature. The physician decides whether or not to treat the patient; nature decides on illness or health. This situation can be represented by a simple decision matrix (see Table 3.1).

Table 3.1 Consequences of alternative acts and states

		States	
		$i = 1$	$i = 2$
Actions	$a = 1$	h_1^1	h_2^1
	$a = 2$	h_1^2	h_2^2

The menu of actions, $a = (1, 2)$, is presented in the rows, the possible states of nature, $i = (1, 2)$, in the columns. The center of the table shows the consequences h_i^a that follow from the actions a chosen by the individual and the states of nature i. With two possible actions and two possible states, the consequence matrix has four elements. In the medical context, the states $i = 1$ and $i = 2$ might represent sick and healthy states, and the possible actions $a = 1$ and $a = 2$ 'treatment' and 'no treatment', respectively. The consequences are assumed to represent the patient's resulting health state (i.e., after treatment or after no treatment). For the moment, we think of h as being a scalar.

More generally, under uncertainty the individual's decision problem will contain the following elements:

1. A set of actions $(1, \ldots, a, \ldots A)$ available to him,
2. A set of states $(1, \ldots, i, \ldots I)$ available to nature,
3. A consequence function $h(a, i)$ showing outcomes for all combinations of actions and states,
4. A probability function $p(i)$ expressing beliefs on the likelihood of nature realizing each state,
5. An elementary utility function $u(h)$ measuring the desirability to the individual of all possible consequences.

We will show that the expected utility rule integrates all elements of the decision situation and allows the individual to choose the most advantageous action. This clarifies how the individual can derive a subjective ordering of his possible actions from his preference scaling of all consequences.

We assume that individuals are able to express their beliefs regarding the likelihood of different states of the world in a subjective probability distribution. Assuming discrete and mutually exclusive states of the world, the individual is thus taken to be able to assign to each state i a belief about its realization p_i between 0 and 1 which sum to unity $(\Sigma_i p_i = 1)$. In the extreme case, where the individual is certain that a particular state i will occur, he would assign $p_i = 1$ to state i, and zero probability to every other state.

3.3   The Elementary Utility Function and the Expected Utility Rule

Utility refers directly to health states and only derivatively to actions. Let $u(h)$ represent an individual's elementary utility function over the health states h and let $EU(a)$ denote his derived preference ordering over his actions a. The analytical challenge is to explain and justify this derivation, i.e., to show how, given his direct preferences over health states, the individual can order the actions available to him according to their desirability.

To choose an action is to choose one of the rows of the consequences matrix (see Table 3.1). Each row of the matrix can be regarded as a prospect associated with an action a, the uncertain health states $h^a = (h_1^a, h_2^a, \ldots, h_I^a)$ which occur with the respective probabilities $p = (p_1, p_2, \ldots, p_I)$. Hence, we can write

$$a \equiv (h_1^a, h_2^a, \ldots, h_I^a; p_1, p_2, \ldots, p_I) \text{ with } \sum_i p_i = 1.$$

The crucial step is to connect the elementary utility function $u(h)$ for the health states with the utility ordering $EU(a)$ of the actions. The classic expected utility rule of John von Neumann and Oskar Morgenstern provides the solution:

$$EU(a) \equiv E[u(h_i^a)] = p_1 u(h_1^a) + p_2 u(h_2^a) + \ldots + p_I u(h_I^a)$$
$$\equiv \sum_i p_i u(h_i^a). \tag{3.2}$$

The utility $EU(a)$ of action a is thus the sum of the probability-weighted elementary utilities $u(h_i^a)$ of the associated health states. Equation (3.2) is additive over states of the world, which means that health states h_i^a realized in any one state i have no effect on the utility function $u(h_j^a)$ in any other state of the world j $(j \neq i)$. Furthermore, Eq. (3.2) is also linear in the probabilities, which again is both very special and simple.

Von Neumann and Morgenstern (1947) showed that the expected utility rule is applicable, provided that certain axioms of rational choice hold and if, and only if, the elementary utility function $u(h)$ relating to consequences is cardinal.

A cardinal variable is one which can be measured quantitatively; e.g., altitude, air pressure or temperature. While measurement might be taken in different units and scales, these scales may diverge only in their zero point and unit intervals. Temperature, for example, can be measured in Celsius or Fahrenheit; 32 °F equals 0 °C, and one degree on the Celsius scale corresponds to 1.8° Fahrenheit. Positive linear transformation ensures that the relative magnitudes of the differences remain unchanged.

When dealing with choices under certainty, standard economic theory treats utility as an ordinal rather than a cardinal variable, as we saw in the last section. In contrast, for choices under uncertainty, the expected utility rule is only applicable if the elementary utility function satisfies cardinality, which is a more restrictive requirement than ordinality. If $u(h)$ describes the ordering of consequences in a satisfactory way, then this will also hold for $\tilde{u}(h) = \alpha + \beta u(h)$, where α is any constant and β is any positive constant. In our temperature example, α is 32 and β is 1.8, such that $F = 32 + 1.8 \cdot C$.

What explains the different requirements for preference scaling functions under certainty and uncertainty? In the riskless case, there is a one-to-one relationship between actions and consequences: an action leads directly to a consequence. It follows that if someone can rank consequences in terms of preferences, he has already determined the preference ordering of his actions—which is all that is needed for the purpose of decisions. Risky choices are different. A ranking of actions does not necessarily follow from an ordering of consequences, since each action itself implies a probabilistic mix of consequences. Von Neumann and Morgenstern's seminal contribution showed that, given plausible assumptions about individual preferences, it is possible to construct a $u(h)$ function—cardinal in that only positive linear transformations of it are permissible—which when used jointly with the expected utility rule Eq. (3.2) will lead to the correct ordering of actions.

We provide an informal illustration of the joint use of a cardinal preference function and the expected utility rule. h represents an individual's current health state, and $\underline{h}$ is the worst health state he can end up in with a positive probability. For most individuals, this will be death, although some can imagine health states worse than death. Accordingly, $\overline{h}$ is the best possible state; i.e., perfect health. A better health state is always preferred to a worse health state, so that the individual initially has an ordinal utility function. The difficulty now is to show that it is possible to assign numerical values to the degree of preference associated with each health state. These values will have to rise with increasing (improving) health so as to be consistent with ordinal preferences. But the chosen scale must also lead to correct answers when used with the expected utility rule. The method leading to a cardinal scale is called the 'reference lottery technique'.

Consider any health state $\widetilde{h}$ between $\overline{h}$ and $\underline{h}$. Imagine that the patient is confronted with the choice between $\widetilde{h}$ and the uncertain prospect $\left(\overline{h}, \underline{h}; p, 1 - p\right)$; that is, the choice between being in health state $\widetilde{h}$ for certain, and a gamble yielding either the best possible health state $\overline{h}$ with probability p or the worst possible outcome $\underline{h}$ with probability $1 - p$. We can assume that the patient will prefer the gamble if p is sufficiently large. On the other hand, if p becomes very small, the patient will surely prefer the certain health state $\widetilde{h}$. Consequently, there must be some probability $\widetilde{p}$ of achieving perfect health in the reference lottery at which the patient is exactly indifferent between the certain health state $\widetilde{h}$ and the gamble prospect of $\left(\overline{h}, \underline{h}; \widetilde{p}, 1 - \widetilde{p}\right)$. We assume the patient can, in fact, specify this $\widetilde{p}$, which is a cardinal measure for the utility level that the individual derives from the health state $\widetilde{h}$. That is: $u\left(\widetilde{h}\right) = \widetilde{p}$, or more elaborately:

$$u\left(\widetilde{h}\right) = EU\left(\overline{h}, \underline{h}; \widetilde{p}, 1 - \widetilde{p}\right) \equiv \widetilde{p}. \tag{3.3}$$

A patient who proceeds to assign cardinal preference values to health states in this way will generate a utility function $u(h)$ over the range $\underline{h} \leq h \leq \overline{h}$, which can be employed to order alternative actions using the expected utility rule Eq. (3.2).

For an illustration, consider the following hypothetical situation. Let $\underline{h} = 0$ and $\overline{h} = 100$ (see Fig. 3.2) represent the extremes of a range of health states. For a specific health state $\widetilde{h} = 25$, assume that the patient will accept the reference lottery if the probability of the perfect outcome is $\widetilde{p} = 0.5$. The patient is thus indifferent between a certain health state equal to 25 and the lottery offering a 50 % chance of

Fig. 3.2 Preference scaling function

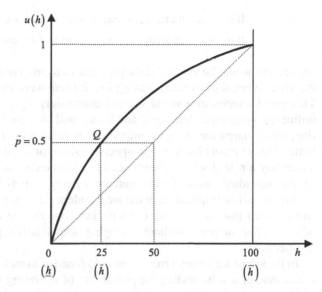

perfect health and a 50 % chance of death. The utility value that can be assigned to the certain health state 25 is then 0.5. This reasoning determines the point Q along the $u(h)$ curve. A repetition of this process generates the entire $u(h)$ curve between $\underline{h} = 0$ and $\overline{h} = 100$.

A comprehensive justification for deriving a cardinal scale in this way requires extensive formal analysis, which is beyond the scope of this text. We provide an intuition instead. The essential point is that the $u(h)$ measure obtained with the help of the reference lottery technique takes the form of a probability, so that the expected utility rule Eq. (3.2) becomes equivalent to the standard formula for compounding probabilities.

3.4 The Axiom of Independence and the Expected Utility Rule

We do not provide full formal proof of the expected utility rule. Instead, our goal is to clarify the crucial element in the proof, the principle of the non-complementarity of health in different states.

Axiom of independence. Assume that an individual is indifferent between two actions or prospects, a_1 and a_2. Then, for any other prospect a_3 and any fixed probability π, the individual will be indifferent between a first compound lottery in which he reaches a_1 with probability π, and a_3 otherwise, and a second compound lottery yielding a_2 with probability π, and a_3 otherwise. Moreover, if he strictly prefers a_1 to a_2, he will strictly prefer the first compound lottery to the second. Thus, using the symbol ~ to indicate indifference and the symbol ≻ for strong preference, we can state the following:

$$\text{If } a_1 \sim a_2, \text{ then } (a_1, a_3; \pi, 1 - \pi) \sim (a_2, a_3; \pi, 1 - \pi);$$
$$\text{If } a_1 \succ a_2, \text{ then } (a_1, a_3; \pi, 1 - \pi) \succ (a_2, a_3; \pi, 1 - \pi).$$

This axiom would be violated if the presence of a_3 in a compound prospect affected the attractiveness of a_1 relative to a_2; i.e., if there were any complementary effect. This could happen in a world without uncertainty if a_1 and a_2 were amounts of ordinary commodities like bread and butter, and a_3 were a commodity like margarine, since margarine is a consumption complement to bread and a substitute for butter. However, in compound prospects, positive or negative complementarity can never play a role since the occurrence of a_1 in one case or a_2 in the other rules out a_3. An individual can never simultaneously enjoy both a_1 and a_3 or both a_2 and a_3.

An immediate implication of the independence axiom is that for two lotteries, a_1 and a_2, such that $a_1 \sim a_2$, we can substitute one for the other in any prospect in which either appears without changing the relative preference ordering of prospects.

In the reference lottery process, the $u(h)$ function associated with any health state h was determined by finding the probability of achieving the best health state that makes the reference lottery equally preferred to the certain reference health state:

$$\text{If } h \sim (\overline{h}, \underline{h}; p, 1 - p), \text{ then } u(h) = p.$$

For simplicity, we introduce the notation $\ell^*(p)$ to represent the reference lottery in which $\overline{h}$ is the outcome with probability p, and $\underline{h}$ is the outcome with probability $1 - p$:

$$\ell^*(p) = (\overline{h}, \underline{h}; p, 1 - p).$$

Now consider two health states h_1 and h_2, and their equivalent reference lotteries $\ell^*(p_1)$ and $\ell^*(p_2)$. Then, $u(h_1) = p_1$ and $u(h_2) = p_2$.

Suppose we wanted to find the preference equivalent for a lottery $(h_1, h_2; \pi, 1 - \pi)$ involving health states h_1 and h_2 with respective probabilities π and $1 - \pi$. Substituting the preference-equivalent prospects yields

$$h_1 \sim \ell^*(p_1) \Rightarrow (h_1, h_2; \pi, 1 - \pi) \sim (\ell^*(p_1), h_2; \pi, 1 - \pi).$$

Moreover,

$$h_2 \sim \ell^*(p_2) \Rightarrow (\ell^*(p_1), h_2; \pi, 1 - \pi) \sim (\ell^*(p_1), \ell^*(p_2); \pi, 1 - \pi).$$

Combining these implies

$$(h_1, h_2; \pi, 1 - \pi) \sim (\ell^*(p_1), \ell^*(p_2); \pi, 1 - \pi). \tag{3.4}$$

Fig. 3.3 Decision tree for a compound lottery

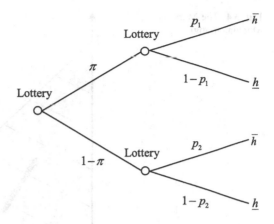

The lottery on the right-hand side of Eq. (3.4) is depicted as a tree diagram in Fig. 3.3. Each node represents a point at which nature determines a move. Outcomes are indicated at the end of each branch.

At the initial node, nature randomly determines which of the two reference lotteries will be realized. This lottery is then played. Note that there are only two possible outcomes of this compound lottery, $\overline{h}$ and $\underline{h}$. Adding probabilities, outcome $\overline{h}$ is reached with probability $\pi p_1 + (1 - \pi)p_2$. The compound lottery is now itself equivalent to the reference lottery:

$$(\ell^*(p_1), \ell^*(p_2); \pi, 1 - \pi) = \ell^*(\pi p_1 + (1 - \pi)p_2). \tag{3.5}$$

Combining Eqs. (3.4) and (3.5), it follows that the individual is indifferent between $(h_1, h_2; \pi, 1 - \pi)$ and a reference lottery in which the probability of reaching perfect health is $\pi p_1 + (1 - \pi)p_2$. Since $p_1 \equiv u(h_1)$ and $p_2 \equiv u(h_2)$, it follows that

$$EU(h_1, h_2; \pi, 1 - \pi) = \pi p_1 + (1 - \pi)p_2$$
$$= \pi u(h_1) + (1 - \pi)u(h_2).$$

The axiom of independence thus leads directly to the von Neumann-Morgenstern expected utility rule.

The significance of the independence axiom can be illustrated by the Marschak-Machina triangle. Consider three possible health states h_1, h_2 and h_3 with $h_1 < h_2 < h_3$ and p_1, p_2 and p_3 denoting their respective probabilities. Different lotteries assign different values to these probabilities $l(p_1, p_2, p_3) = (h_1, h_2, h_3; p_1, p_2, p_3)$. Since $p_1 + p_2 + p_3 = 1$, lotteries are uniquely determined by the values of p_1 and p_3 and are represented by points in the triangle 0AB of Fig. 3.4.

Fig. 3.4 The Marschak-
Machina triangle

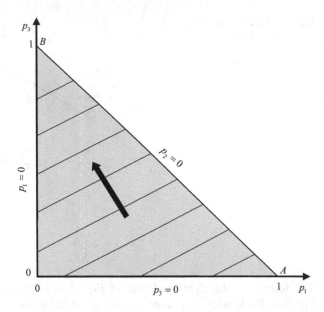

Fig. 3.4 The Marschak-Machina triangle

If the expected utility theory holds, preferences can be represented by $EU(l) = p_1 u(h_1) + (1 - p_1 - p_3)u(h_2) + p_3 u(h_3)$, whose indifference curves satisfy the following condition:

$$p_3 = \frac{EU(l) - u(h_2)}{u(h_3) - u(h_2)} + \frac{u(h_2) - u(h_1)}{u(h_3) - u(h_2)}p_1,$$

This is an equation for a straight line with variables p_1 and p_3. Therefore, the indifference curves must be parallel straight lines. Since $u(h_3) > u(h_2) > u(h_1)$, expected utility increases from the angle $p_1 = 1, p_3 = 0$ to the angle $p_1 = 0, p_3 = 1$.

The slope of the indifference line is $(u(h_2) - u(h_1))/(u(h_3) - u(h_2))$. This slope can also be calculated by the marginal rate of substitution between health states 1 and 3, which takes the form

$$
\begin{aligned}
MRS_{13} &= \frac{\partial EU/\partial h_1}{\partial EU/\partial h_3} \\
&= \frac{p_1 \, \partial u/\partial h_1}{p_3 \, \partial u/\partial h_3}.
\end{aligned}
\tag{3.6}
$$

This MRS only depends on the health states 1 and 3, but not on state 2. Thus, the independence axiom guarantees that the indifference curves in the Marschak-Machina triangle are straight and parallel lines.

Although the utility function is cardinal under the expected utility theory, marginal utility has no behavioral content. Choice behavior only reveals information about how a decision maker ranks different uncertain prospects. The marginal rate of substitution in Eq. (3.6) informs us how the patient would be willing—at the given respective probabilities—to trade health between states 1 and 3.

3.5 The QALY Concept

Medical services are never a goal per se, nor do patients benefit directly from treatment. Rather, the utility a patient derives from the application of a medical service comes from the improvement in his health state. Diagnostic and treatment decisions in medical care are thus always directed towards the outcome they produce for the patient.

In order to formalize and facilitate choices in health care, the concept of a QALY (quality adjusted life year) was developed in the 1970s (while Klarman et al. (1968) introduced the concept, Weinstein and Stason (1977) coined the term). Its general formula is:

$$QALYs(a) \equiv EU(a) = \sum_i p_i T_i^a u(h_i^a),$$ (3.7)

where a is the action taken by the individual, i is the state of nature and p_i the probability that i occurs. h_i^a describes the health state of the patient depending on the choice of action and the course of nature. Finally, the new variable T_i^a stands for the time a health state will last. Note that the duration of a health state and the preference for this health state are separate; i.e., the utility the patient derives from a certain health state does not depend on how long it lasts. This is a strong assumption which has been subject to much debate (see, among others, Miyamato 1999).

The definition of a QALY follows the expected utility rule presented in the last section, but extends it to include time. In the QALY concept, expected utility theory abstracts from commodities other than health which would also enter the elementary preference function in a more general approach to decisions under uncertainty. The QALY is therefore considered to be an extra-welfarist concept (see Culyer 1989).

The QALY literature offers two approaches to valuating health states which are rooted in expected utility theory. The first one is called the standard gamble and is equivalent to the reference lottery technique introduced in the last section. The preference scaling of a given health state thus follows from a reference lottery involving $\underline{h}$ for the worst health outcome, possibly death, and $\bar{h}$ for perfect health. The utility of the worst outcome is assumed to be zero, and that of the best outcome, one. Since we know that cardinality of the elementary utility function allows for any positive linear transformation, this normalization does not affect the preference ordering of actions.

In the standard gamble approach, a respondent is faced with an illness that leaves him in health state h_i and a treatment which would either cure him with probability p or lead to immediate death with probability $1 - p$. The success probability p is then varied until the respondent is indifferent between the certain state in which he is not treated and the gamble implied by the treatment. This procedure thus exactly mimics the reference lottery technique.

The second approach to eliciting $u(h)$ is the time trade-off method developed by Torrance et al. (1972). Here, individuals are confronted with a (non-perfect) health state h_i, the remaining time T_i that they will spend in this state and a treatment option which would restore full health $\bar{h}$. Unlike the standard gamble, treatment here does not involve a mortality risk, but only the shortening of the remaining life expectancy t_i. Life expectancy t_i is then varied until the respondent is indifferent between 'treatment' and 'no treatment'. Normalizing the preference scale for perfect health to one, the point of indifference $\widetilde{t}_i$ determines the utility of the given health state according to $u(h_i) = \widetilde{t}_i / T_i$.

Figure 3.5 illustrates the time trade-off method. The utility of living for T_i years in state h_i is given by the area of the rectangle $0T_iBA$. The same utility can be achieved by living $\widetilde{t}_i$ years in perfect health $\left(T_i \cdot \overline{AB} = \widetilde{t}_i \cdot \overline{CD}\right)$.

The time trade-off illustrates the QALY concept well. The number of QALYs corresponding to T_i years in state h_i is given by $\widetilde{t}_i$; i.e., from $T_i u(h_i) = T_i(t_i/T_i) = \widetilde{t}_i$. Since $h_i < \bar{h}$, we have $\widetilde{t}_i < T_i$. The time trade-off thus leads directly to the QALY, as it multiplicatively combines duration and quality of life. But this advantage comes at a price. The time trade-off requires the elementary utility function to be linear in time. By contrast, the standard gamble method is more general, as it does not pose this requirement.

Box 3.1: Methodology and the Performance of QALYs

Empirical studies indicate that on average respondents rate a given health state higher if the standard gamble is used than under the time trade-off method (see, for instance, Torrance 1976, and Read et al. 1984). The assessment method can therefore have implications for policy and should be considered carefully.

Bleichrodt and Johannesson (1997) compare the results of eliciting QALYs with the standard gamble and the time trade-off method using an experimental design. Both approaches were compared to individual preferences which were measured by direct ranking of health profiles. 172 students of the Stockholm School of Economics and the Erasmus University Rotterdam participated in the experiment. Health states referring to common types of back pain and rheumatism were taken from the Maastricht Utility Measurement Questionnaire. To measure individual preference directly, students had to rank health profiles printed on a set of cards. Additionally, respondents

(continued)

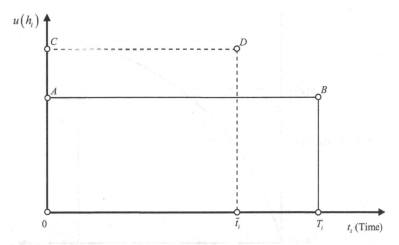

Fig. 3.5 The proportional time trade-off method

3.6 Risk Aversion

The concept of risk aversion is linked to the idea of a fair bet. A fair bet is an
uncertain prospect with an expected yield of zero. An individual is risk-averse if he
never accepts a fair bet. An individual is called a risk lover if he always accepts a
fair bet. If an individual is always indifferent between accepting a fair bet and
rejecting it, he is called risk-neutral.[3]

   In order to conceptualize risk aversion in a medical context, we return to Fig. 3.2
where we stated that the individual is indifferent between a certain health state of

---

[3]Note that individuals need not belong to any of these three categories. An individual may accept a
coin toss where he receives €1 if heads comes up and pays €1 if tails comes up, but reject a gamble
where the amount is raised to €1000. This individual is a risk lover for small bets and risk-averse
for large bets. There have been different explanations for this puzzle. The Friedman-Savage
Hypothesis (Friedman and Savage 1948) suggests that the preference scaling function is doubly
inflected. Another explanation is that most individuals regard gambling as a recreational activity,
so the pure joy of gambling will lead them to accept a fair gamble even though they are risk-averse
regarding income.

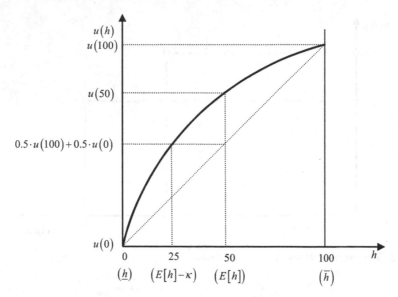

Fig. 3.6 Utility and risk aversion

25 and an uncertain prospect offering either perfect health $(\bar{h} = 100)$ or death $(\underline{h} = 0)$ with a probability of 0.5 each.

The form of the utility function $u(h)$, displayed again in Fig. 3.6, also implies

$$u(50) > 0.5 \cdot u(100) + 0.5 \cdot u(0).$$

Thus, the individual prefers a health state of 50 for certain over the uncertain prospect of achieving the same health state in expected terms $(50 = 0.5 \cdot 100 + 0.5 \cdot 0)$. This corresponds to an individual who rejects a fair bet. Risk aversion can be formally represented with the help of expected utility theory and the assumption that the elementary utility function is concave.

A concave utility function by definition implies

$$u(\lambda h_1 + (1 - \lambda)h_2) > \lambda u(h_1) + (1 - \lambda)u(h_2) \quad \text{for any } 0 < \lambda < 1.$$

If the utility function is concave, the marginal utility of health decreases with increasing health. Consequently, an individual values a marginal improvement in health at a high level less than the same improvement at a low level. This decreasing marginal valuation of health is essential for many results which we will derive in the following chapters.

A risk-neutral individual, by comparison, does not care about his initial level of health. His utility function is linear in health. In the situation displayed in Fig. 3.6, he would be indifferent between a certain health state of 50 and the prospect of a 0.5 probability for either perfect health or death.

Risk-averse individuals are prepared to forego some of their health if they can thereby reduce uncertainty over their health state. Risk aversion can explain, for instance, why a patient agrees to undergo a diagnostic procedure that has harmful side effects. Provided that the expected utility of the test exceeds the utility of his expected health state, including the adverse health effects of the test, a risk-averse patient will opt for the test. In the example given in Fig. 3.6, he would be willing to forgo 25 units of health compared to the situation with an expected health state of 50 in order to achieve a certain health state of 25 units. This is called the cost of risk or the risk premium. The cost of risk κ is defined as follows:

$$u(E[h] - \kappa) = EU(a) = \sum_i p_i u(h_i^a),$$
(3.8)

where $E[h]$ is the expected health state and $E[h] - \kappa$ is the certain health state yielding the same utility as risky action a. In order to receive a measure for κ, we approximate both sides of Eq. (3.8) using the Arrow-Pratt approximation. Assuming that k is sufficiently small, we can approximate the left-hand side with a Taylor series around $E[h]$. Ignoring terms of second and higher orders, we derive

$$u(E[h] - \kappa) \cong u(E[h]) - \frac{du(E[h])}{dh} \kappa.$$
(3.9)

We thus employ a linear approximation of the utility function. This is not possible for the right-hand side of Eq. (3.8), since health states here might be far from $E[h]$. We thus employ a second-order approximation:

$$u(h) \cong u(E[h]) + \frac{du(E[h])}{dh}(h - E[h]) + \frac{1}{2}\frac{d^2u(E[h])}{dh^2}(h - E[h])^2.$$

It follows, then, that

$$\sum_i p_i u(h_i^a) \cong u(E[h]) + \frac{du(E[h])}{dh}\sum_i p_i(h_i^a - E[h])$$
$$+ \frac{1}{2}\frac{d^2u(E[h])}{dh^2}\sum_i p_i(h_i^a - E[h])^2$$
$$= u(E[h]) + \frac{du(E[h])}{dh} \cdot 0 + \frac{1}{2}\frac{d^2u(E[h])}{dh^2} \cdot Var(E[h]).$$
(3.10)

Using

$$u'(E[h]) = \frac{du(E[h])}{dh} \text{ and } u''(E[h]) = \frac{d^2u(E[h])}{dh^2},$$

Equations (3.8), (3.9) and (3.10) give

$$\kappa \cong -\frac{1}{2}\frac{u''(E[h])}{u'(E[h])} Var(E[h]) = \frac{1}{2}A(E[h])Var(E[h]).$$
(3.11)

This shows that the approximate cost of risk depends on preferences (the first and second derivatives of the utility function) and on the variance of the uncertain prospect. The first term in the approximation

$$A(E[h]) \equiv -u''(E[h])/u'(E[h]) \tag{3.12}$$

is known as the Arrow-Pratt coefficient of absolute risk aversion and is a useful measure of the (second-order) preference towards risk.

Box 3.2: The Founding Father of the Expected Utility Theory

In 1738, the Swiss mathematician and physicist Daniel Bernoulli published the seminal essay "Specimen Theoriae Novae de Mensura Sortis" (Bernoulli 1738) in which he studied decision making under uncertainty and introduced the concept of expected utility. Until then, the expected value theory was used where gains and losses are multiplied by their respective probabilities of occurrence to inform optimal decision making. Bernoulli, however, argued that "a poor man generally obtains more utility than a rich man from an equal gain" (p. 24). This notion corresponds to a concave utility function and the concept of risk aversion.

To illustrate his point, Daniel Bernoulli referred to his cousin Nicolas Bernoulli—like Daniel Bernoulli also a professor at the University of Basel at the time—who had submitted five problems to the mathematician Montmort, including the so-called St. Petersburg paradox. This paradox considers a lottery in which a fair coin is tossed. The game starts with one ducat and is doubled every time a head appears. Once a tail appears, the game ends and the player wins whatever is in the pot. If a head is tossed in the first round and a tail in the second round, the player wins one ducat. If a head appears in the first two rounds followed by a tail in the third round, the player wins two ducats. Four ducats result if a head appears in the first three rounds before a tail in the fourth round. While the probability that the coin shows heads at the first toss is 1:2 (½), the probability reduces to 1:4 (¼) for two consecutive throws. The question is what would be the fair price for this lottery.

Now, with probability ½ the player wins 1 ducat, with probability ¼ he wins 2 ducats, with probability 1:8 (⅛) he wins 4 ducats, and so on. The expected value of the lottery, if the coin is tossed an infinite number of times, is thus ½ · 1 + ¼ · 2 + ⅛ · 4 + ... = ½ + ½ + ½ + ... = ∞. Although the expected profit of this lottery is infinite, it turned out that nobody was willing to pay a moderately high price to play it. Daniel Bernoulli (1738) argued that the discrepancy between the expected value theory and actual behavior can be explained when taking risk preferences into account. Assuming a concave utility function for wealth, the willingness to purchase a lottery ticket will increase with the individual's wealth, but at a decreasing rate. According to

---

(continued)

> **Box 3.2** (continued)
> Bernoulli, who used a logarithmic utility function, an individual with no wealth would be willing to pay 2 ducats, while an individual owning 10 (100) ducats would be willing to pay 3 (4) ducats. Despite the fact that an individual owning nothing would not have the possibility to purchase a lottery ticket for 2 ducats (unless he borrowed the money), Bernoulli's approach to solving the St. Petersburg paradox is based on the finiteness of the individual's wealth.
>
> Bernoulli did not solve the paradox in general; however, Menger (1934) proved that a solution requires the assumption of an upper bound of the utility function. Still, he showed that the concept of decreasing marginal utility and thus risk aversion can explain the individual's behavior when expected values are finite—which is true for all realistic decision problems, Bernoulli can be seen as the founding father of the expected utility theory, which was later formalized by von Neumann and Morgenstern (1947).

If the patient is risk-averse $(u''(E[h]) < 0)$, $A(E[h])$ is positive. $A(E[h])$ depends on the particular health state and may increase or decrease as health varies. Larger Arrow-Pratt coefficients lead to a higher cost of risk. Although $A(E[h])$ appears as part of an approximation of the cost of risk, its usefulness does not depend on the accuracy of this approximation. As we will see later on, making assumptions about $A(E[h])$ enables us to predict how the decision maker will respond to changes in his uncertain environment even when the risks are large and Eq. (3.11) would not be a useful approximation.

The willingness to give up some health in exchange for certainty is thus proportional to the variance of the health states. More generally, the cost of risk κ includes the objective risk of the uncertain prospect in the form of $Var(E[h])/2$, as well as the subjective measure of risk aversion in the form of $-u''/u'$. A riskier prospect will lead to a higher cost of risk κ, although it does not change the individual's subjective risk preference.

An alternative measure of risk aversion is called the Arrow-Pratt coefficient of relative risk aversion and is defined as follows:

$$R(E[h]) \equiv - \frac{u''(E[h])E[h]}{u'(E[h])}. \tag{3.13}$$

An individual with a constant degree of absolute risk aversion will consider any uncertain prospect independently of his initial health state. If he shows a constant relative degree of risk aversion, he will be less risk-averse in absolute terms, the higher his actual health state is.

$R(E[h])$ is the negative of the elasticity of marginal utility of health and measures the responsiveness of marginal utility to changes in the health state in a way which is independent both of the particular utility function used to represent preferences and of the units in which health is measured.

Risk aversion can also be illustrated in the Marschak-Machina triangle of Fig. 3.4. The slope of the indifference line is equal to $(u(h_2) - u(h_1))/(u(h_3) - u(h_2))$. This gradient can be interpreted as a measure of attitude to risk. Since the domain of the utility function is a set of three discrete points, we cannot talk about its degree of concavity, but given that $h_1 < h_2 < h_3$, the ratio between $u(h_2) - u(h_1)$ and $(u(h_3) - u(h_2))$ is a natural analogue of a measure of concavity.

Along an indifference curve, movements in north-east direction represent increasing risk. The steeper indifference curves are, the more risk-averse the individual is, and the more compensation is required for increasing risk.

3.7 Prudence

The concept of absolute risk aversion, which follows from equalizing the total utility of a certain prospect and the total expected utility of an uncertain prospect, is useful for the comparative statics analysis presented in this section. It helps, for instance, to understand how the degree of risk aversion affects a decision maker's optimal test strategy.

It turns out, however, that in more complex situations risk aversion is no longer sufficient to describe decisions under uncertainty. If there are multiple risks, one must apply not only the risk premium, but also the prudence premium, which was introduced by Kimball (1990) to characterize precautionary savings by individuals facing uncertainty over their future income.

In the medical context, the risk of comorbidity is a background risk related to the sick health state. Unlike the diagnostic risk, the comorbidity risk is exogenous to the decision maker. Suppose that health in the sick state takes on the values $h_s + m$ and $h_s - m$ with equal probability so that $E[m] = 0$ and $E[h_s] = h_s$. The expected marginal utility of health in the sick state is now

$$0.5 \cdot u'(h_s + m) + 0.5 \cdot u'(h_s - m),$$

whereas it was $u'(h_s)$ without the comorbidity risk. The valuation at the margin of health in the sick state will increase due to the comorbidity risk if

$$\frac{1}{2}u'(h_s + m) + \frac{1}{2}u'(h_s - m) > u'(h_s). \tag{3.14}$$

This inequality holds only if $u'(h_s)$ is convex, or $u''' > 0$. The slope of the marginal utility curve is decreasing in h, but at a decreasing rate, so that $u''' > 0$ (see Fig. 3.7). The marginal value of health in the sick state is thus higher if there is a comorbidity risk than if there is none. Patients with $u''' > 0$ are said to be prudent. We will show that in the presence of comorbidity risk, prudent patients test earlier, i.e., at a lower a-priori probability of illness.

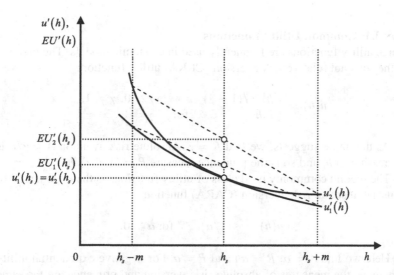

Fig. 3.7 Marginal utility and prudence

As we saw in the last section, risk aversion is equivalent to concavity of the utility function $u(h)$, but it has no implications for the concavity or convexity of the marginal utility function $u'(h)$. However, assumptions about how absolute risk aversion $A = -u''/u'$ varies with health can determine the sign of u'''. It can be shown that individuals with decreasing absolute risk aversion must have $u''' > 0$ (see Exercise 3.4(a)).

Figure 3.7 illustrates the importance of the shape of the decision maker's marginal utility function for the evaluation of health in the sick state. Individual 1 has the marginal utility function $u_1'(h)$ and individual 2 has $u_2'(h)$. Without comorbidity risk, the valuation of health in the sick state h_s is the same for both individuals, as $u_1'(h_s) = u_2'(h_s)$. Now we introduce a comorbidity risk to health in the sick state for both individuals. Health may be greater or smaller by an amount m with equal probability, so that it is either $h_s + m$ or $h_s - m$ in our example. Individual 2 has a more convex marginal utility curve, and the expected value of his marginal utility of health is thus greater than that of individual 1. Hence, individual 2 has a larger expected benefit from an improvement in his health state in the sick state than individual 1. His expected marginal benefit from treatment, conditioned on being sick, is greater than that of individual 1.

To measure the curvature of the marginal utility function, or P for prudence, we use

$$P \equiv -\frac{u'''}{u''}. \tag{3.15}$$

Prudence is unaffected by the particular numerical representation of preferences. We say a risk-averse decision maker is prudent if $P > 0$. P has the same sign as u''' and is positive in our example if comorbidity risk leads to an increase in the expected marginal utility of health in the sick state.

Box 3.3: Common Utility Functions

Three utility functions are frequently used in economic models. The first one is the constant relative risk aversion (CRRA) utility function:

$$u(h) = \begin{cases} h^{1-\gamma}/(1-\gamma) & \text{for} \quad \gamma > 0, \gamma \neq 1, \\ \ln h & \text{for} \quad \gamma = 1. \end{cases}$$

As the name suggests, we find $R = \gamma$. Absolute risk aversion $A = \gamma/h$ is decreasing in h, and so is the prudence measure $P = (1+\gamma)/h$.

The second commonly used class of utility functions is the exponential or constant absolute risk aversion (CARA) function

$$u(h) = -(1/\alpha)e^{-\alpha h} \text{ for } \alpha > 0.$$

Here we find $A = \alpha$, $R = \alpha h$ and $P = \alpha$. For negative exponential utility functions, the measures of absolute risk aversion and prudence are the same and constant. CARA is usually considered a less plausible description of risk aversion than CRRA, though the CARA specification is sometimes more convenient analytically than CRRA, which justifies its inclusion in the standard tool kit.

The third frequently used class of utility functions is the quadratic function:

$$u = a + 2bh - ch^2 \text{ with } h < b/c.$$

For quadratic utility functions, provided $h < b/c$, the degrees of absolute and relative risk aversion increase with h, $A = -c/(b-ch)$ and $R = ch/(b-ch)$. This contradicts general intuition, as one might expect an individual to become less risk-averse with increasing health. The third derivative of the quadratic utility function is zero, which implies that marginal utility is not affected by an increase in risk if the mean is held constant. Since $P = 0$, the individual would not react to the presence of a background risk.

In the nineteenth century, Fechner (1860) and Weber (1846) pioneered psychophysics by proposing specific shapes of a 'sensation function' that describes the relationship between a stimulus intensity and its subjective magnitude. These psychophysical laws have implication for the shape of the preference function of rational decision makers. When Weber's relativity law, which posits that equal relative stimulus changes seem equally important, equally intensive, and are perceived as being equal, is applied to risk preferences, it implies a CRRA utility function. Fechner's logarithmic law, which posits that equal relative changes of a stimulus bring about equal absolute changes of sensation, on the other hand, implies a CARA utility function (for details, see Sinn 1985).

In the last section, we found risk-averse decision makers to have a positive coefficient of absolute risk aversion. This coefficient is closely related to the risk premium, as it marks the amount of health an individual would be willing to give up to achieve a lower health state for certain. We can extend the analogy between prudence and absolute risk aversion to introduce the prudence premium ψ, which is the reduction of health in the sick state by the same amount as the effect of incorporating the comorbidity risk on the decision maker's marginal utility.

$$u'(h_s - \psi) = EU'(h_s + \tilde{m}), \qquad (3.16)$$

where $\tilde{m}$ is the comorbidity risk written as a random variable. While the risk premium κ indicates how much compensation the individual requires to maintain his total utility, ψ measures the compensation that preserves his expected marginal utility.

Box 3.4: Prudent or Imprudent—That Is the Question

Prudence has been shown to impact saving decisions (e.g., Leland 1968; Sandmo 1970; Kimball 1990; Eeckhoudt et al. 2005), asset allocation (e.g., Gomes and Michaelides 2005), auctions (e.g., Esö and White 2004), bargaining (e.g., White 2008), insurance demand (e.g., Fei and Schlesinger 2008), public goods provision (e.g., Bramoullé and Treich 2009) and risk sharing (Gollier 1996). In the medical context, the concept of prudence has been used to analyze optimal prevention levels (see Courbage and Rey 2006, and Eeckhoudt and Gollier 2005) and treatment decisions (e.g., Eeckhoudt 2002 and Felder and Mayrhofer 2014). But while prudence has proved an important concept in decision theory, evidence on whether individuals are, in fact, prudent has only been studied recently.

Almost all studies use economic laboratory experiments to elicit prudence preferences (see Tarazona-Gómez 2004; Deck and Schlesinger 2010, 2014; Ebert and Wiesen 2011, 2014, Maier and Rüger 2012, as well as Krieger and Mayrhofer 2012, 2016, and Heinrich and Mayrhofer 2014). All of these studies observe that a majority of choices are risk-averse and prudent. Interestingly, most of these experiments find a higher share of prudent responses compared to risk-averse choices. This is in line with the concepts of mixed risk-averse (Brocket and Golden 1987, and Caballé and Pomansky 1996) and mixed risk-loving behavior (Crainich et al. 2013). Under mixed risk aversion, the derivatives of utility functions exhibit alternating signs and thus imply risk aversion as well prudent behavior. This is the case for most of the commonly used utility functions (e.g., $\ln(x)$ and $x^{0.5}$). For mixed risk lovers, the derivatives of their utility functions are positive. Thus, they distinguish themselves from mixed risk averters regarding the signs of the even derivatives of their utility function, while they accord with mixed risk averters regarding the signs of all odd derivatives. Therefore, both, mixed risk-averse as well as mixed risk-loving individuals are prudent.

(continued)

Box 3.4 (continued)

Noussair et al. (2014) go one step further. They experimentally elicit prudence preferences from a representative sample of the Dutch population. They, too, observe most choices to be risk-averse and prudent. Moreover, Noussair et al. (2014) correlate individual lottery choices with individual field behavior. While they do not find any correlation of risk aversion with financial decisions in the field, they observe more prudent individuals to have less credit card debt.

Altogether this implies that prudence is not only important for economic theory, but can also be found in actual behavior.

The prudence premium has several convenient properties. One is derived by decomposing ψ into its component parts in the same way we decomposed κ: we apply a Taylor series approximation to each side of Eq. (3.16), to the first order on the left-hand side and to the second order on the right-hand side. We derive

$$\psi \cong -\frac{1}{2} Var(\widetilde{m}) \frac{u'''(h_s)}{u''(h_s)} = P\frac{1}{2} Var(\widetilde{m}). \tag{3.17}$$

Hence, the change in the decision maker's action caused by the introduction of comorbidity risk depends on his preferences, as measured by prudence, and the risk, as measured by the variance.

A second property of ψ deals with its relationship with κ. It can be shown (see Exercise 3.5b) that if the risk premium κ is positive and decreasing in h, then $\psi > \kappa$. This shows that prudence is as important to consider as risk aversion.

3.8 Non-Expected Utility Theories

The expected utility theory (EUT) suggests that the utility function is linear in probabilities—see Eq. (3.2). Experimental research has cast doubts on the validity of EUT. It often fails to explain the decisions of individuals involved in decision making under uncertainty. This led to a search for alternative theories of choice under uncertainty. Most of the non-expected utility theories suggest that the expected utility function is basically non-linear in probabilities. The weighted utility function may be written as

$$NEU(a) = \sum_i w(p_i)u(h_i^a), \tag{3.18}$$

where $w(p_i)$ continuously maps the unit interval onto itself. The subjectively weighted utility theory is able to explain observed behavior in contradiction to EUT. On the other hand, it does not satisfy the so-called first-order stochastic

Fig. 3.8 Fanning out of indifference curves

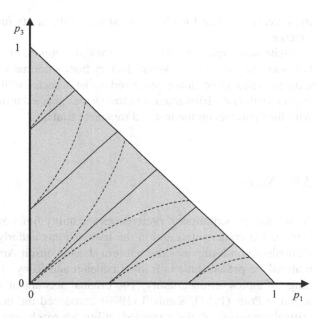

dominance property.[4] The concept of weighted utility was used by Kahneman and Tversky (1979) to formulate the prospect theory. A typical probability weighting in prospect theory has the property that $w(p)$ is greater than p for $p < p^*$ and less than p for $p > p^*$. The transition point p^* is subjective, except that $p^* < 0.5$. This probability weighting function assumes that individuals overweigh low probability events, which is supported by empirical evidence.

Another proposed alternative theory, the rank-dependent expected utility theory, independently developed by Allais (1987), Quiggin (1982) and Yaari (1987), suggests that subjective weights applied to utilities are different from the probabilities of events occurring. This theory applies the weighting to the cumulative distribution function $F(h_i^a)$ to obtain:

$$NEU_{RD}(a) = \sum_i \left[w\big(F(h_i^a)\big) - w\big(F(h_{i-1}^a)\big) \right] u\big(h_i^a\big). \qquad (3.19)$$

In case of two outcomes, $NEU_{RD}(a) = w(p)u\big(h_1^a\big) + (1 - w(p))u\big(h_2^a\big)$, where p is the probability of the worse outcome h_1. Features like overweighing of small probabilities and risk aversion can be captured in the Marschak-Machina triangle through variations in the shape of the weighting function $w(\cdot)$. Indifference curves in this triangle are no longer linear. They may fan out as suggested by Machina (1982) and illustrated in Fig. 3.8. Risk aversion, as reflected by the slope of the

---

[4]First order stochastic dominance implies that shifting probability mass from an outcome to a preferred outcome should lead to a preferred prospect. In other words, the more health the better.

indifference curve, is founded in the shapes of the utility function and the weighting function.

While non-expected utilities theories are important for explaining observed behavior, they are much less satisfactory from a normative point of view. Medical guidelines should be elaborated based on the expected utility theory, and we should expect medical decision makers to follow the expected utility theory when deciding with their patients on the test and treatment strategy.

3.9 Notes

A thorough presentation of preferences and utility functions is provided by Varian (1992). The reader interested in the basic axioms underlying the expected utility theorem of von Neumann-Morgenstern should consult Arrow (1971). Some of the material we present here is from Hirshleifer and Riley (1992), who cover a wide range of topics on uncertainty. The original account of Arrow-Pratt measures is found in Pratt (1964). Kimball (1990) introduced the notion of prudence. For a critical appraisal of the expected utility approach and some alternatives, see Machina (1987) and Wakker (2010). Miyamato (1999) provides a general presentation of the QALY approach under expected and non-expected utility theories.

Exercises

1. Prove that indifference curves can never cross!
2. A decision maker with a QALY utility function is often said to be risk-neutral. Under which assumptions is this true, under which, wrong?
3. An individual has a utility function according to the QALY model. His health can take on the states 1 and 2 with respective longevities T_1 and T_2 and respective probabilities p and $1 - p$. The following table summarizes the initial situation, including utility weights for the two health states:

y	$u(h_i)$	p_i	T_y
1	0.6	0.8	10
2	0.9	0.2	15

   (a) Calculate the QALYs and expected life years for the initial situation.
   (b) Which lifespan with perfect health is equivalent to the initial situation?
   (c) Assume that life expectancy with perfect health is 8 years. Calculate the probability of death $(1 - \pi)$ that is equivalent to the initial situation.
   (d) Calculate the change in QALYs if remaining life expectancy increases by 1 year in state 1 and by 2 years in state 2.

4. The utility weights in the following table are taken from a study where randomly chosen individuals responded to time trade-off questions (see Sackett and Torrance 1978).

Health state h_i	Utility weight $u(h_i)$ for one year
Inability to work due to TBC	0.68
Stationary dialysis	0.65
Breast amputation due to breast cancer	0.48

Use this information to solve the following problems:

(a) How many QALYs are produced by a treatment with dialysis which increases life expectancy by 8 years?
(b) How many QALYs are gained if one TBC case is prevented which would otherwise last 3 months and require treatment at home?
(c) A breast cancer patient undergoes a breast amputation and lives on for another 6 years. Screening 1 year earlier would have detected the cancer, led to an immediate operation and thus increased life expectancy by an additional 2 years (i.e., 9 years after screening) (assume that the utility weight without operation for the first year is 1). Calculate the utility gain from screening.

5. Prudence

(a) Show that individuals with decreasing risk aversion $A(h) = -u''(h)/u'(h)$ must also be prudent, i.e., $u'''(h) > 0$.
(b) Prove that $\psi > \kappa$ if $\frac{\partial \pi}{\partial h} < 0$.

References

Allais, M. (1987). *The general theory of random choices in relation to invariant cardinal utility function and the specific probability function: The (U, Θ) Model—a general overview*. Paris: Centre National de la Recherche Scientific.

Arrow, K. J. (1971). *Essays in the theory of risk-bearing*. London: North-Holland.

Bernoulli, D. (1738). Specimen Theoriae Novae de Mensura Sortis. Commentarii Academiae Scientiarum Imperialis Petropolitanae, Translated from Latin into English by L. Sommer (1954). Exposition of a new theory on the measurement of risk. *Econometrica, 22*, 23–36.

Bleichrodt, H., & Johannesson, M. (1997). Standard Gamble, time trade-off and rating scale: Experimental results on the ranking properties of QALYs. *Journal of Health Economics, 16*(2), 155–175.

Bramoullé, Y., & Treich, N. (2009). Can uncertainty alleviate the commons problem? *Journal of the European Economic Association, 7*(5), 1042–1067.

Brocket, P. L., & Golden, L. L. (1987). A class of utility functions containing all the common utility functions. *Management Science, 33*(8), 955–964.

Caballé, J., & Pomansky, A. (1996). Mixed risk aversion. *Journal of Economic Theory, 71*(2), 485–513.

Courbage, C., & Rey, B. (2006). Prudence and optimal prevention for health risks. *Health Economics, 15*(12), 1323–1327.

Crainich, D., Eeckhoudt, L., & Trannoy, A. (2013). Even (mixed) risk-lovers are prudent. *American Economic Review, 103*(4), 1529–1535.

Culyer, A. J. (1989). The normative economics of health care finance and provision. *Oxford Review of Economic Policy, 5*(1), 34–58.

Deck, C., & Schlesinger, H. (2010). Exploring higher order risk effects. *Review of Economic Studies, 77*(4), 1403–1420.

Deck, C., & Schlesinger, H. (2014). Consistency of higher order risk preferences. *Econometrica, 82*(5), 1913–1943.

Ebert, S., & Wiesen, D. (2011). Testing for prudence and skewness seeking. *Management Science, 57*(7), 1334–1349.

Ebert, S., & Wiesen, D. (2014). Joint measurement of risk aversion, prudence, and temperance. *Journal of Risk and Uncertainty, 48*(3), 231–252.

Eeckhoudt, L. (2002). *Risk and medical decision making*. Boston: Kluwer.

Eeckhoudt, L., & Gollier, C. (2005). The impact of prudence on optimal prevention. *Economic Theory, 26*(4), 989–994.

Eeckhoudt, L., Gollier, C., & Treich, N. (2005). Optimal consumption and the timing of the resolution of uncertainty. *European Economic Review, 49*(3), 761–773.

Esö, P., & White, L. (2004). Precautionary bidding in auctions. *Econometrica, 72*(1), 77–92.

Fechner, G. G. (1860). *Elemente der Psychophysik*. Leipzig: Breitkopf and Härtel.

Fei, W., & Schlesinger, H. (2008). Precautionary insurance demand with state-dependent background risk. *Journal of Risk and Insurance, 75*(1), 1–16.

Felder, S., & Mayrhofer, T. (2014). Risk preferences: Consequences for test and treatment thresholds and optimal cutoffs. *Medical Decision Making, 34*(1), 33–41.

Friedman, M., & Savage, L. J. (1948). The utility analysis of choices involving risk. *Journal of Political Economy, 56*(4), 279–304.

Gollier, C. (1996). Decreasing absolute prudence: Characterization and applications to second-best risk sharing. *European Economic Review, 40*(9), 1799–1815.

Gomes, F., & Michaelides, A. (2005). Optimal life-cycle asset allocation: Under-standing the empirical evidence. *Journal of Finance, 60*(2), 869–904.

Heinrich, T., & Mayrhofer, T. (2014). *Higher-order risk preferences in social settings*. Ruhr Economic Paper No. 508.

Hirshleifer, J., & Riley, J. G. (1992). *The analytics of uncertainty and information*. Cambridge: Cambridge University Press.

Kahneman, D., & Tversky, A. (1979). Prospect theory: An analysis of decision under risk. *Econometrica, 47*, 263–291.

Kimball, M. S. (1990). Precautionary saving in the small and in the large. *Econometrica, 58*(1), 53–73.

Klarman, H., Francis, J., & Rosenthal, G. (1968). Cost-effectiveness analysis applied to the treatment of chronic renal disease. *Medical Care, 6*(1), 48–56.

Krieger, M., & Mayrhofer, T. (2012). *Patient preferences and treatment thresholds under diagnostic risk—An Economic Laboratory Experiment*. Ruhr Economic Papers No. 321.

Krieger, M., & Mayrhofer, T. (2016). Prudence and prevention: An economic laboratory experiment. *Applied Economics Letters*. doi:10.1080/13504851.2016.1158909.

Leland, H. E. (1968). Saving and uncertainty: The precautionary demand for saving. *Quarterly Journal of Economics, 82*(3), 465–473.

Machina, M. J. (1982). 'Expected Utility' analysis without the independence axiom. *Econometrica, 50*(2), 277–323.

Machina, M. J. (1987). Choices under uncertainty: Problems solved and unsolved. *Journal of Economic Perspectives, 1*(1), 112–152.

Maier, J., & Rüger, M. (2012). *Experimental evidence on higher-order risk preferences with real monetary losses*. Working Paper.

Menger, K. (1934). Das Unsicherheitsmoment in der Wertlehre—Betrachtungen im Anschluß an das sogenannte Petersburger Spiel. *Zeitschrift für Nationalökonomie (Journal of Economics), 5* (4), 459–485.

Miyamato, J. M. (1999). Quality-adjusted Life Years (QALY) Utility models under expected utility and rank-dependent utility assumptions. *Journal of Mathematical Psychology, 43*(2), 201–237.

Noussair, C. N., Trautmann, S. T., & van de Kuilen, G. (2014). Higher order risk attitudes, demographics, and financial decisions. *Review of Economic Studies, 81*(1), 325–355.

Pratt, J. W. (1964). Risk aversion in the small and in the large. *Econometrica, 32*(1–2), 122–136.

Quiggin, J. (1982). A theory of anticipated utility. *Journal of Economic Behavior and Organization, 3*, 323–343.

Read, J. L., Quinn, R. J., Berwick, D. M., Fineberg, H. V., & Weinstein, M. C. (1984). Preference for health outcomes: Comparison of assessment methods. *Medical Decision Making, 4*(3), 315–329.

Sackett, D. L., & Torrance, G. W. (1978). The utility of different health states as perceived by the general public. *Journal of Chronic Disease, 31*(11), 697–704.

Sandmo, A. (1970). The effect of uncertainty on saving decisions. *Review of Economic Studies, 37* (3), 353–360.

Sinn, H. W. (1985). Psychophysical laws in risk theory. *Journal of Economic Psychology, 6*, 185–206.

Tarazona-Gómez, M. (2004). *Are individuals prudent? An experimental approach using lottery choices*. Working Paper, Laboratoire d'Economie des Ressources Naturelles (LERNA).

Torrance, G. W. (1976). Social preferences for health states—an empirical evaluation of three measurement techniques. *Socio-Economic Planning Sciences, 10*(3), 129–136.

Torrance, G. W., Thomas, W. H., & Sackett, D. L. (1972). A utility maximization model for evaluation of health care programs. *Health Services Research, 7*(2), 118–133.

Varian, H. R. (1992). *Microeconomic analysis* (3rd ed.). New York: Norton.

Von Neumann, J., & Morgenstern, O. (1947). *Theory of games and economic behavior* (2nd ed.). Princeton, NJ: Princeton University Press.

Wakker, P. P. (2010). *Prospect theory: For risk and ambiguity*. Cambridge, UK: Cambridge University Press.

Weber, E. W. (1846). *Die Lehre vom Tastsinne und Gemeingefühle auf Versuche gegründet*. Braunschweig: Vieweg & Sohn.

Weinstein, M. C., & Stason, W. B. (1977). Foundations of cost-effectiveness analysis for health and medicine practice. *New England Journal of Medicine, 296*, 716–721.

White, L. (2008). Prudence in bargaining: The effect of uncertainty on bargaining outcomes. *Games and Economic Behavior, 62*(1), 211–231.

Yaari, Y. (1987). The dual theory of choice under risk. *Econometrica, 55*(1), 95–115.

Chapter 4
Treatment Decisions Without Diagnostic Tests

Fort de la théorie et de l'expérience, j'ai le droit de soupçonner
le premier venu d'être un porteur des germes.

Jules Romains[1]

Consider a situation that calls for a medical decision for which no diagnostic test is available to the physician. The physician knows the particular illness and how to treat it, but is uncertain whether the patient is in fact sick or not. From the medical literature the physician has information on the prevalence rate, i.e., the a priori probability that any one member of the general population suffers from the illness, and the benefits and possible side effects of the treatment. Additionally, he may know certain characteristics of the patient which have a particular influence on his personal probability of developing an illness.

Under these circumstances of diagnostic risk, the physician must decide whether to treat the patient or abstain from treatment. As in the previous chapter, we assume that the physician is a perfect agent and acts in the best interest of his principal, the patient. To aid his decision, we derive a threshold probability or lower bound for the a priori probability of an illness which necessitates the physician's treatment. This probability is called the treatment threshold. We then analyze the effect of the decision maker's risk aversion on the treatment threshold. We show that risk aversion reduces it. Choosing treatment can be regarded as an insurance against the low level of health that would occur in the sick und untreated state. Furthermore, we consider the cost of treatment and analyze its effect on the treatment threshold. This analysis requires that we monetize the utility outcome of treatment.

In the second section of this chapter, we focus on the impact of therapeutic risk, which refers to the outcome of a treatment, on the physician's decision to treat. The therapeutic risk is captured by a probability that the treatment is successful. Again,

---

[1] 'By virtue of theory and experience, I have the right to suspect the first who comes along to be a carrier of germs.'—Romains, J.—*Knock ou le triomphe de la medicine*—Gallimard, Paris—1923, p. 74.

© Springer-Verlag GmbH Germany 2017
S. Felder, T. Mayrhofer, *Medical Decision Making*,
DOI 10.1007/978-3-662-53432-8_4

a threshold probability is inferred where the physician is indifferent between treatment and no treatment. The distinction between diagnostic risk and therapeutic risk is important for the treatment decision. In terms of diagnostic uncertainty, treatment reduces the spread between health states and therefore the diagnostic risk, whereas the decision to treat is riskier in terms of therapeutic uncertainty, since the patient's health will deteriorate if treatment fails. This difference explains why risk-averse decision makers react differently to these two types of risk. In the second section we also analyze the role of the treatment cost on the physician's decision.

In the third section, we combine the diagnostic risk and the therapeutic risk. While the thresholds in this extended model are similar to the ones where only one risk is considered, we can study how the diagnostic risk and therapeutic risk are intertwined in the physician's treatment decision. Moreover, we show that the models in the first and the second section are special cases of the general model where both the diagnostic risk and the therapeutic risk are present.

4.1   The Treatment Decision Under Diagnostic Risk

4.1.1   The Treatment Threshold

In the following chapter, we will assume a certain sickness that can be treated. The diagnostics of the illness, however, produces uncertain results and the physician must decide whether to treat or not to treat the patient. A sick patient will benefit, whereas a healthy patient will suffer from the treatment.

The decision tree in Fig. 4.1 illustrates the situation. It shows the patient's utility u depending on the realized health state h. Indices distinguish the different possible health states: h for healthy, s for sick. The signs indicate the physician's decision: plus denotes 'treatment', minus 'no treatment'.

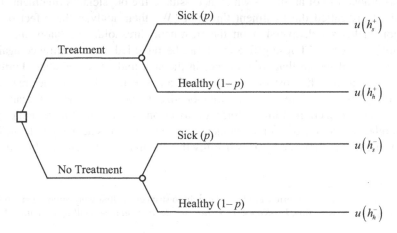

Fig. 4.1 Decision tree for the situation without a diagnostic test

The expected utility of the decision 'treatment' can be derived from the upper branch of the decision tree in Fig. 4.1. It adds the utilities of the two health states, weighted with their respective probabilities of occurrence:

$$EU^+(p) = p \cdot u(h_s^+) + (1-p)u(h_h^+).$$ (4.1)

In order to understand the effect of the a priori probability of an illness on the expected utility of treatment, we transform Eq. (4.1) to obtain

$$EU^+(p) = u(h_h^+) + p[u(h_s^+) - u(h_h^+)].$$

If treating the sick patient restores him to full health, the utility difference between a treated sick individual and a treated healthy individual is positive, i.e., $u(h_s^+) - u(h_h^+) > 0$. In this case, the expected utility of treatment will increase with the probability of illness. However, in many cases one would assume the difference in utility is negative, which would imply that the expected utility of treatment is then decreasing in the a priori probability of an illness. Hence, we cannot definitively determine the sign of the slope of the expected utility function regarding treatment:

$$\frac{\partial EU^+(p)}{\partial p} = u(h_s^+) - u(h_h^+) \gtrless 0.$$ (4.2)

The expected utility of 'no treatment' is calculated based on the lower branch of the decision tree:

$$EU^-(p) = p \cdot u(h_s^-) + (1-p)u(h_h^-).$$ (4.3)

Again, rewriting Eq. (4.3) in order to isolate the effect of the a priori probability of an illness gives

$$EU^-(p) = u(h_h^-) - p[u(h_h^-) - u(h_s^-)].$$

This function has a negative slope, as we can safely assume that the utility level of an untreated sick individual is lower than that of an untreated healthy individual, i.e., $u(h_h^-) - u(h_s^-) > 0$. The option 'no treatment' becomes less attractive the higher the a priori probability of suffering from an illness is:

$$\frac{\partial EU^-(p)}{\partial p} = -[u(h_h^-) - u(h_s^-)] < 0.$$ (4.4)

Figure 4.2 displays the expected utility of the physician's decision as a function of the a priori probability of an illness p. The line $EU^-(p)$ is the expected utility if he decides not to treat, and $EU^+(p)$ represents his expected utility from treating.

Fig. 4.2 The treatment
threshold as a decision rule

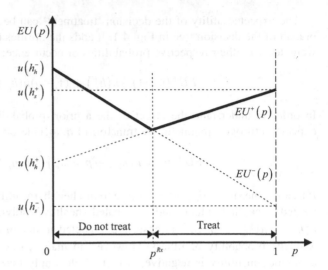

Assuming that the physician follows the expected utility rule and chooses the option
with the higher value, his expected utility as a function of the a priori probability of
an illness will be represented by the thick upper line.

If there were no sick individuals in the population (i.e., $p = 0$), it would always
be advisable not to treat, so that the expected utility of this decision equals the
utility level of a healthy individual: $EU(p = 0) = u(h_h^-)$. If all individuals are ill
(i.e., $p = 1$), treatment is always indicated and the expected utility of treatment
corresponds to the utility level of a treated sick patient: $EU(p = 1) = u(h_s^+)$. This
suggests that the physician will abstain from treatment at low a priori probabilities
of an illness and treat at high probabilities. Moreover, there should be an intermediate a priori probability at which the physician is indifferent between 'treatment'
and 'no treatment'. This is called the treatment threshold, which we denote as p^{Rx},
where 'Rx' stands for treatment (see Fig. 4.2).

In order to further characterize the physician's decision, we write the difference
between the expected utilities of 'treatment' and 'no treatment' using Eqs. (4.1) and
(4.3). This is formulated as follows:

$$EU^+(p) - EU^-(p) = p[u(h_s^+) - u(h_s^-)] \\ + (1 - p)[u(h_h^+) - u(h_h^-)]. \tag{4.5}$$

The differences in the two brackets will be crucial to our further analyses. We
define a sick individual's utility gain from treatment as g and the utility loss of a
healthy individual from (unnecessary) treatment as l:

$$g \equiv u(h_s^+) - u(h_s^-) > 0 \tag{4.6}$$

and

$$l \equiv u(h_h^-) - u(h_h^+) > 0. \tag{4.7}$$

While the signs of the utility differences determining the slopes of the expected utility lines in Fig. 4.2 are not always clear, the signs of the differences Eqs. (4.6) and (4.7) are definite. A precondition for a patient to undergo treatment is that treatment is effective, meaning that the utility of a sick patient increases through treatment. It is also safe to assume that a healthy individual would suffer from treatment, in particular if it is invasive.

Inserting the utility differences g and l into Eq. (4.5) yields

$$EU^+(p) - EU^-(p) = p \cdot g - (1 - p)l. \tag{4.8}$$

This equation reveals the trade-off involved in the physician's decision on treatment. If he opts for treatment, the sick will benefit, while the healthy will suffer a utility loss. If he abstains from treatment, the healthy will benefit, while the sick will suffer a utility loss.

From Eq. (4.8), we derive that the attractiveness of treating as compared to not treating increases linearly with the a priori probability of an illness:

$$\frac{\partial EU^+(p) - \partial EU^-(p)}{\partial p} = g + l > 0, \tag{4.9}$$

since both g and l are positive.

The treatment threshold is where 'treatment' and 'no treatment' lead to the same expected utility: $EU^+(p) = EU^-(p)$ and thus $p \cdot g = (1 - p)l$. At this point, the utility gain from treating a sick individual multiplied by the a priori probability of the illness is equal to the utility gain from not treating a healthy individual multiplied by the probability of the individual being healthy. Solving for p gives the treatment threshold p^{Rx}:

$$p^{Rx} = \frac{l}{g + l} = \frac{1}{1 + g/l}. \tag{4.10}$$

Since $g, l > 0$, we have $0 < p^{Rx} < 1$. The treatment threshold lies at the intersection of the expected utility curves for 'treatment' and 'no treatment' in Fig. 4.2. For a priori probabilities of an illness below the treatment threshold, the expected utility of 'no treatment' exceeds the expected utility of 'treatment'. The physician should therefore not treat in the range of $0 \leq p < p^{Rx}$. With increasing a priori probability of an illness, the expected utility of 'treatment' increases, while the expected utility of 'no treatment' falls. For probabilities above this threshold, expected utility from 'treatment' is higher than expected utility from 'no treatment'. The physician should thus treat patients in the range of $p^{Rx} \leq p \leq 1$.

The decision maker's maximum expected utility curve as a function of the a priori probability of illness consists of the upper envelope of the expected utility lines, i.e., $EU^-(p)$ for $0 \leq p < p^{Rx}$ and $EU^+(p)$ for $p^{Rx} \leq p \leq 1$. The other sections of the expected utility lines are not relevant for a utility-maximizing decision maker, since they imply suboptimal decisions.

Box 4.1: The Treatment Threshold
The following example is taken from Pauker and Kassirer (1975). Consider a 15-year-old boy who has been complaining of increasing abdominal pain over the past 2 days. A urine analysis gives no remarkable results, although the count of white blood cells is somewhat elevated. Further results suggest an appendicitis, but other typical disease patterns can be excluded. The physician must now decide how to proceed, e.g., whether to perform an appendectomy.

Assumptions
- The mortality rate for appendectomies is 0.1 %. In other words, if 1000 of a cohort of boys of this age and this health state are operated on, one will die due to the invasive treatment.
- The survival rate without invasive treatment for a perforated cecum is 99 % for this cohort.
- A healthy boy will survive with 100 % probability without an operation and with 99.9 % probability with an operation.

In this example, the utility gains and losses are measured in probabilities:

$$g = u\left(h_s^+\right) - u\left(h_s^-\right) = 99.9\% - 99\% = 0.9\%,$$
$$l = u\left(h_h^-\right) - u\left(h_h^+\right) = 100.0\% - 99.9\% = 0.1\%.$$

The treatment threshold can be calculated as follows:

$$p^{Rx} = \frac{0.1\%}{0.9\% + 0.1\%} = 0.1.$$

Results:
- At a 10 % a priori probability that the patient suffers from an appendicitis, the physician should be indifferent between 'treatment' and 'no treatment' ($p^{Rx} = 0.1$).
- Up to an a priori probability of 10 %, the expected utility of 'treatment' is below the expected utility of 'no treatment'. Thus the physician should not treat the patient.
- By contrast, for an a priori probability larger than 10 %, the expected utility of 'treatment' exceeds the expected utility of 'no treatment'; the physician should treat the patient.

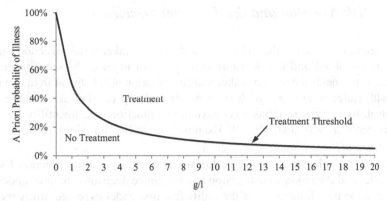

Fig. 4.3 The treatment threshold and the g/l ratio

The treatment threshold is determined by the relative sizes of utility gain g and utility loss l from treatment. If g and l are equal in absolute terms, the treatment threshold is 0.5. If the ratio is 4 to 1, the threshold decreases to 0.2. Figure 4.3 shows how the treatment threshold depends on an increasing ratio of utility gains to losses from treatment. The function is a watershed, dividing a priori illness probabilities into those where treatment is indicated and those where it is not.

Note that the physician's decision is invariant to positive linear transformations of the utility function. It is not the absolute values of g and l which determine the treatment threshold, but their relative value g/l. The relative value is independent of linear transformations of the utility function, and so are the treatment threshold and the decisions on treatment.

Generally, it is assumed that treatment involves a higher utility gain for the sick than the utility loss for the healthy: $g > l$.[2] This condition is a prerequisite for the use of many medical services. For instance, market access is only granted for drugs, if their use does not endanger the healthy. Furthermore, liability considerations will often lead physicians to administer only those services which are more beneficial to the sick than harmful to the healthy.

We can summarize the physician's decision rules in a situation without a diagnostic test as follows: If the a priori probability of an illness is below the treatment threshold, i.e., $p < p^{Rx}$, the physician should not treat the patient. If the a priori probability exceeds the threshold, i.e., $p > p^{Rx}$, treatment is the dominant choice.

---

[2]Situations arise, however, where the harm to the healthy is greater than the gain for the sick. One example is serum used to treat snake bites. Treatment may help a sick individual to survive, while it could be deadly if given to a healthy individual.

4.1.2   Risk Aversion and the Treatment Decision

In this section, we study the effect of the decision maker's risk aversion on the treatment threshold and the decision to treat or not to treat. As seen in the last Chapter, a risk-neutral decision maker's utility function $u(h)$ is linear in the level of the health state: $u(h) = a + b \cdot h$ with $b > 0$ and any constant a. A risk-averse individual, by comparison, has a concave utility function, i.e., his utility function satisfies both $u' > 0$ and $u'' < 0$. Examples of utility functions featuring risk aversion are $u(h) = \sqrt{h}$ and $u(h) = \ln(h)$.

Figure 4.4 displays the respective linear and a concave utility function for the risk-neutral and the risk-averse decision makers. Since decisions are independent of positive linear transformations of the utility function under expected utility theory, we can assume without loss of generality that risk-averse (A) and risk-neutral (N) individuals value the health states h_s^- und h_h^- equally:

$$u_A\left(h_s^-\right) = u_N\left(h_s^-\right) \quad \text{and} \quad u_A\left(h_h^-\right) = u_N\left(h_h^-\right). \tag{4.11}$$

The concavity of the utility function then implies that $u_A\left(h_s^+\right) > u_N\left(h_s^+\right)$ and $u_A\left(h_h^+\right) > u_N\left(h_h^+\right)$ (see Fig. 4.4). The risk-averse individual experiences a larger utility gain from treatment than the risk-neutral individual. For the latter, marginal utility of health is constant, while for the former it is decreasing in the level of health. The risk-averse decision maker values a marginal improvement in his health more at a low health level than at a high health level. In other words, for the same expected health state the risk-averse individual prefers a minimal spread between the possible outcomes, while the risk-neutral individual is indifferent to this spread. Since treatment reduces the spread of the health states, the utility gain from treatment is larger for the risk-averse individual than for the risk-neutral individual.

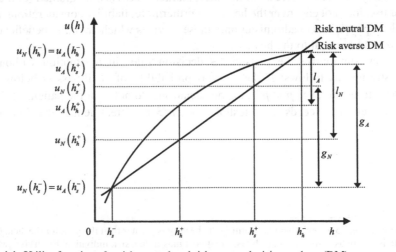

Fig. 4.4 Utility functions for risk-neutral and risk-averse decision makers (DM)

Furthermore, the concavity of the utility function implies that the utility changes ascribed to treatment which is conditioned on factual health states differ for risk-averse and risk-neutral individuals. Recall our definitions in the last section: $g \equiv u(h_s^+) - u(h_s^-)$ for the sick and $l \equiv u(h_h^-) - u(h_h^+)$ for the healthy. Figure 4.4 shows that while the utility gain is greater for a risk-averse individual, $g_A > g_N$, his utility loss is smaller than that of a risk-neutral individual, $l_A < l_N$.

How will the risk aversion of the decision maker, then, affect the treatment threshold? There is a short answer and a more detailed answer to this question. For the short answer, we just differentiate the equation for the treatment threshold Eq. (4.10) with respect to g/l, the ratio of utility gain to utility loss from treatment for the sick and the healthy, to arrive at

$$\frac{\partial p^{Rx}}{\partial (g/l)} = -\frac{1}{(1 + g/l)^2} = -\left(p^{Rx}\right)^2 < 0. \tag{4.12}$$

The treatment threshold thus decreases with an increase in the utility gain from treatment for the sick. In other words, the larger the gains from treatment for the sick, the sooner the physician will treat. The utility loss the healthy suffer from treatment works in the opposite direction. If this loss l increases, the threshold increases. As the utility loss from treatment experienced by the healthy increases, the physician will perform treatment only if the a priori probability of illness exceeds a particular threshold.

Since $g_A/l_A > g_N/l_N$, it follows from Eq. (4.12) that

$$p_A^{Rx} < p_N^{Rx}. \tag{4.13}$$

The treatment threshold is thus lower for a risk-averse individual than it is for a risk-neutral individual.

For the detailed answer, we start with Eqs. (4.1) and (4.3) for the expected utility of the decision to treat or not to treat. For $i = A, N$ we have

$$EU_i^+(p) = p \cdot u_i(h_s^+) + (1 - p)u_i(h_h^+)$$

and

$$EU_i^-(p) = p \cdot u_i(h_s^-) + (1 - p)u_i(h_h^-).$$

We then compare the expected utilities of risk-averse and risk-neutral individuals for the two options. For the 'no treatment' option we find

$$EU_A^-(p) - EU_N^-(p) = p\left[u_A\left(h_s^-\right) - u_N\left(h_s^-\right)\right]$$
$$+ (1-p)\left[u_A\left(h_h^-\right) - u_N\left(h_h^-\right)\right]$$
$$= 0.$$

This difference equals zero, due to the normalization of the utility function performed in Eq. (4.11). Hence, the expected utility of 'no treatment' is the same for risk-averse and risk-neutral decision makers.

The following holds for the 'treatment' option:

$$EU_A^+(p) - EU_N^+(p) = p\left[u_A\left(h_s^+\right) - u_N\left(h_s^+\right)\right]$$
$$+ (1-p)\left[u_A\left(h_h^+\right) - u_N\left(h_h^+\right)\right].$$

Using the normalization of Eq. (4.11) again, we can extend this difference to

$$EU_A^+(p) - EU_N^+(p) = p\left[u_A\left(h_s^+\right) - u_A\left(h_s^-\right) - u_N\left(h_s^+\right) + u_N\left(h_s^-\right)\right]$$
$$+ (1-p)\left[u_A\left(h_h^+\right) - u_A\left(h_h^-\right) - u_N\left(h_h^+\right) + u_N\left(h_h^-\right)\right].$$

The differences in the brackets correspond to the utility gains and losses of treatment for the sick and the healthy [see Eqs. (4.6) and (4.7)]. We obtain

$$EU_A^+(p) - EU_N^+(p) = p[g_A - g_N] + (1-p)[l_N - l_A]. \tag{4.14}$$

Since $g_A > g_N > 0$ and $l_N > l_A > 0$, it follows that $EU_A^+(p) - EU_N^+(p) > 0$. In other words, the 'treatment' option is more attractive for the risk-averse than for the risk-neutral decision maker. Since there is no difference in their evaluations of the 'no treatment' option, we expect the risk-averse individual to opt for treatment earlier, i.e., at a lower a priori probability of an illness, than the risk-neutral individual.

We conclude our argumentation with Fig. 4.5, which displays the expected utility of the two decision options ('treatment' and 'no treatment') as a function of the a priori probability of an illness p for risk-neutral and risk-averse decision makers.

If the decision is not to treat, the expected utility lines of risk-averse and risk-neutral individuals fall together due to the normalization of utility. If the decision is to treat, the expected utility function of the risk-averse individual lies above that of the risk-neutral individual.[3] Given the negative slope of the expected utility curve for the 'no treatment' option, this implies a lower treatment threshold for risk-averse individuals.[4] Physicians can thus be said to treat their patients more often under risk aversion than under risk neutrality.

---

[3]In Fig. 4.4, the difference in expected utility from treatment between risk-averse and risk-neutral decision makers increases with increasing p. This holds only if $g_A - g_N > l_N - l_A$.

[4]Note that the negative slope of the $EU_i^-(p)$ line—see Eq. (4.4)—is in fact the decisive factor for the result. Even if the $EU_i^+(p)$ line had a negative slope the treatment threshold would still be lower for a risk-averse decision maker than for a risk-neutral one.

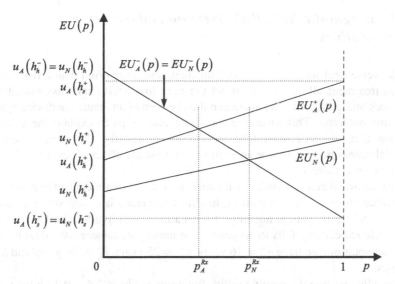

Fig. 4.5 The treatment threshold for risk-averse and risk-neutral individuals

---

Box 4.2: Why Does Treatment Reduce the Diagnostic Risk?
Let us start with the following example:

- Option A 'treatment': $h_s^+ = 30$, $h_h^+ = 20$
- Option B ' no treatment': $h_s^- = 10$, $h_h^- = 40$

Note that the expected health state is the same for both decision options. The difference between the best and the worst outcomes in the two options is, then,

- With treatment: $h_s^+ - h_h^+ = 30 - 20 = 10$
- Without treatment: $h_h^- - h_s^- = 40 - 10 = 30$

The decision between the two options is similar to a choice between two lotteries in which the odds are constant and the expected outcome is the same. The relative risks of the two lotteries can be measured by the difference between the best and the worst outcomes. The higher the spread, the riskier the lottery.

Treatment is similar to an insurance policy: One trades in health in a good state in order to improve health in a bad state. Regarding the diagnostic risk, risk-averse decision makers will thus undertake treatment more often than risk-neutral decision makers.

4.1.3 Diagnostic Risk, Risk Aversion and the Severity of Illness

A risk-averse decision maker will opt for treatment more often than a risk-neutral one, as treatment allows him to avoid the very low health state associated with being sick and untreated. Treatment can thus be seen as an insurance device against the worst outcome. This insurance metaphor also helps to explain the common intuition that someone should be treated more urgently, the more severe his potential illness is. We provide an example to show the effect of severity of illness on the treatment decision.

Assume first that a sick patient who does not receive treatment can expect to live for another 16 years. With treatment, his life expectancy is assumed to increase to 25 years. A healthy patient not subject to treatment will live for another 36 years, but his life expectancy falls to 30 years if he undergoes unnecessary treatment. In the usual notation, we have $h_s^- = 16$ years, $h_s^+ = 25$ years, $h_h^- = 36$ years and $h_h^+ = 30$ years.

Secondly, assume the specific utility functions $u_N(h) = 2.4 + 0.1 \cdot h$ for a risk-neutral and $u_A(h) = \sqrt{h}$ for a risk-averse patient. Both utility functions are normalized so that the same utility levels arise for the situations h_s^- and h_h^- without treatment $\left(u_N\left(h_s^-\right) = u_A\left(h_s^-\right) = 4\right)$. The treatment threshold can be calculated using the sick patient's utility gain from treatment g_i and the healthy individual's utility loss from treatment l_i for $i = A, N$.

For the risk-neutral decision maker we obtain

$$
\begin{aligned}
p_N^{Rx} &= \frac{l_N}{g_N + l_N} \\
&= \frac{u_N\left(h_h^-\right) - u_N\left(h_h^+\right)}{u_N\left(h_s^+\right) - u_N\left(h_s^-\right) + u_N\left(h_h^-\right) - u_N\left(h_h^+\right)} \\
&= \frac{(0.1 \cdot 36 + 2.4) - (0.1 \cdot 30 + 2.4)}{[(0.1 \cdot 25 + 2.4) - (0.1 \cdot 16 + 2.4)] + [(0.1 \cdot 36 + 2.4) - (0.1 \cdot 30 + 2.4)]} \\
&= \frac{3.6 - 3}{(2.5 - 1.6) + (3.6 - 3.0)} = \frac{0.6}{0.9 + 0.6} = 0.4.
\end{aligned}
\tag{4.15}
$$

Accordingly, the treatment threshold of the risk-averse patient is

$$
p_A^{Rx} = \frac{l_A}{g_A + l_A} = \frac{\sqrt{36} - \sqrt{30}}{\left(\sqrt{25} - \sqrt{16}\right) + \left(\sqrt{36} - \sqrt{30}\right)} = \frac{0.52}{1 + 0.52} = 0.34.
\tag{4.16}
$$

Since $g_A > g_N$ (1.0 > 0.9) and $l_N > l_A$ (0.60 > 0.52), it follows from Eqs. (4.15) and (4.16) that the treatment threshold for risk-averse patients is smaller than that for risk-neutral patients: $p_A^{Rx} = 0.34 < 0.40 = p_N^{Rx}$.

Now assume that the severity of the illness increases: For a given h_h^-, the untreated health status h_s^- decreases. In our example, the severity of the illness reduces life expectancy by 5 years from 16 years to 11 years. The effectiveness of the treatment remains constant, so that h_s^+ must decrease from 25 to 20 years, too. The severity of the illness thus influences only the utility gain from treatment for the sick g. What are the effects on the treatment threshold? For the risk-neutral decision maker we find

$$p_N^{Rx;new} = \frac{l_N}{g_N + l_N} = \frac{3.6 - 3}{(2 - 1.1) + (3.6 - 3)} = \frac{0.6}{0.9 + 0.6} = 0.4. \qquad (4.17)$$

Since utility is linear in health for the risk-neutral patient and the effectiveness of treatment is unchanged, g_N is not affected. In turn, the treatment threshold remains constant.

For the risk-averse patient, however, the treatment threshold changes as follows:

$$p_A^{Rx;new} = \frac{l_A}{g_A + l_A} = \frac{\sqrt{36} - \sqrt{30}}{(\sqrt{20} - \sqrt{11}) + (\sqrt{36} - \sqrt{30})} = \frac{0.52}{1.16 + 0.52} = 0.31.$$

$$(4.18)$$

The concave shape of u_A thus implies that the utility gain from treatment g_A increases with a decreasing initial health state h_s^-. The physician who is a risk-averse decision maker assigns a higher degree of risk to the new situation with a more severe illness than the physician who is a risk-neutral decision maker. Thus, the former's willingness to opt for treatment increases (i.e., his threshold p_A^{Rx} decreases). We can therefore conclude that the greater the severity of an illness, the lower the treatment threshold, and the more likely a risk-averse physician is to treat a patient. By contrast, a risk-neutral physician will not react to the severity of illness in his decision to treat, provided that the expected gain in health remains constant.

4.1.4   Introducing the Cost of Treatment

Our analysis so far has not considered the aspect of scarce medical resources in medical decision making. Under time and other restrictions, however, decisions do have opportunity costs. Treating one patient might imply for the physician that he has not the time to treat another patient. A budget or a capacity constraint such as the number of available hospital beds can also restrict a physician's treatment options. The shadow value, then, is the utility of the best alternative action that a decision maker cannot choose due to his constraint. On the societal level, it is the shadow value of the health budget. If revealed it corresponds to the societal marginal willingness to pay for citizens' health.

When the cost of treatment is incorporated, we need to monetize utility. The most general approach would be to use the willingness to pay for any change in utility that is under consideration. Instead, we use the QALY approach and assume that the utility gain from treatment in the sick state has been measured as q_g. Correspondingly, q_l denotes the utility loss from treatment in the healthy state. Then, we assume that λ represents the patient's willingness to pay for a QALY. Let c^{Rx} be the cost of treatment.

The additional expected net benefit from treatment, as compared to no treatment, as a function of the a priori probability of illness then is:

$$ENB(p) = p \cdot \lambda \cdot q_g - (1-p)\lambda \cdot q_l - c^{Rx}. \tag{4.19}$$

Setting $ENB(p)$ equal to zero and solving for p yields the treatment threshold for which the physician is indifferent between treatment and no treatment:

$$
\begin{aligned}
p_m^{Rx} &= \frac{\lambda \cdot q_l + c^{Rx}}{\lambda \cdot \left(q_l + q_g\right)} \\
&= \frac{1 + c^{Rx}/(\lambda \cdot q_l)}{1 + q_g/q_l}.
\end{aligned}
\tag{4.20}
$$

$0 < p_m^{Rx} < 1$ requires that $c^{Rx} < \lambda \cdot q_g$: i.e., the cost is smaller than the benefit of treatment in the sick state. If this condition is not met, treatment will never be an optimal decision. Equation (4.20) also reveals that the cost of treatment in the calculation of the treatment threshold is just as important as the monetized utility loss from treatment in the healthy states.

Comparing with the threshold in the model without treatment cost, we obtain:

$$p_m^{Rx} > p^{Rx} = \frac{1}{1 + q_g/q_l}. \tag{4.21}$$

Not surprisingly, the consideration of treatment cost increases the treatment threshold. Thus, taking into account its monetary cost decreases the attractiveness of the treatment option.

4.2   The Treatment Decision Under Therapeutic Risk

In the last section, we demonstrated that risk-averse patients opt for treatment more often than risk-neutral patients. On the other hand, one might expect risk-averse patients to be reluctant to undergo treatment due to the danger of complications and the uncertainty of the outcome. After all, operations are said to be risky and should be avoided if possible.

The presumed contradiction is solved if one distinguishes the diagnostic risk, which we have dealt with so far, from the therapeutic risk. While treatment reduces the diagnostic risk, it increases the therapeutic risk. Statements about operations or other risky treatments being dangerous usually refer not to the diagnostic risk but to the therapeutic risk.

4.2.1 The Treatment Success Probability Threshold

Therapeutic risk exists due to the uncertainty of the outcome of a treatment. An invasive treatment, for instance, may fail and not restore a patient's full health, or it may even lead to poorer outcomes, death in the worst case.

Since we want to isolate the effect of therapeutic risk on the physician's treatment decision, we ignore diagnostic risk for now, assuming in this section that the physician knows for certain whether the patient is sick or not. As he will treat the patient only if he is sick, we can confine the analysis to sick patients. Without treatment, the patient's health state is h_s^-. Treatment will be successful with a probability of π and lead to the health level h_s^{+s}. The probability of failure is $(1 - \pi)$ and results in the health status h_s^{+f}. The indices s and f stand for success and failure. We assume that $h_s^{+s} > h_s^- \geq h_s^{+f}$. The decision tree in Fig. 4.6 characterizes the situation.

Note again that the decision tree shows only the case of a sick individual. In contrast to the last section, the outcome of treatment is no longer certain (although it is different for the sick and the healthy), but involves the therapeutic risk. Similar to our treatment of the diagnostic risk, we define the difference in utility arising from successful treatment and from 'no treatment' as

$$s \equiv u\left(h_s^{+s}\right) - u\left(h_s^-\right) > 0. \tag{4.22}$$

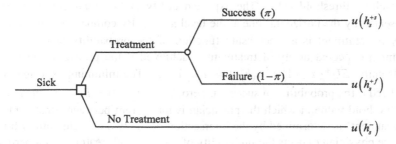

Fig. 4.6 Decision tree under therapeutic risk

Accordingly, we define the utility loss between unsuccessful treatment and 'no treatment' as

$$f \equiv u(h_s^-) - u(h_s^{+f}) \geq 0. \tag{4.23}$$

If the treatment does no harm, the loss will be zero; otherwise we expect a positive sign for f. We formulate the expected utility from treatment (see the decision tree in Fig. 4.6) as

$$EU^+(\pi) = \pi \cdot u(h_s^{+s}) + (1 - \pi)u(h_s^{+f}). \tag{4.24}$$

Inserting the expressions for s and f into Eq. (4.21) yields

$$EU^+(\pi) = \pi[u(h_s^-) + s] + (1 - \pi)[u(h_s^-) - f]. \tag{4.25}$$

The utility of 'no treatment' is given by $u(h_s^-)$, corresponding to the certain outcome of not treating. If we set the utility level of 'no treatment' equal to the expected utility of 'treatment', we can derive a threshold success rate for which the physician is indifferent between the two actions:

$$\pi^{Rx} = \frac{f}{s+f} = \frac{1}{1 + s/f}. \tag{4.26}$$

Since $s, f > 0$, we have $0 < \pi^{Rx} < 1$. In accordance with the treatment threshold, we interpret this threshold as the success probability threshold. Exactly as with the treatment threshold regarding the a priori illness probability, the physician should opt for treatment if the probability of success is above the threshold. The success probability threshold decreases if s (the utility gain from successful treatment) increases or if f (the utility loss from a failure) decreases:

$$\frac{\partial \pi^{Rx}}{\partial(s/f)} = -(\pi^{Rx})^2 < 0. \tag{4.27}$$

Figure 4.7 displays the expected utility as a function of the success probability and the resulting threshold value. The expected utility of 'no treatment' is constant, represented by the horizontal line at the level $u(h_s^-)$. By comparison, the expected utility of treatment is an increasing function of the probability of success. The maximum expected utility of treatment is achieved if the probability of success equals unity, $EU^+(\pi = 1) = u(h_s^{+s}) = u(h_s^-) + s$. The minimum expected utility is realized if the probability of success is zero, $EU^+(\pi = 0) = u(h_s^{+f}) = u(h_s^-) - f$. The threshold value at which the physician is indifferent between 'treatment' and 'no treatment' is determined by the intersection of the two expected utility lines.

If the physician expects the probability of a successful treatment of a particular patient to be below the threshold, $\pi < \pi^{Rx}$, he should not treat the patient.

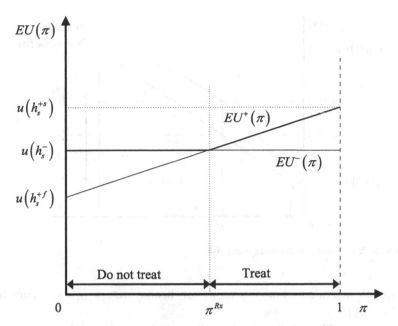

Fig. 4.7 The success probability threshold as a decision rule

Accordingly, if the success probability is estimated to be above the threshold, $\pi > \pi^{Rx}$, the patient should be treated. Again, the physician's relevant expected utility function can be formulated by aligning these two inequalities to form an envelope condition (represented by thick lines in Fig. 4.7): $EU^-(\pi)$ for $0 < \pi < \pi^{Rx}$ and $EU^+(\pi)$ for $\pi^{Rx} < \pi < 1$, where not treating is indicated in the first part and treatment is indicated in the second part.

4.2.2   The Role of Risk Aversion

In contrast to the case of diagnostic risk, treatment in the present situation increases the risk that the decision maker faces (without treatment the outcome is certain, with treatment the outcome is uncertain). Risk-averse decision makers will thus be more reluctant to opt for treatment than risk-neutral individuals.

We can use linear transformation to normalize the utility functions for risk-averse and risk-neutral individuals such that $u_N\left(h_s^{+s}\right) = u_A\left(h_s^{+s}\right)$ and $u_N\left(h_s^{+f}\right) = u_A\left(h_s^{+f}\right)$. Figure 4.8 shows the respective utility functions for risk-neutral and risk-averse physicians facing therapeutic risk. The health state of the sick patient, h_s^-, represents a certain outcome. With treatment, health states h_s^{+s} or h_s^{+f} will be achieved, hence treatment involves a risk. The risk-averse decision maker values the certain alternative of 'no treatment', h_s^-, more highly than the

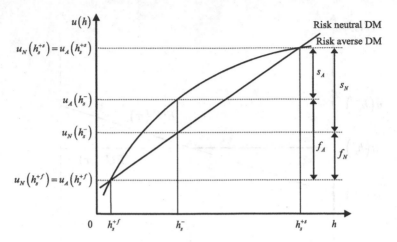

Fig. 4.8 Risk aversion and the therapeutic risk

risk-neutral individual. For the utility of health status h_s^-, we thus have $u_A(h_s^-) > u_N(h_s^-)$.

Furthermore, Fig. 4.8 displays the utility gain from successful treatment s_i and the utility loss from a failed treatment f_i for decision makers $i = A, N$. Due to the concavity of his utility function, the risk-averse decision maker values the utility gain from successful treatment less than the risk-neutral decision maker: $s_A < s_N$. By contrast, in the case of an unsuccessful treatment, the risk-averse decision maker weights the utility loss more heavily than his risk-neutral counterpart: $f_A > f_N$. We thus expect the risk-averse physician to be more reluctant to treat his patient than the risk-neutral physician.

For the success probability threshold we derive

$$\pi_A^{Rx} > \pi_N^{Rx} \tag{4.28}$$

from Eq. (4.27), noting that $s_A/f_A < s_N/f_N$. As expected, the success probability threshold is higher for a risk-averse physician than for a risk-neutral physician.

This result is visualized in Fig. 4.9. Contrary to the situation under diagnostic risk, the expected utility of 'no treatment' under therapeutic risk differs between risk-neutral and risk-averse physicians. Since the risk-averse decision maker values the certain outcome h_s^- more highly, his expected utility from 'no treatment' is greater than that gained by the risk-neutral decision maker. Given that the expected utility of 'treatment' is the same for both types, the threshold is higher for the risk-averse individual.

The fact that $\pi_A^{Rx} > \pi_N^{Rx}$ can also be interpreted as the cost of risk as introduced in Chap. 2. While risk-neutral decision makers will opt for treatment as soon as the expected value of the outcome is non-negative ($E(\Delta h) \geq 0$), risk-averse ones will

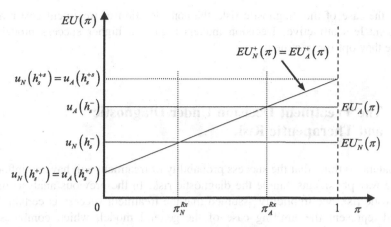

Fig. 4.9 Expected utility: risk-averse versus risk-neutral individuals

treat only if they receive compensation for the shift from the certain situation 'no treatment' to the uncertain situation 'treatment'.

4.2.3 Considering the Cost of Treatment

As in the case with a diagnostic risk, we can include the cost of treatment in the analysis of the therapeutic risk and study its effect on the threshold. The monetized expected additional net benefit of treatment then is

$$ENB(\pi) = \pi \cdot \lambda \cdot q_s - (1 - \pi)\lambda \cdot q_f - c^{Rx}. \tag{4.29}$$

where q_s and q_f are the respective QALYs of treatment in the successful and the failure cases. Setting this expression equal to zero, we obtain the successful probability threshold:

$$\pi_m^{Rx} = \frac{\lambda q_f + c^{Rx}}{\lambda(q_s + q_f)} = \frac{1 + c^{Rx}/\lambda q_f}{1 + q_s/q_f}. \tag{4.30}$$

This threshold is higher compared to the situation where treatment cost are not considered, as can easily be shown by comparing Eqs. (4.30) with (4.26), where the latter has been transformed to include QALYs instead of utility gains:

$$\pi_m^{Rx} > \pi^{Rx} = \frac{1}{1 + q_s/q_f}. \tag{4.31}$$

As in the case of the diagnostic risk, the consideration of treatment cost renders treatment less attractive: Decision makers require a higher success probability before they opt for treatment.

4.3 The Treatment Decision Under Diagnostic and Therapeutic Risk

It is natural to think that the success probability of treatment will have an influence on the way physicians handle the diagnostic risk. In the previous analysis of the diagnostic risk, we implicitly assumed that the treatment success is certain. This should represent the limiting case of the general model, which combines the diagnostic and the therapeutic risk.

To analyze this in greater detail, we can write the expected utility of treatment in the presence of both the diagnostic and the therapeutic risk:

$$EU^+(p, \pi) = \pi\big(p \cdot u(h_s^{+s}) + (1 - p)u(h_h^{+s})\big) \\ + (1 - \pi)\Big(p \cdot u(h_s^{+f}) + (1 - p)u\big(h_h^{+f}\big)\Big). \tag{4.32}$$

The expected utility of no treatment remains unchanged:

$$EU^-(p) = p \cdot u(h_s^-) + (1 - p)u(h_h^-). \tag{4.3}$$

The difference between the two amounts to

$$EU^+(p, \pi) - EU^-(p) = \pi\big[p(u(h_s^{+s}) - u(h_s^-)) + (1 - p)(u(h_h^{+s}) - u(h_h^-))\big] \\ - (1 - \pi)\Big[p(u(h_s^-) - u(h_s^{+f})) + (1 - p)\Big(u(h_h^-) - u\big(h_h^{+f}\big)\Big)\Big]. \tag{4.33}$$

Let $s_s = u(h_s^{+s}) - u(h_s^-) > 0$ and $f_s = u(h_s^-) - u(h_s^{+f}) > 0$ denote the utility gain from a successful treatment and the utility loss from a failed treatment, respectively, in the sick state. We assume that $s_s > f_s$. In the healthy state, we expect a utility loss in both possible outcomes of treatment compared to the no treatment case: $s_h = u(h_h^-) - u(h_h^{+s}) > 0$ and $f_h = u(h_h^-) - u\big(h_h^{+f}\big) > 0$. We assume that $f_h > s_h$. By inserting these expressions into Eq. (4.33), we obtain the equation

$$EU^+(p, \pi) - EU^-(p) = \pi(p \cdot s_s - (1 - p)s_h) \\ - (1 - \pi)(p \cdot f_s + (1 - p)f_h). \tag{4.34}$$

Setting this difference to zero and solving for p, yields the a priori probability of an illness where the physician is indifferent between treatment and no treatment:

$$\tilde{p}^{Rx} = \frac{(1-\pi)f_h + \pi s_h}{\pi(s_s + s_h) - (1-\pi)(f_s - f_h)}$$

$$= \frac{1}{1 + \dfrac{\pi s_s - (1-\pi)f_s}{\pi s_h + (1-\pi)f_h}}. \tag{4.35}$$

The denominator in the first line of Eq. (4.35) can be written as $\pi s_s - (1-\pi)f_s + (\pi s_h + (1-\pi)f_h)$. Thus, the existence of an intermediate threshold (i.e. $0 < \tilde{p}^{Rx} < 1$) requires that the expected utility gain from treatment in the sick state is larger than the expected change in utility from treatment in the healthy state. Note that for $\pi = 1$, we have $\pi s_h + (1-\pi)f_h = s_h = l$ and $\pi s_s - (1-\pi)f_s = s_s = g$, so that $\tilde{p}^{Rx} = l/(l+g)$. This confirms that the general model contains the model with diagnostic risk only as a limiting case. If the treatment success is certain, the threshold is determined by the benefit-loss ratio of treatment g/l. If treatment prospects are uncertain, the certain benefit-loss ratio is replaced by the ratio between expected utility gain and expected utility loss of treatment.

Since $\pi s_s - (1-\pi)f_s \leq g$ and $(1-\pi)f_h + \pi s_h \geq l$, the ratio is smaller when the therapeutic risk is present as well, which in turn implies:

$$\tilde{p}^{Rx} = \frac{1}{1 + \frac{\pi s_s - (1-\pi)f_s}{(1-\pi)f_h + \pi s_h}} \geq \frac{1}{1 + \frac{g}{l}} = p^{Rx}. \tag{4.36}$$

Therefore, if the therapeutic risk is added to the diagnostic risk, the a priori probability threshold where treatment is indicated increases.

Using Eq. (4.34) and solving for π when the difference is zero, we derive the successful treatment threshold where the physician is indifferent between treatment and no treatment as follows:

$$\tilde{\pi}^{Rx} = \frac{pf_s + (1-p)f_h}{p(s_s + f_s) + (1-p)(f_h - s_h)} = \frac{1}{1 + \dfrac{p \cdot s_s - (1-p)s_h}{p \cdot f_s + (1-p)f_h}}. \tag{4.37}$$

The treatment option only is in the choice set of the physician (i.e., $\tilde{\pi}^{Rx} < 1$) if the expected utility net utility of a successful treatment exceeds the expected utility loss of a failed treatment.

For $p = 1$, we derive $\tilde{\pi}^{Rx} = f_s/(f_s + s_s) = \pi^{Rx}$ (see (Eq. 4.26)). Again, our general model entails the model with therapeutic risk only as a special case.

Furthermore, we find

$$\tilde{\pi}^{Rx} = \frac{1}{1 + \frac{s_s - s_h/\Omega}{f_s + f_h/\Omega}} \geq \frac{1}{1 + \frac{s_s}{f_s}}, \tag{4.38}$$

given that $s_s, f_s, s_h, f_h > 0$. The treatment success threshold also increases if we add the diagnostic risk to the model of the therapeutic risk.

The physician's treatment decision in the presence of a diagnostic risk and a therapeutic risk can be characterized as follows. The physician will only treat if $p \geq \tilde{p}^{Rx}$ and $\pi \geq \tilde{\pi}^{Rx}$ is satisfied at the same time, i.e., if one of these inequalities is not satisfied, $p < \tilde{p}^{Rx}$ or $\pi < \tilde{\pi}^{Rx}$, he will not treat the patient.

Moreover, we can study the cross-effects. For the a priori probability threshold we find:

$$\frac{\partial \tilde{p}^{Rx}}{\partial \pi} = -\frac{s_h f_s + s_s f_h}{(\pi(s_s + s_h) + (1 - \pi)(f_h - f_s))^2} < 0. \tag{4.39}$$

Since $s_s, f_s, s_h, f_h > 0$, the treatment threshold decreases if the probability of a successful treatment increases. This result is intuitively appealing: The higher the success rate of the treatment is, the more likely it is that the physician treats the patient with a given a priori probability of illness.

For the success probability threshold, we derive:

$$\frac{\partial \tilde{\pi}^{Rx}}{\partial p} = -\frac{s_h f_s + s_s f_h}{(p(s_s + f_s) + (1 - p)(f_h - s_h))^2} < 0. \tag{4.40}$$

The inequalities $s_s, f_s, s_h, f_h > 0$ again ensure that the cross-effect is negative: An increase in the a priori probability of illness lowers the treatment success threshold. The decision maker will react to a lower a priori probability and increase the success threshold at which he starts the treatment.

Finally, consider the effect of risk aversion on the a priori probability threshold of illness and the probability threshold of successful treatment, respectively. These effects cannot be signed without strong assumptions on the level of the different health states. For instance, it is important whether the sick patient's health outcome will be lower if untreated or with a failed treatment. If the latter holds, a risk-averse decision maker is reluctant to treat, although the patient would benefit from a successful treatment. If the former holds, the risk-averse decision maker might be ready to treat in order improve the sick patient's low health status. Additionally, the success probability also impacts the decision. If it is high (low), the treatment option becomes more (less) attractive, ceteris paribus.

4.4 Notes

The treatment threshold where the decision maker is indifferent between 'treatment' and 'no treatment' was introduced by Pauker and Kassirer (1975). Eeckhoudt (2002) analyzes the diagnostic risk (Chap. 2) and the therapeutic risk (Chap. 4).

Exercises

1. This exercise is adopted from Eeckhoudt (2002), p. 21. After a physician has thoroughly examined a patient, he must decide for or against treatment. Assume that the patient's utility can be measured in QALYs. If the patient is sick and does not undergo treatment, he obtains 10 QALYs. If the sick patient is treated, his utility increases by 15 QALYs. There is, however, a chance that the patient does not actually suffer from the particular illness. In this case, he obtains 50 QALYs if he is not treated. If the physician treats the patient despite his good health, a utility loss of 5 QALYs will ensue.

   (a) How large are g and l in this situation?
   (b) Calculate the treatment threshold.
   (c) Imagine that this is not a single case, but that a physician's practice features 100 patients from one population group with an a priori disease prevalence rate of 0.1, 200 patients from another group with a prevalence rate of 0.2, and 50 patients from a third group with an a priori rate of 0.6.

      (1) How many patients will receive treatment if the physician follows the threshold rule?
      (2) How large is the expected number of QALYs in the entire patient population if

         • No patient gets treatment?
         • All patients get treatment?
         • The physician follows the threshold rule?

   (d) Assume that the effectiveness of treatment increases such that a sick patient undergoing treatment obtains 28 QALYs and a healthy patient obtains 47 QALYs after treatment.

      (1) How does this affect the treatment threshold?
      (2) How many patients are treated now?
      (3) Calculate the new number of QALYs if

         • No patient gets treatment.
         • All patients get treatment.
         • The physician follows the threshold rule.

(e) Draw the equivalent of Fig. 4.2 for the situations before and after the improved treatment.

2. Show that even if the $EU_i^+(p)$ line has a negative slope, the treatment threshold is lower for a risk-averse decision maker than for a risk-neutral one.

3. The following values are given for these health states: $h_s^{+s} = 36$; $h_s^- = 25$; $h_s^{+f} = 16$. A risk-neutral decision maker has the utility function $u(h) = 0.1 \cdot h + 2.4$. The utility function of the risk-averse decision maker is $u(h) = \sqrt{h}$.

   (a) Calculate the utility gains from successful treatment and the utility loss from a failure for both types of decision maker.
   (b) At which success probability will the risk-neutral physician start to treat? What is the threshold for the risk-averse physician?
   (c) Draw Fig. 4.9 for the above values.

References

Eeckhoudt, L. (2002). *Risk and medical decision making*. Boston: Kluwer.
Pauker, S. G., & Kassirer, J. P. (1975). Therapeutic decision making: A cost benefit analysis. *New England Journal of Medicine, 293*(5), 229–234.

Chapter 5
Treatment Decisions with Diagnostic Tests

> The value of information may be thought of as the
> difference between the payoff when he [the decision maker]
> is not informed and the payoff when he is informed.
> John P. Gould[1]

In the last chapter, we assumed that the physician decides about treatment under uncertainty. Uncertainty characterizes the physician's knowledge of the patient's health state—that he is in fact sick or not. We called this the diagnostic risk. A wrong treatment decision can lead to the unnecessary treatment of a healthy patient or to the failure to treat a sick patient, while a right decision is to the advantage of both.

In this chapter, we analyze how the availability of new information from diagnostic testing affects the treatment decision. We define the value of information from a test as the additional expected utility resulting from its optimal use. We differentiate between a perfect and an imperfect test. A perfect test provides an informational value greater than zero over the whole range of the a priori probability of illness, while the value of information of an imperfect test is negative at the boundaries of the a priori probability range. This gives rise to two probability thresholds, the test threshold and the test-treatment threshold, which confine the range within which testing is indicated. The test threshold marks the minimal value of the a priori probability of illness at which testing is called for. At probabilities above the test-treatment threshold, the decision maker should treat immediately without prior testing.

In Sect. 5.2, we analyze the effect of risk attitude on the test and test-treatment thresholds. We examine whether a more risk-averse decision maker will test sooner (i.e., at lower a priori probabilities of illness) and more often (i.e., across a wider range of probabilities) than a risk-neutral one. In Sect. 5.3, we investigate the thresholds in

---

[1]Gould, J. P.—Risk, Stochastic Preference, and the Value of Information—*Journal of Economic Theory*, 8: 64–84, 1974, p. 64.

© Springer-Verlag GmbH Germany 2017
S. Felder, T. Mayrhofer, *Medical Decision Making*,
DOI 10.1007/978-3-662-53432-8_5

the general model where the diagnostic and the therapeutic risk are present. In Sect. 5.4, we focus on the harm that a test may cause a patient and show how this affects the a priori probability of illness range for testing. Finally, in Sect. 5.5, we introduce costs of testing and treatment and study their effect on the thresholds.

5.1 The Value of Information of a Diagnostic Test

5.1.1 The Perfect Test

A perfect test is able to perfectly separate the sick from the healthy within a population. In other words, the test detects both the sick and the healthy with certainty. Hence, its sensitivity and specificity are both one. The decision tree for a situation in which a diagnostic test is available includes a third branch (see Fig. 5.1): in addition to 'treatment' and 'no treatment', the decision maker can choose to test the patient and decide on treatment depending on the test outcome. With a perfect test, a positive test result is perfectly correlated with the presence of the specific illness (and a negative test result is perfectly correlated with the absence of the illness).

Given an a priori probability of illness p, a positive test result can be expected with probability p and a negative test result with probability $1 - p$. The decision maker will treat the patient if the test result is positive and abstain from treatment if the result is negative. Furthermore, the perfect test represents a certain alternative to the options 'treatment' and 'no treatment', which both involve a diagnostic risk. If the test itself does the patient no harm—as per our assumption—we expect the physician to always use diagnostics before deciding on treatment. To demonstrate

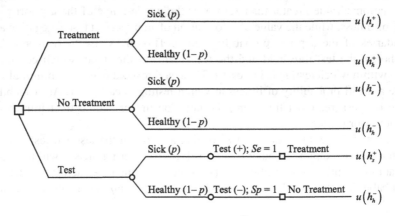

Fig. 5.1 Decision tree for the situation with a perfect test[2]

---

[2]The decision tree is of the prune type, since alternatives which will not be chosen are not presented. For instance, 'no treatment' following a positive test result is principally an option, too.

this, we calculate the expected utility of testing and compare it to the expected utilities of the alternative options.

We use the decision tree to calculate the expected utility of a perfect test:

$$EU^{pt}(p) = p \cdot u(h_s^+) + (1-p)u(h_h^-). \tag{5.1}$$

The index pt indicates that the test is perfect. The expected utility of the test is linear in the a priori probability of illness. Given that the health state of a healthy patient without treatment is not below that of a sick patient after treatment, the expected utility has a non-positive slope: $\partial EU^{pt}/\partial p = u(h_s^+) - u(h_h^-) \leq 0$.

For the comparison, we define the expected utility gain from the (perfect) test as the difference in expected utilities between testing and not testing $VI^P(p)$, known in the literature as the value of information. If no test is available, the decision follows the threshold rule: Treat if the a priori probability of an illness is above the treatment threshold, abstain from treatment if it is below. Thus we can distinguish two cases: $p \in [0, p^{Rx}[$ and $p \in [p^{Rx}, 1]$.

In the first case where $0 \leq p < p^{Rx}$, the physician decides not to treat in the situation without a test. The expected utility of no treatment is $EU^-(p) = p \cdot u(h_s^-) + (1-p)u(h_h^-)$. The value of perfect information as a function of the a priori probability of an illness is then

$$
\begin{aligned}
VI^P(p)\big|_{p<p^{Rx}} &= EU^{pt}(p) - EU^-(p) \\
&= p \cdot u(h_s^+) + (1-p)u(h_h^-) - [p \cdot u(h_s^-) + (1-p)u(h_h^-)] \\
&= p \underbrace{\left(u(h_s^+) - u(h_s^-)\right)}_{g} \\
&= p \cdot g.
\end{aligned}
\tag{5.2}
$$

The perfect test will correctly identify the sick and the healthy. The sick will undergo treatment and achieve a utility gain equal to g, while for the healthy utility remains constant. The expected utility gain from the test, then, is g times the a priori probability of an illness. It thus increases proportionally with the a priori probability. Note also that $VI^P(p)\big|_{p<p^{Rx}}$ is strictly non-negative, making it always optimal to test before deciding on treatment.

For a priori probabilities in the range of $p^{Rx} \leq p \leq 1$, the physician will treat the patient in the situation without a test. The expected utility of treating without prior testing is $EU^+(p) = p \cdot u(h_s^+) + (1-p)u(h_h^+)$, giving rise to

$$
\begin{aligned}
VI^P(p)\big|_{p \geq p^{Rx}} &= EU^{pt}(p) - EU^+(p) \\
&= p \cdot u(h_s^+) + (1-p)u(h_h^-) - (p \cdot u(h_s^+) + (1-p)u(h_h^+)) \\
&= (1-p) \underbrace{\left(u(h_h^-) - u(h_h^+)\right)}_{l} \\
&= (1-p)l.
\end{aligned}
\tag{5.3}
$$

In the upper range of the a priori probability of an illness nothing changes for the sick patients, as they undergo treatment both with and without the test. Healthy patients, however, benefit to the extent of l, the utility loss they would suffer from treatment in the situation without the test. Hence, it is not surprising that the test's value of information is a function of l, the utility loss healthy patients suffer from treatment. The weighting factor here is $1 - p$, the probability of the healthy state. The utility gain then decreases proportionally with the a priori probability of illness. As $VI^p(p)|_{p \geq p^{Rx}}$ is strictly non-negative, testing is also the dominant option in the range of $p^{Rx} \leq p \leq 1$.

In summary, we can write the utility gain from a perfect test as a function of the a priori probability of an illness p

$$VI^p(p) = \begin{cases} p \cdot g & \text{for} \quad 0 \leq p < p^{Rx}, \\ (1-p)l & \text{for} \quad p^{Rx} \leq p \leq 1. \end{cases} \tag{5.4}$$

Figure 5.2 displays the expected utility of 'treatment' and 'no treatment', $EU^+(p)$ and $EU^-(p)$, as well as the expected utility of a perfect test, $EU^{pt}(p)$, as a function of p. The expected utility function of the perfect test corresponds to the

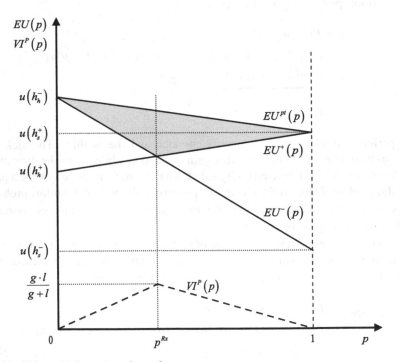

Fig. 5.2 Value of information of a perfect test

connecting line between $EU^-(p = 0) = u(h_h^-)$ and $EU^+(p = 1) = u(h_s^+)$.[3] A triangle emerges between the expected utility line for the best decisions if no test is available, $EU^-(p)$ for $0 \leq p < p^{Rx}$ and $EU^+(p)$ for $p^{Rx} \leq p \leq 1$, and the expected utility line for the utility gain of the test, $EU^{pt}(p)$.

In the graph, the triangle is mirrored above the abscissa, where the outer dashed lines indicate the value of perfect information $VI^P(p)$. The value is zero for $p = 0$ and rises proportionally to p with a slope of g until it reaches a maximum $g \cdot l/(g + l)$ at $p = p^{Rx}$. Once the a priori probability exceeds the treatment threshold, the value of perfect information decreases in proportion to the rising p with a slope of l and reaches zero at $p = 1$.

We conclude that the informational value of a perfect test as a function of the a priori probability of an illness is strictly positive, except at the boundaries where it is zero. Hence, if a perfect test exists, it is always a dominant strategy to test first before deciding on treatment. This result will no longer hold if the test is imperfect, if it involves harm to the patient or if testing or treatment is costly.

5.1.2 The Imperfect Test

In most cases a test is not perfect, meaning that it cannot perfectly separate the sick from the healthy; the test's sensitivity or specificity is less than one ($Se \leq 1$; $Sp \leq 1$). With probability Se (the sensitivity) the test correctly detects a sick patient (true positive result). With complementary probability $1 - Se$ the test misses a sick patient (false negative result). Accordingly, the test correctly identifies a healthy patient with probability Sp (the specificity; true negative test result) and wrongly labels him as sick with the complementary probability $1 - Sp$ (false positive result).

Depending on the test result and the corresponding treatment decisions (treat if the test result is positive, do not treat if it is negative), we can assign a patient's health state as follows:

$$
\begin{array}{ll}
\text{true positive :} & h_s^+ \\
\text{false positive :} & h_h^+ \\
\text{true negative :} & h_h^- \\
\text{false negative :} & h_s^-
\end{array}
$$

The decision tree in Fig. 5.1 is extended by further nodes in the test branch (see Fig. 5.3).

---

[3]Note that Eq. (5.1) can be rewritten as $EU^{pt} = u(h_h^-) - p\left[u(h_h^-) - u(h_s^+)\right]$.

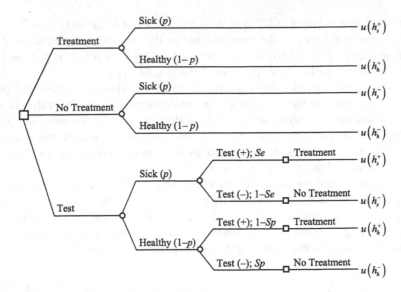

Fig. 5.3 Decision tree for the situation with an imperfect test

The expected utility of the test can then be written as follows:

$$
\begin{aligned}
EU^{t}(p) &= p\big[Se \cdot u(h_s^+) + (1 - Se)u(h_s^-)\big] \\
&\quad + (1-p)\big[Sp \cdot u(h_h^-) + (1 - Sp)u(h_h^+)\big] \\
&= p\big[u(h_s^-) + Se \cdot g\big] + (1-p)\big[u(h_h^+) + Sp \cdot l\big].
\end{aligned}
\tag{5.5}
$$

We can compare the expected utility of an imperfect test—Eq. (5.5)—with that of a perfect test—Eq. (5.1)—to find

$$
\begin{aligned}
EU^{pt}(p) - EU^{t}(p) &= p\big[u(h_s^+) - u(h_s^-) - Se \cdot g\big] \\
&\quad + (1-p)\big[u(h_h^-) - u(h_h^+) - Sp \cdot l\big] \\
&= p(1 - Se)g + (1-p)(1 - Sp)l > 0.
\end{aligned}
$$

Hence, and not surprisingly, the expected utility of a perfect test is always higher than the expected utility of an imperfect one.

Comparing $EU^{t}(p)$ to the optimal choices at the boundaries of the a priori probability range in the situation without a test—see the expressions in the last paragraph—we can derive probabilities at which testing is not indicated. For $p = 0$ it is evident that 'no treatment' is the optimal option, while for $p = 1$ it is optimal to treat in any case. Unlike the case of the perfect test, there are intervals at the edges of the a priori probability of illness interval where an imperfect diagnostic test should not be employed. This gives rise to two thresholds which mark the ranges (in increasing order of the a priori probability) within which it is optimal not to treat at all, to test before treating, and to treat without prior testing. The first point is the test threshold p', the second the test-treatment threshold p^{tRx}.

To derive these thresholds, we first define the value of information of the test as a function of the a priori probability of an illness as in the previous section. Within $0 \leq p < p^{Rx}$ abstaining from treatment is the best choice in the situation without a test. With $EU^{-}(p) = p \cdot u(h_s^-) + (1-p)u(h_h^-)$ we then find

$$
\begin{aligned}
VI(p)\big|_{p < p^{Rx}} &= EU^t(p) - EU^-(p) \\
&= p\big[u(h_s^-) + Se \cdot g\big] + (1-p)\big[u(h_h^+) + Sp \cdot l\big] \\
&\quad - \big[p \cdot u(h_s^-) + (1-p)u(h_h^-)\big] \\
&= p \cdot Se \cdot g - (1-p)(1-Sp)l.
\end{aligned}
\tag{5.6}
$$

Note that if we set both sensitivity and specificity in Eq. (5.6) to unity, we can derive the value of information of the perfect test: $VI^p(p) = p \cdot g$ —see Eq. (5.2).

The first term in Eq. (5.6), $p \cdot Se \cdot g$, which is the utility gain in the sick health state, is multiplied not only by the a priori probability of the illness as in Eq. (5.2) but also by the sensitivity, since the test does not detect all sick patients. Only true positive cases gain utility from the test, while false negative cases experience no change in utility.

The second term, $-(1-p)(1-Sp)l$, reflects the utility loss of the healthy who would not be treated in the situation without a test and now undergo treatment due to a false positive test result. Their utility loss, l, is thus weighted with one minus specificity.

Moving towards the treatment threshold, the utility gain increases proportionally to the a priori probability of illness at the rate of $g \cdot Se + (1-Sp)l$, where $g > 0$ and $l > 0$ ensure the positive slope.

Within $p^{Rx} \leq p \leq 1$, the reference option in the situation without a test is treatment, with an expected utility of $EU^+(p) = p \cdot u(h_s^+) + (1-p)u(h_h^+)$. We obtain

$$
\begin{aligned}
VI(p)\big|_{p \geq p^{Rx}} &= EU^t(p) - EU^+(p) \\
&= p\big[u(h_s^-) + Se \cdot g\big] + (1-p)\big[u(h_h^+) + Sp \cdot l\big] \\
&\quad - \big[p \cdot u(h_s^+) + (1-p)u(h_h^+)\big] \\
&= -p \cdot g(1-Se) + (1-p)Sp \cdot l.
\end{aligned}
\tag{5.7}
$$

The first term, $-p \cdot g(1-Se)$, regards sick patients who are misclassified by the test. Without the test they would have been treated and would have obtained a utility gain equal to g. Since the test is imperfect, sick patients are wrongly classified as healthy and not treated with probability $1 - Se$ (false negative test result). These patients' utility gain from the test is thus lowered by the corresponding amount.

The second term, $(1-p)Sp \cdot l$, reflects the utility gain of the healthy who would be treated in the situation without a test and are now spared treatment due to their true negative test result. This utility gain is weighted with the specificity.

Beyond the treatment threshold, the utility gain decreases proportionally at the rate of $-(1-Se)g - Sp \cdot l$, where $g > 0$ and $l > 0$ again ensure the negative slope.

Altogether, we can summarize the test's value of information as

$$VI(p) = \begin{cases} p \cdot Se \cdot g - (1-p)(1-Sp)l & \text{for} \quad 0 \le p < p^{Rx}, \\ -p \cdot g(1-Se) + (1-p)Sp \cdot l & \text{for} \quad p^{Rx} \le p \le 1. \end{cases} \qquad (5.8)$$

$VI(p = 0) = -(1 - Sp)l < 0$ and $VI(p = 1) = -(1 - Se)g < 0$ now hold at the boundaries of the a priori probability range; hence testing in fact leads to negative value of information in these areas.[4]

At the treatment threshold $VI(p = p^{Rx}) = g \cdot l(Se - (1 - Sp))/(g + l)$. If the test has discriminatory power, $Se - (1 - Sp) > 0$, then $VI(p = p^{Rx}) > 0$. Hence there must be two points left and right of the treatment threshold at which $VI(p) = 0$. Setting both equations of (5.8) to zero, we obtain

$$p^t = \frac{(1 - Sp)l}{Se \cdot g + (1 - Sp)l} = \frac{1}{1 + LR^+ g/l} \qquad (5.9)$$

and

$$p^{tRx} = \frac{Sp \cdot l}{(1 - Se)g + Sp \cdot l} = \frac{1}{1 + LR^- g/l}, \qquad (5.10)$$

where $LR^+ = Se/(1 - Sp)$ is the positive and $LR^- = (1 - Se)/Sp$ is the negative likelihood ratio. These two thresholds were first introduced in the medical literature by Pauker and Kassirer (1980).

Equation (5.9) marks the test threshold where the optimal strategy transitions from not testing and not treating to testing and deciding on treatment depending on the test outcome. Testing is not optimal below this threshold, since the possible utility gain for the true positive cases weighted by the a priori probability of the illness $(p \cdot Se \cdot g)$ does not exceed the utility loss for the false positive cases weighted by one minus the a priori probability $(-(1 - p)(1 - Sp)l)$. If specificity converges to one, the positive test threshold becomes zero. Hence, the test threshold will disappear if the test produces no false positive cases, as the optimal strategy at a lower a priori probability of illness range is to abstain from treatment if no test is available.

Equation (5.10) denotes the test-treatment threshold, which marks the transition of the physician's optimal strategy from testing first to treating immediately. Testing is not indicated beyond this threshold, since the utility loss for false negative cases multiplied by the a priori probability of the illness $(-p(1 - Se)g)$ exceeds the utility gain for true negative cases multiplied by one minus the a

---

[4]Strictly speaking the value of information is non-negative, as an information technology is only employed if it is useful. The precise equation for the value of information is $VI(p) = \max(0, EU^t(p) - EU^+(p))$. For the sake of simplicity, we abstract from this (important) complication.

priori probability $((1-p)Sp \cdot l)$. If sensitivity converges to one, the test-treatment threshold becomes one. A sensitivity of one implies that the test misses no sick individual (zero false negative cases); since the reference strategy without a test is treatment, $Se = 1$ is sufficient to allow the test-treatment threshold disappear.

Comparing Eq. (4.10) with Eqs. (5.9) and (5.10), respectively, we find

$$p^t < p^{Rx} < p^{tRx} \text{ if } LR^+ > 1 \text{ and } LR^- < 1. \tag{5.11}$$

$LR^+ > 1$ and $LR^- < 1$ are both satisfied if $Se - (1 - Sp) > 0$, which in turn is the minimal condition under which the test is useful at all.

For the distance between the two thresholds we obtain

$$p^{tRx} - p^t = \frac{1}{1 + LR^- g/l} - \frac{1}{1 + LR^+ g/l} > 0, \text{ if } LR^+ > LR^-. \tag{5.12}$$

The minimal condition for gainfully employing the test then opens up the a priori probability range which is larger, the better the discriminatory power of the test is.

In fact, if the discriminatory power of a test increases—due either to increased sensitivity or increased specificity—the positive likelihood ratio increases as well ($\partial LR^+/\partial Se > 0$ and $\partial LR^+/\partial Sp > 0$), while the negative likelihood ratio decreases ($\partial LR^-/\partial Se < 0$ and $\partial LR^-/\partial Sp < 0$), so that the range in which testing is indicated broadens.

Formally, Eqs. (5.9) and (5.10) provide us with

$$\frac{\partial p^t}{\partial LR^+} = -(p^t)^2 \frac{g}{l} < 0, \tag{5.13}$$

and

$$\frac{\partial p^{tRx}}{\partial LR^-} = -(p^{tRx})^2 \frac{g}{l} < 0. \tag{5.14}$$

Thus, if a test becomes more precise due to an increase in either sensitivity or specificity, the a priori probability range for testing increases.

Box 5.1: A Test's Value of Information: An Example

Pauker and Kassirer (1980) calculated the diagnostic utility of a test for ulcers. The test's sensitivity is 0.96, the specificity 0.98. Treatment following a positive test result provides a utility gain of 0.33 for the sick and a loss of 0.02 for the healthy. Both g and l are measured in terms of a change in the survival probability. For the treatment threshold this implies

(continued)

Box 5.1 (continued)

$$p^{Rx} = \frac{l}{g+l} = \frac{0.02}{0.33+0.02} = 0.057.$$

Without diagnostics the physician's optimal decision is therefore to treat patients with an a priori probability of illness larger than 0.057 and not to treat patients with an a priori probability smaller than 0.057.

What is the informational value of the test? We expect the value to be negative for an a priori probability of the illness of zero:

$$VI(p = 0) = -(1 - Sp)l = -0.02 \cdot 0.02 = -0.004.$$

As the a priori probability of an illness increases, the informational value of the test increases as well and becomes positive at the test threshold. In order to calculate the test threshold, we set the first part of Eq. (5.8) equal to zero and solve for the a priori probability:

$$0 = p^t Se \cdot g - (1 - p^t)(1 - Sp)l$$
$$\Leftrightarrow p^t = \frac{(1 - Sp)l}{Se \cdot g + (1 - Sp)l} = 0.0013.$$

The test reaches its maximum informational value at the treatment threshold:

$$VI\left(p = p^{Rx}\right) = \frac{g(Se + Sp - 1)}{1 + g/l} = 0.018.$$

Beyond the treatment threshold, the informational value of the test declines and returns to zero at the test-treatment threshold. It can be calculated by setting the second part of Eq. (5.8) equal to zero:

$$0 = -p^{tRx} \cdot g(1 - Se) + (1 - p^{tRx})Sp \cdot l$$
$$\Leftrightarrow p^{tRx} = \frac{Sp \cdot l}{g(1 - Se) + Sp \cdot l} = 0.5976.$$

At an a priori probability of the illness equal to one the informational value of the test will be negative:

$$VI(p = 1) = -(1 - Se)g = -0.04 \cdot 0.33 = -0.0132.$$

The implication for the physician is to test at a priori probabilities between 0.0013 and 0.5976. Above probabilities of 0.5976 he should abstain from testing and treat the patient immediately.

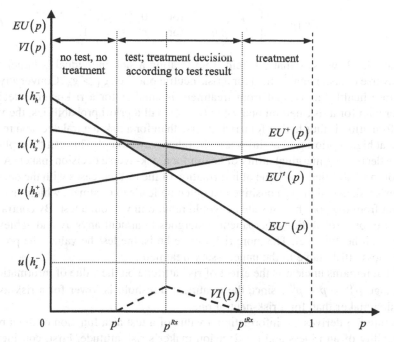

Fig. 5.4 Value of information of an imperfect test

Figure 5.4 displays the expected utilities of the imperfect test and the alternatives and illustrates the value of information of the test as well as the two thresholds. The triangle indicating the value of information of the imperfect test is smaller than that for the perfect test. At very low and very high a priori probabilities, the value of information is negative (zero in the figure); testing is therefore not advised in these ranges. At the treatment threshold p^{Rx}, the expected utility gain from the test reaches its maximum.

Employing a diagnostic test outside the testing interval can produce more harm than good. Contrary to common belief, a test does not always lead to a welfare gain. Especially cases that involve screenings and thus low a priori probabilities often do not pass the test threshold. However, a physician might be reassured knowing that he can refer to a test result to justify his actions, particularly if liability poses a threat (we will discuss this situation in the last chapter of this book).

5.2 Risk Attitude and the Test and Test-Treatment Thresholds

5.2.1 The Perfect Test

We stated the value of information provided by a perfect test as

$$VI^p(p) = \begin{cases} p \cdot g & \text{for} \quad 0 \le p < p^{Rx}, \\ (1-p)l & \text{for} \quad p^{Rx} \le p \le 1. \end{cases} \qquad (5.4)$$

In Sect. 4.1.2, we saw that the gain from treating a sick individual is larger for a risk-averse decision maker than for a risk-neutral one, i.e., $g_A > g_N$. Conversely, the loss to a healthy individual from treatment is smaller for a risk-averse decision maker than for a risk-neutral one: $l_A < l_N$. At small a priori probabilities, the value of information is thus higher for a risk-averse than for a risk-neutral decision maker, while at high a priori probabilities it is the other way around. This can be explained by the decreasing marginal utility of health for a risk-averse decision maker. At low a priori probabilities, the value of information of the test increases with the decision maker's risk aversion, as a positive test outcome leads to treatment which saves the patient from the poor health state he would remain in without a test. By contrast, at high a priori probabilities the patient undergoes treatment anyway and achieves a fairly high health level. The more risk-averse he is, the less he values the possible utility loss attributable to the unnecessary treatment.

What remains unclear is the effect of risk attitude on the value of information in the range $p_A^{Rx} < p < p_N^{Rx}$, since the treatment threshold is lower for a risk-averse decision maker than for a risk-neutral one.

Figure 5.5 derives the informational value of a test as a function of the a priori probability of an illness and the decision maker's risk attitude. First, consider the expected utilities from 'treatment', from 'no treatment' and from the perfect test for

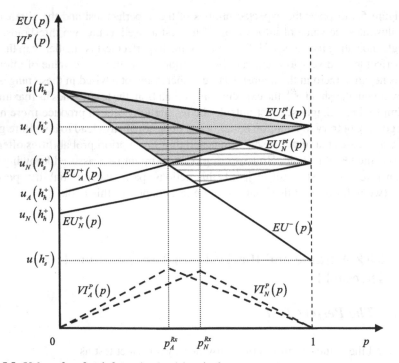

Fig. 5.5 Value of perfect information by risk attitude

risk-neutral and risk-averse decision makers. The informational value of the test is represented by the difference between the expected value of the test and the expected utility of the best decision without a test. The grey area marks the informational value of the test for the risk-averse decision maker, the hatched area marks the equivalent for the risk-neutral decision maker.

The figure confirms our earlier results: the line representing the informational value for the risk-averse decision maker is steeper at low a priori probabilities and flatter at high probabilities than it is for the risk-neutral decision maker. Within the range $p_A^{Rx} < p < p_N^{Rx}$ no clear statement can be made about the relative advantage of the test for the two types of decision makers, since the value of information is already decreasing for the risk-averse individual, while still increasing for the risk-neutral one.

We illustrate the effect of risk attitude on the value of information of a test using three lotteries. Consider the range $p < p_A^{Rx}$, within which treatment without testing is not indicated, and the possible health states $h_s^- = 16$, $h_s^+ = 25$ and $h_h^- = 36$, $h_h^+ = 30$ (all in remaining life years).

In the situation without a test, the patient is sick with probability p and has a health state of $h_s^- = 16$. With probability $1 - p$ he is healthy and has a health state of $h_h^- = 36$. In the situation in which a (perfect) test is available, the ill patient is detected and receives treatment. The sick individual achieves a higher health level than in the first lottery: $h_s^+ = 25 > h_s^- = 16$. The healthy individual does not undergo treatment following the test and thus remains at $h_h^- = 36$.

Which of the two lotteries (illustrated in Fig. 5.6) will be chosen? As long as utility increases with health, the decision maker will always opt for the test, i.e., the second lottery. Both risk-averse and risk-neutral individuals derive a positive value of information from the test, since it increases utility in the sick state and leaves utility in the healthy state constant. But due to its decreasing marginal utility, the informational value of the test will be higher for the risk-averse decision maker. His higher marginal utility in the sick state implies that the risk-averse decision maker draws a higher expected utility from lottery 2 than the risk-neutral one, whose utility is linear in health. We can also say that lottery 1 involves a higher risk, since the potential difference in health for the sick is 20 years in lottery 1 and 11 years in lottery 2. In the range $p < p_A^{Rx}$, the informational value of the test is thus higher for the risk-averse than for the risk-neutral individual.

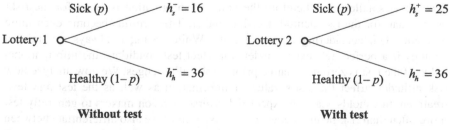

Fig. 5.6 Lotteries for $p < p_A^{Rx}$

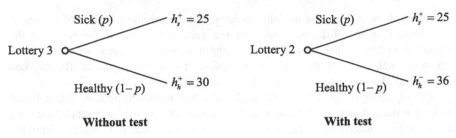

Fig. 5.7 Lotteries for $p > p_N^{Rx}$

Decreasing marginal utility is also responsible for the switch in the relative informational value for risk-averse and risk-neutral decision makers in the range $p > p_N^{Rx}$, where treatment is the optimal decision in the situation without a test (see Fig. 5.7). We now include a third lottery in which 6 years are lost in the healthy state if the decision maker abstains from testing and treats immediately.

Note that the situation with a test (lottery 2) dominates the situation without a test (lottery 3): Since the healthy state improves due to the test—unnecessary treatment is avoided—and the sick state remains constant, every decision maker whose utility function is increasing in health will choose to test.

The risk-averse decision maker will also consider the spread between the two health states. This is 11 years for lottery 2, but only 5 years for lottery 3. The risk is therefore smaller in the situation without a test than in the situation with a test. While the risk is of no concern to the risk-neutral decision maker, the risk-averse decision maker is confronted with two opposite effects: On the one hand, the increase in expected health with the test is positive, on the other hand the higher risk of the test is negative. The value of information in the range $p > p_N^{Rx}$ is thus lower for the risk-averse decision maker than for the risk-neutral one.

5.2.2 The Imperfect Test

In the last section, we showed that a risk-averse decision maker values a diagnostic test more than a risk-neutral decision maker only in the low a priori probability of an illness range. For high a priori probabilities, the risk involved in the treatment decision is smaller, and therefore the value of information is lower for the risk-averse than for the risk-neutral decision maker. These results become even more relevant when considering imperfect tests: While testing is always a dominant strategy if a perfect test exists, under imperfect test conditions the informational value of the test is zero in certain a priori probability ranges. We now analyze how risk attitudes affect the test's value of information as well as the test and test-treatment thresholds. Can we expect risk-averse decision makers to generally test more often than risk-neutral decision makers, or must we also differentiate between low and high a priori probability ranges?

In Sect. 5.1.2, we obtained the following value of information for an imperfect test:

$$VI(p) = \begin{cases} p \cdot Se \cdot g - (1-p)(1-Sp)l & \text{for} \quad 0 \leq p < p^{Rx}, \\ -p(1-Se)g + (1-p)Sp \cdot l & \text{for} \quad p^{Rx} \leq p \leq 1. \end{cases} \tag{5.8}$$

Concavity of the utility function, i.e., the decision maker's risk aversion, implies $g_A > g_N$ and $l_A < l_N$. From the last section we know that no definite statements can be made for the range $p_A^{Rx} < p < p_N^{Rx}$. Regarding the difference in a test's value of information for risk-averse and risk-neutral decision makers,

$$VI_A(p) - VI_N(p) = \begin{cases} > 0 & \text{for} \quad 0 \leq p \leq p_A^{Rx}, \\ \gtrless 0 & \text{for} \quad p_A^{Rx} < p < p_N^{Rx}, \\ < 0 & \text{for} \quad p_N^{Rx} \leq p \leq 1, \end{cases} \tag{5.15}$$

follows from Eq. (5.8). The relative size of the informational value of the imperfect test is thus analogous to the perfect test: At low a priori probabilities risk-averse decision makers value a test more than risk-neutral decision makers while at high probabilities risk-averse decision makers value a test less than risk-neutral decision makers.

How are the test and treatment thresholds affected by the decision makers' risk attitudes? The shortest way to answer this question is to differentiate the thresholds with respect to the ratio (g/l), since this ratio increases with the degree of risk aversion. For the test threshold, Eq. (5.9) provides

$$\frac{\partial p^t}{\partial (g/l)} = -LR^+(p^t)^2 < 0. \tag{5.16}$$

The test threshold thus decreases with an increase in the utility gain of the sick from treatment and increases with an increase in the utility loss of the healthy from treatment. The higher g is, the more important it is to test in order to identify the sick who can then undergo treatment. By comparison: with an increase in l, false positive cases receive more weight and the decision maker will be more reluctant to use the test.

Since $g_A/l_A > g_N/l_N$, the difference in the test threshold between risk-averse and risk-neutral decision makers is characterized by

$$p_A^t < p_N^t. \tag{5.17}$$

The risk-averse decision maker will thus test sooner.

For the test-treatment threshold, Eq. (5.10) provides

$$\frac{\partial p^{tRx}}{\partial (g/l)} = -LR^{-}\left(p^{tRx}\right)^{2} < 0. \tag{5.18}$$

This threshold also falls with an increase in g and rises with an increase in l. If the utility gain from treating the sick increases, then false negative cases become more important. Hence the decision maker will choose treatment sooner. By analogy, an increase in the utility loss from treating the healthy will defer treatment, as true negative cases weigh more heavily. With $g_A/l_A > g_N/l_N$, the difference in the test-treatment threshold between the risk-averse and the risk-neutral decision maker is specified by

$$p_A^{tRx} < p_N^{tRx}. \tag{5.19}$$

The risk-averse decision maker will thus switch from testing first to treating directly earlier than the risk-neutral decision maker. Intuitively, the informational value of the test is less important for the risk-averse decision maker, as 'treatment' is the risk-reducing strategy and is the best option in a situation without a test.

Figure 5.8 illustrates the change in the test's value of information and the shifts of the two thresholds for risk-neutral and risk-averse decision makers. The triangle indicating the area of the positive value of information shifts to the left for the risk-averse decision maker. Hence, decision makers can indeed be said to test earlier if they are risk-averse. However, it is unclear whether they test more often, since they also switch their strategy to direct treatment earlier.

The a priori probability of an illness range for testing is determined by the change in the height and the slopes of the $VI(p)$ lines. Without further assumptions on the relative sizes of g and l for risk-averse and risk-neutral decision makers we cannot make definite statements regarding the relative size of their testing ranges.

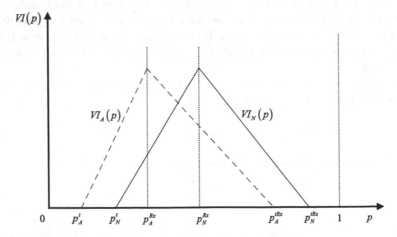

Fig. 5.8 Risk attitude and the informational value of an imperfect test

Since both the test threshold and the test-treatment threshold shift to the left, the probability that a patient undergoes treatment increases. This effect not only stems from the leftward shift of the test-treatment threshold but also from the fact that the test is used at lower a priori probabilities, resulting in more positive tests. We see that treatment becomes more attractive if decision makers are risk-averse. Patients are willing to accept a possible utility loss from treatment (if they are in fact healthy) in order to avoid ending up in the low-utility health state of sickness.

5.3 The Test and Test-Treatment Threshold When Both the Diagnostic and the Therapeutic Risk Are Present

As in Sect. 4.3, we can extend the model to include the therapeutic risk as well. With probability π the treatment is successful and the patient achieves utility $u(h_s^{+s})$ if sick and utility $u(h_h^{+s})$ if healthy. With probability $1 - \pi$ the treatment fails and the utility consequences would be $u(h_s^{+f})$ or $u\left(h_h^{+f}\right)$, depending on the health state. Taking into account therapeutic risk for patients with a positive test outcome, expected utility of testing can be written as follows:

$$EU^t(p, \pi) = p\left[Se\left(\pi \cdot u(h_s^{+s}) + (1 - \pi)u(h_s^{+f})\right) + (1 - Se)u(h_s^{-})\right]$$
$$+ (1 - p)\left[Sp \cdot u(h_h^{-}) + (1 - Sp)\left(\pi \cdot u(h_h^{+s}) + (1 - \pi)u\left(h_h^{+f}\right)\right)\right].$$

$$(5.20)$$

Before deciding on whether to test the patient or not, the physician will have to check that the probability of a successful treatment is sufficiently high, given the a-priori probability of an illness and the test characteristics.

Setting Eq. (5.20) to zero and solving for the success probability, we find the corresponding threshold:

$$\tilde{\pi}^{tRx} = \frac{p \cdot Se \cdot f_s + (1 - p)(1 - Sp)f_h}{p \cdot Se(s_s + f_s) - (1 - p)(1 - Sp)(s_h + f_h)}$$

$$= \frac{1}{1 + \dfrac{p \cdot Se \cdot s_s - (1 - p)(1 - Sp)s_h}{p \cdot Se \cdot f_s + (1 - p)(1 - Sp)f_h}}$$

$$= \frac{1}{1 + \dfrac{\Omega \cdot LR^+ s_s - s_h}{\Omega \cdot LR^+ f_s + f_h}}.$$

$$(5.21)$$

The physician will start diagnostics or directly treat the patient only if $\pi_i > \tilde{\pi}^{tRx}$. Compared to the threshold when the presence of the illness is certain, (see (Eq. 4.32)), we find:

$$\tilde{\pi}^{tRx} \geq \tilde{\pi}^{Rx} = \frac{1}{1 + \frac{\Omega \cdot s_s - s_h}{\Omega \cdot f_s + f_h}}, \tag{5.22}$$

provided that $s_s f_h + s_h f_s > 0$, which is satisfied, given that $s_h, s_s, f_s, f_h > 0$. Therefore, with an imperfect test, the success probability threshold increases.

Once the principal treatment decision is settled, the physician then has to decide whether he needs to make a diagnosis first, based on the concept of the value of information. From Chap. 4, the a-priori probability threshold, where the physician is indifferent between treatment and non treatment amounts to

$$\tilde{p}^{Rx} = \frac{1}{1 + \frac{\pi s_s - (1-\pi)f_s}{\pi s_n - (1-\pi)f_n}}, \tag{4.35}$$

and the expected utility of no treatment is

$$EU^-(p) = p \cdot u(h_s^-) + (1-p)u(h_h^-). \tag{4.3}$$

The value of information in the lower range of the a priori probability of illness then is

$$
\begin{aligned}
VI(p,\pi)\big|_{p < \tilde{p}^{Rx}} &= EU^t(p,\pi) - EU^-(p,\pi) \\
&= \pi\big[p \cdot Se(u(h_s^{+s}) - u(h_s^-)) + (1-p)(1-Sp)(u(h_h^{+s}) - u(h_h^-))\big] \\
&\quad -(1-\pi)\big[p \cdot Se(u(h_s^-) - u(h_s^{+f})) + (1-p)(1-Sp)\big(u(h_h^-) - u(h_h^{+f})\big)\big].
\end{aligned}
\tag{5.23}
$$

Inserting the definitions from Sect. 4.3 yields

$$
\begin{aligned}
VI(p,\pi)\big|_{p < \tilde{p}^{Rx}} &= \pi(p \cdot Se \cdot s_s + (1-p)(1-Sp)s_h) \\
&\quad -(1-\pi)(p \cdot Se \cdot f_s + (1-p)(1-Sp)f_h)
\end{aligned}
\tag{5.24}
$$

Setting the value of information equal to zero and solving for p gives the test threshold in the extended model

$$\tilde{p}^t = \frac{1}{1 + LR^+ \cdot \frac{\pi s_s - (1-\pi)f_s}{\pi s_h + (1-\pi)f_h}}. \tag{5.25}$$

Since $\pi s_s - (1-\pi)f_s \leq g$ and $(1-\pi)f_h + \pi s_h \geq l$, we have from Eq. (5.9)

$$\tilde{p}^t \geq p^t = \frac{1}{1 + LR^+ g/l}. \tag{5.26}$$

Thus, the test threshold increases if a therapeutic risk is added to the diagnostic risk.

For the upper a priori probability of illness range, the expected utility for the best alternative without a diagnostic test is treatment which depends not only on the a priori probability of illness but also on the success probability

$$EU^+(p, \pi) = \pi\left(p \cdot u\left(h_s^{+s}\right) + (1-p)u\left(h_h^{+s}\right)\right)$$
$$+ (1-\pi)\left(p \cdot u\left(h_s^{+f}\right) + (1-p)u\left(h_h^{+f}\right)\right). \tag{4.32}$$

Therefore, the value of information in the upper range of the a priori probability of illness changes to

$$VI(p,\pi)\big|_{p>\tilde{p}^{Rx}} = EU^t(p,\pi) - EU^+(p,\pi)$$
$$= -\pi\left[p(1-Se)\left(u\left(h_s^{+s}\right) - u\left(h_s^-\right)\right) + (1-p)Sp\left(u\left(h_h^{+s}\right) - u\left(h_h^-\right)\right)\right]$$
$$+ (1-\pi)\left[p(1-Se)\left(u\left(h_s^-\right) - u\left(h_s^{+f}\right)\right) + (1-p)(Sp)\left(u\left(h_h^-\right) - u\left(h_h^{+f}\right)\right)\right], \tag{5.27}$$

and, after inserting the definitions from Sect. 4.3, to

$$VI(p)\big|_{p>\tilde{p}^{Rx}} = -\pi(p(1-Se)s_s + (1-p)Sp \cdot s_h)$$
$$+ (1-\pi)(p(1-Se)f_s + (1-p)Sp \cdot f_h). \tag{5.28}$$

We can derive the test-treatment threshold, by setting the value of information equal to zero. We find:

$$\tilde{p}^{tRx} = \frac{1}{1 + LR^- \cdot \frac{\pi s_s - (1-\pi)f_s}{\pi s_h + (1-\pi)f_h}}. \tag{5.29}$$

The inequalities $\pi s_s - (1-\pi)f_s \leq g$ and $(1-\pi)f_h + \pi s_h \geq l$ guarantee that the threshold increases if a therapeutic risk is added to the diagnostic risk:

$$\tilde{p}^{tRx} \geq p^{tRx} = \frac{1}{1 + LR^- g/l}. \tag{5.30}$$

The presence of the therapeutic risk, thus, shifts the testing range to the right: the no-test-no-treatment range increases, while the treatment range shrinks.

Regarding the effect of risk aversion on the threshold, we have no clear result. Treatment becomes more attractive in the presence of risk-averse decision makers, if the utility loss from a failed treatment is too high in the sick state compared to the utility gain from a successful treatment. This would tend to lower both the test-treatment threshold and the treatment threshold. But it is also possible that risk aversion works in the other direction. If the utility loss from failed treatment is high and the probability of a successful treatment low, the thresholds will increase.

Note that the test and treatment decision becomes somewhat involved in the extended model where both the diagnostic risk and the therapeutic risk are present, as two thresholds have to be taken into account. In the range $0 \leq p < \tilde{p}^t$ no testing and no treatment is indicated, irrespective of the probability of a successful treatment. In the range $\tilde{p}^t \leq p < \tilde{p}^{tRx}$ testing occurs and treatment is advised provided that the test outcome is positive and that $\pi \geq \tilde{\pi}^{tRx}$. For $p \geq \tilde{p}^{tRx}$ treatment is indicated if $\pi \geq \tilde{\pi}^{tRx}$.

5.4   Potential Harm from a Test

So far, we have assumed that testing itself involves no harm to the patient. However, this is not always realistic. Tests that require a blood or tissue sample cause the patient discomfort. Some tests may even lead to complications: for example, an injury of the intestinal wall during a colonoscopy. Moreover, the harm from a test depends on the health status of the patient. The probability of an infection following a tissue sample is higher for a sick patient than for a healthy one. In the following we differentiate the harm to health d from a test according to the test outcome (positive or negative). The corresponding utility loss due to testing, l^t, is then

$$l^i_j = u\left(h^i_j\right) - u\left(h^i_j - d^i_j\right) > 0 \quad i = +, - \; ; j = h, s. \tag{5.31}$$

The expected utility of the test changes to (see the decision tree in Fig. 5.9)

$$EU^t(p) = p\left[Se\left(u(h_s^+) - l_s^{t^+}\right) + (1 - Se)\left(u(h_s^-) - l_s^{t^-}\right)\right]$$
$$+ (1 - p)\left[Sp(u(h_h^-) - l_h^{t^-}) + (1 - Sp)\left(u(h_h^+) - l_h^{t^+}\right)\right]. \tag{5.32}$$

The possible harm from testing established in Eq. (5.32) can be summarized to form the expected loss from the test, depending on the a priori probability of an illness:

$$l^t(p) = p\left[Se \cdot l_s^{t^+} + (1 - Se)l_s^{t^-}\right]$$
$$+ (1 - p)\left[Sp \cdot l_h^{t^-} + (1 - Sp)l_h^{t^+}\right]. \tag{5.33}$$

The expected utility of the test, using g, l and $l^t(p)$, then becomes

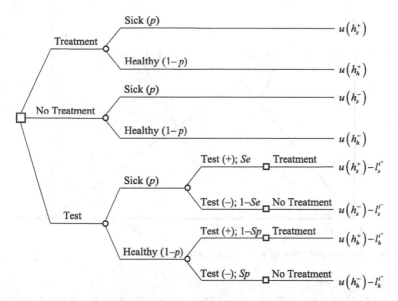

Fig. 5.9 Decision tree for an imperfect and harmful test

$$EU^t(p) = p\left[u(h_s^-) + Se \cdot g\right] + (1-p)\left[u(h_h^+) + Sp \cdot l\right] - l^t(p). \qquad (5.34)$$

The test's value of information is obtained analogously to Eq. (5.8):

$$VI(p) = \begin{cases} p \cdot Se \cdot g - (1-p)(1-Sp)l - l^t(p) & \text{for} \quad 0 \le p < p^{Rx}, \\ -p(1-Se)g + (1-p)Sp \cdot l - l^t(p) & \text{for} \quad p^{Rx} \le p \le 1. \end{cases} \qquad (5.35)$$

If the test causes harm to the patient, its informational value is reduced by the expected utility loss.

For a perfect test (sensitivity and specificity are both one), the informational value considering the harm from testing reduces to

$$VI^P(p) = \begin{cases} p \cdot g - l^t(p) & \text{for} \quad 0 \le p < p^{Rx}, \\ (1-p)l - l^t(p) & \text{for} \quad p^{Rx} \le p \le 1. \end{cases} \qquad (5.36)$$

Figure 5.10 displays the informational gain from the perfect test with and without the harm it causes. Including the harm from testing shifts the informational value downwards and changes the slope of the lines, since the expected harm from the test also depends on the a priori probability of illness. Although the test is perfect, the harm it causes implies that it should not be used at the boundaries of the a priori probability interval.

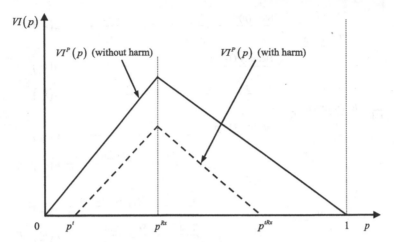

Fig. 5.10 Informational value of a perfect and a harmful test

---

Box 5.2: Harm from Testing and the a Priori Probability Thresholds

We return to the example of Pauker and Kassirer (1980) from Box 5.1, now taking into account that the test causes harm equivalent to a mortality rate of 0.00005. The sensitivity of the test is 0.96 and the specificity is 0.98. The utility gain remains 0.33 and the utility loss 0.02. The treatment threshold refers to the situation without a test and is thus independent of any potential harm:

$$p^{Rx} = \frac{l}{g+l} = \frac{0.02}{0.33 + 0.02} = 0.057.$$

Previously, we calculated a test threshold at 0.0013 and a test-treatment threshold at 0.5976. How does the expected harm from testing affect these two thresholds?

For the test threshold we obtain

$$0 = p^t \cdot Se \cdot g - (1 - p^t)(1 - Sp)l - l^t(p)$$
$$\Leftrightarrow p^t = \frac{(1 - Sp)l + l^t(p)}{Se \cdot g + (1 - Sp)l} = 0.0014.$$

Accordingly, for the test-treatment threshold we obtain

$$0 = -p^{tRx} \cdot g(1 - Se) + (1 - p^{tRx})Sp \cdot l - l^t(p)$$
$$\Leftrightarrow p^{tRx} = \frac{Sp \cdot l - l^t(p)}{g(1 - Se) + Sp \cdot l} = 0.5960.$$

The effects, thus, are as expected: the range of the a priori probability of illness where testing is indicated decreases if potential harm from testing is taken into account.

5.5 Considering Costs of Treatment and Testing

In Chap. 4 we introduced the cost of treatment and derived the corresponding treatment threshold. This threshold can be used to derive $INB(p)$, the incremental expected net benefit of the test compared to the situation without test:

$$
INB(p) = \begin{cases} p \cdot Se\left(\lambda \cdot q_g - c^{Rx}\right) \\ -(1-p)(1-Sp)(\lambda \cdot q_l + c^{Rx}) - c^t & \text{for} \quad 0 \le p < p_m^{Rx}, \\[2mm] -p(1-Se)\left(\lambda \cdot q_g - c^{Rx}\right) \\ +(1-p)Sp(\lambda \cdot q_l + c^{Rx}) - c^t & \text{for} \quad p_m^{Rx} \le p \le 1, \end{cases} \tag{5.37}
$$

where c^t and c^{Rx} is the cost of testing and of treatment, respectively.

In the lower range of the a priori probability of illness, no treatment is the baseline strategy. Therefore, applying a test leads to an additional cost of testing for everyone, while treatment costs are only imputed for patients with positive test outcomes. Setting incremental net benefits equal to zero, yields the test threshold:

$$
\begin{aligned} p_m^t &= \frac{(1-Sp)(\lambda \cdot q_l + c^{Rx}) + c^t}{(1-Sp)(\lambda \cdot q_l + c^{Rx}) + Se\left(\lambda \cdot q_g - c^{Rx}\right)} \\ &= \frac{1 + c^t/(1-Sp)(\lambda \cdot q_l + c^{Rx})}{1 + LR^+\left(\lambda \cdot q_g - c^{Rx}\right)/(\lambda \cdot q_l + c^{Rx})}. \end{aligned} \tag{5.38}
$$

$c^{Rx} < \lambda \cdot q_g$ ensures that $p_m^t > 0$. Compared to the test threshold where the treatment cost is not considered, we find:

$$
p_m^t > p^t = \frac{1}{1 + LR^+ q_g/q_l}. \tag{5.39}
$$

Taking into account the costs of testing and treatment, thus, increases the test threshold, which in turn implies that testing and treatment become less attractive.

In the upper range, treatment is the baseline strategy. Again, applying a diagnostic test leads to an additional cost of testing for all patients. However, patients with negative test outcomes are spared the cost of treatment. Setting incremental net benefit equal to zero, yields the test-treatment threshold:

$$
\begin{aligned} p_m^{tRx} &= \frac{Sp(\lambda \cdot q_l + c^{Rx}) - c^t}{Sp(\lambda \cdot q_l + c^{Rx}) + (1-Se)\left(\lambda \cdot q_g - c^{Rx}\right)} \\ &= \frac{1 - c^t/Sp(\lambda \cdot q_l + c^{Rx})}{1 + LR^- \cdot \left(\lambda \cdot q_g - c^{Rx}\right)/(\lambda \cdot q_l + c^{Rx})}. \end{aligned} \tag{5.40}
$$

For this threshold to be positive it must hold that $c^t < Sp(\lambda \cdot q_l + c^{Rx})$. Otherwise, treatment is always the dominant strategy.

Compared to the test-treatment threshold in the model without monetary costs, we find:

$$p_m^{tRx} > p^{tRx} = \frac{1}{1 + LR^- q_g/q_l}, \tag{5.41}$$

provided that $c^t < (1 - Se)c^{Rx}$. This inequality, comparing the testing cost with the savings in treatment cost with a false-negative test outcome, will in most cases hold. Thus, the test-treatment threshold also increases when we take into account the cost of testing and treatment.

Furthermore, we can carry out comparative statics, by analyzing the effects of parameter changes on the two thresholds. First, we analyze the effect of an increase in the cost of testing on the two thresholds:

$$\frac{\partial p_m^t}{\partial c^t} = \frac{1}{(1 - Sp)(\lambda \cdot q_l + c^{Rx}) + Se\left(\lambda \cdot q_g - c^{Rx}\right)} > 0, \tag{5.42}$$

$$\frac{\partial p_m^{tRx}}{\partial c^t} = \frac{-1}{Sp(\lambda \cdot q_l + c^{Rx}) + (1 - Se)\left(\lambda \cdot q_g - c^{Rx}\right)} < 0. \tag{5.43}$$

Assuming that $\lambda \cdot q_g > c^{Rx}$ (otherwise the net benefit of treatment would be negative and no treatment would always be the dominant strategy), both equations confirm the result of the last section that the cost involved in testing decreases the a priori probability of the illness range where testing is indicated.

Next, we study the effect of an increase in the treatment cost. Here one finds:

$$\frac{\partial p_m^t}{\partial c^{Rx}} = \frac{(1 - Sp)Se \cdot \lambda\left(q_g + q_l\right) + (Sp + Se - 1)c^t}{\left((1 - Sp)(\lambda \cdot q_l + c^{Rx}) + Se\left(\lambda \cdot q_g - c^{Rx}\right)\right)^2} > 0, \tag{5.44}$$

$$\frac{\partial p_m^{tRx}}{\partial c^{Rx}} = \frac{(1 - Se)Sp \cdot \lambda\left(q_g + q_l\right) + (Sp + Se - 1)c^t}{\left(Sp(\lambda \cdot q_l + c^{Rx}) + (1 - Se)\left(\lambda \cdot q_g - c^{Rx}\right)\right)^2} > 0. \tag{5.45}$$

Given that $Sp + Se > 1$, which is a necessary assumption for a meaningful test, an increase in the cost of treatment increases both the test and the test-treatment thresholds. Thus, the probability of treatment decreases when its cost rises.

Finally, consider the effects of an increase in the willingness to pay for a QALY on the thresholds:

$$\frac{\partial p_m^t}{\partial \lambda} = -\frac{(1-Sp)q_l(Se \cdot c^{Rx} + c^t) + Se \cdot q_g((1-Sp)c^{Rx} + c^t)}{\left((1-Sp)(\lambda \cdot q_l + c^{Rx}) + Se \cdot \left(\lambda \cdot q_g - c^{Rx}\right)\right)^2} < 0, \qquad (5.46)$$

$$\frac{\partial p_m^{tRx}}{\partial \lambda} = -\frac{Sp \cdot q_l((1-Se)c^{Rx} - c^t) + (1-Se)q_g(Sp \cdot c^{Rx} - c^t)}{\left(Sp(\lambda \cdot q_l + c^{Rx}) + (1-Se) \cdot \left(\lambda \cdot q_g - c^{Rx}\right)\right)^2} \gtrless 0. \qquad (5.47)$$

While the test threshold decreases when the willingness to pay for a QALY increases, we do not find a clear-cut answer for the test-treatment threshold. However, if the cost savings of a negative test outcome in the sick state as well as in the healthy state exceeds the cost of the test (i.e., $(1-Se)c^{Rx} > c^t$ and $Sp \cdot c^{Rx} > c^t$)—a condition that should be satisfied in most cases—the test-treatment threshold will then increase with an increase in the willingness to pay for a QALY. Thus, the testing range of the a priori probability of illness most likely widens when willingness to pay for a QALY increases.

The consideration of the monetary cost of test and treatment in the threshold analysis goes beyond the effects of testing and treatment on patient utility. Does this mean that an altruistic physician acting as the patient's agent should not consider monetary costs? To answer this, consider a world where health insurance is absent and patients pay the cost of medical care. In such a world, the costs of testing and treatment would naturally enter into the physician's decision. In the presence of health insurance, patients do not directly pay the cost of medical care. Instead, they pay health insurance premiums, which covers average cost of medical care. This premium, of course, depends on the cost of testing and treatment. In this sense, in an ex ante perspective, patient utility and costs of testing and treatment should enter into the decision calculus as well as inform professional guidelines on testing and treatments.

5.6 Notes

Pauker and Kassirer (1980) developed the threshold analysis. The definition of the value of information, stressing the maximal value of the expected outcome that the decision maker can reach with the aid of the information technology, is from Gould (1974). Weinstein et al. (1980) provide examples of the threshold analysis in different parts of their textbook and Eeckhoudt (2002) analyzes the value of perfect information in detail.

Exercises

1. Prove the rank order of the three thresholds $p^t < p^{Rx} < p^{tRx}$.
2. For the slope of the value of information with respect to the a priori probability of illness Eq. (5.8) leads to

$$\frac{\partial VI}{\partial p} = \begin{cases} Se \cdot g + (1 - Sp)l & \text{for} \quad p < p^{Rx}, \\ -g(1 - Se) - Sp \cdot l & \text{for} \quad p > p^{Rx}. \end{cases}$$

   Compare these slopes for risk-averse and risk-neutral decision makers. What can you say about the conditions that determine the difference between the slopes, given that $g_A > g_N$ and $l_A < l_N$?
3. Assume that there is a specific treatment for an illness from which a sick patient will benefit with 0.4 QALYs. On the other hand, the patient might not actually suffer from the diagnosed illness and experience a loss of 0.1 QALYs from unnecessary treatment. The physician estimates the a priori probability of illness and has to decide whether or not to treat the patient.

   (a) What is the minimal a priori probability of an illness at which the physician should treat the patient?

   A diagnostic test now becomes available to the physician. The test's discriminatory power is given by the sensitivity $Se = 0.6$ and the specificity $Sp = 1$.

   (b) What is the informational value of the test at the treatment threshold?
   (c) Within which range of a priori probabilities is the informational value of the test positive? What does this imply for the physician's decision?
   (d) Use a suitable graph to display the value of information of the test as a function of the a priori probability.

   The physician has initially ignored the fact that the test itself can cause the patient harm. Assume that the harm is equivalent to a mortality risk $l^t = 0.01$ for both the sick and the healthy. Equation (5.8) then changes to

$$VI(p) = \begin{cases} p \cdot Se \cdot g - (1 - p)(1 - Sp)l - l^t & \text{for} \quad 0 \leq p < p^{Rx}, \\ -p \cdot g(1 - Se) + (1 - p)Sp \cdot l - l^t & \text{for} \quad p^{Rx} \leq p \leq 1. \end{cases}$$

   (e) Calculate the treatment threshold, the test and test-treatment thresholds as well as the value of information for the situation in which a harmful test is available.
   (f) Display the situation in a graph.
   (g) How does the treatment decision change?

4. A treatment of an illness increases the patient's utility by 4 QALYs in the sick state, while reducing it by 1 QALY in the healthy state. The willingness to pay

for a QALY is 100 monetary units. A test for detecting the illness has the following characteristics: $Se = 0.8$ and $Sp = 0.6$.

(a) Calculate the treatment, test and test treatment thresholds.

Assume that the respective cost of the test and treatment is 10 and 50 monetary units.

(b) Recalculate the treatment, test and test-treatment thresholds.

5. Assume that there is a perfect diagnostic test and the patient's utility is described by $u(h) = \sqrt{h}$. His four possible health states are $h_s^- = 16$, $h_s^+ = 25$, $h_h^+ = 49$, $h_h^- = 64$.

(a) Calculate the treatment threshold as well as the test and test-treatment thresholds. Calculate the test's value of information at the treatment threshold.
(b) Now assume that the test is invasive and thus involves a potential loss of utility. For simplicity, let this utility loss be constant in all states of the world: $l^t = 0.1$. Calculate the test and test-treatment thresholds.
(c) How do the test and test-treatment thresholds change if the utility loss due to testing increases to $l_s^t = 0.2$ for the sick, but remains at $l_h^t = 0.1$ for the healthy? What is the value of information of this test at the treatment threshold?
(d) Display the situations described in (a), (b) and (c) in a suitable graph.

6. Show that $\tilde{\pi}^{tRx} > \tilde{\pi}^{Rx}$ (see (Eq. 5.22)) and $p_m^{tRx} > p^{tRx}$ (see (Eq. 5.41)).

References

Eeckhoudt, L. (2002). *Risk and medical decision making*. Boston: Kluwer.

Gould, J. P. (1974). Risk, stochastic preference, and the value of information. *Journal of Economic Theory, 8*(1), 64–84.

Pauker, S. G., & Kassirer, J. P. (1980). The threshold approach to clinical decision making. *The New England Journal of Medicine, 302*(20), 1109–1117.

Weinstein, M. C., Fineberg, H. V., Elstein, A. S., Frazier, H. S., Neuhauser, D., Neutra, R. R., et al. (1980). *Clinical decision analysis*. Philadelphia: W.B. Saunders.

Chapter 6
Treatment Decisions Under Comorbidity Risk

The term "prudence" is meant to suggest the propensity to prepare and forearm oneself in the face of uncertainty, in contrast to "risk aversion" which is how much one dislikes uncertainty and would turn away from uncertainty if possible.

Miles S. Kimball[1]

So far, we have assumed that health in the sick state is known with certainty. However, in medicine this might not be the case for several reasons. The disease indicated by a patient's symptoms might be accompanied by other health problems, so that the patient faces a comorbidity risk. In this case, health in the sick state becomes itself a random variable: The health status of a sick patient, h_s^- before and h_s^+ after treatment, is also described by an exogenous risk $\widetilde{m}$ reflecting comorbidity. We assume that $\widetilde{m}$ is a random variable with an expected value of zero: $E[\widetilde{m}] = 0$.

Another interpretation of $\widetilde{m}$ is that it reflects the severity of the (primary) disease. In this case, the efficiency of treatment is assumed to be a function of the initial severity. In order to mitigate the complexity generated by this relationship, we assume that the effect of treatment on health is given and constant. In other words, the treatment of the disease is assumed to have no impact on the presence and the extent of any comorbid conditions.

Our model now includes two different types of risk: The diagnostic risk is still present and can still be addressed by the treatment decision. It is an endogenous risk, since it is affected by the decision maker's choice. In addition, we now have the uncontrollable risk $\widetilde{m}$ which is superposed upon h_s and exogenous to the decision maker.

While $\widetilde{m}$ can be given at least two medical interpretations (comorbidity and severity), economists would use a single term to qualify $\widetilde{m}$, considering it a background risk. This terminology reveals that this additional risk is not affected by the decision maker's behavior. We will see, however, that its presence 'in the

---

[1]Kimball, M.—Precautionary Saving in the Small and in the Large—*Econometrica*, 58(1): 53–73, 1990, p. 54.

© Springer-Verlag GmbH Germany 2017
S. Felder, T. Mayrhofer, *Medical Decision Making*,
DOI 10.1007/978-3-662-53432-8_6

background' has a strong impact on decisions regarding the controllable diagnostic risk.

In this chapter, we study the influence of comorbidities on the physician's treatment decision. In Sect. 6.1, we analyze the effect of prudence on the treatment threshold, dividing the prevalence interval into a 'no treatment' and a 'treatment' range. In Sect. 6.2, we calculate the value of information of a test under comorbidity risk. This allows us to study the impact of prudence on the test threshold and the test-treatment threshold in the final section.

6.1 Prudence and the Treatment Threshold

Figure 6.1 extends the decision tree from Chap. 4 to include a comorbidity risk. The outcomes in the sick state are no longer certain.[2] Instead, $u(h_s^+)$ and $u(h_s^-)$ are replaced by the respective expected utilities $EU(h_s^+ + \widetilde{m})$ and $EU(h_s^- + \widetilde{m})$, where $\widetilde{m}$ is a random variable with $E[\widetilde{m}] = 0$ and variance σ_m^2.

Nothing changes with respect to the utility outcome in the healthy state: Unnecessary treatment leads to a certain utility loss of $l = u(h_h^-) - u(h_h^+) > 0$. By comparison, the utility gain from treatment in the sick state becomes uncertain: $EG_P := EU(h_s^+ + \widetilde{m}) - EU(h_s^- + \widetilde{m}) > 0$, where the index P stands for the presence of prudence.[3]

The decision maker's choice in the situation without a test is still whether to treat or not to treat depending on the a priori probability p. The treatment threshold p_P^{Rx} is the point at which the options 'treatment' and 'no treatment' lead to the same expected utility: $p_P^{Rx} \cdot EG_P = (1 - p_P^{Rx})l$. Solving for p_P^{Rx} gives

$$p_P^{Rx} = \frac{1}{1 + EG_P/l}. \tag{6.1}$$

For a comparison of treatment thresholds with and without comorbidity risk, it is sufficient to consider the respective gains in expected utility from treatment for the sick, g and EG_P, since the utility loss from treatment for the healthy, l, remains unchanged by assumption.

---

[2]Of course, one could also assume that a comorbidity risk impacts all health states, i.e., the sick and the healthy. In this case, prudence is not sufficient for unambiguous results. However, Felder and Mayrhofer (2014) showed that the combination of prudence and temperance (4th order risk aversion) using the concept of risk vulnerability (Gollier and Pratt 1996) also leads to the same qualitative results as the model that considers comorbidity only for the sick health state.

[3]Prudence is defined as a preference for disaggregating a sure loss and zero-mean background risk. In medical decisions, this means that an individual is more willing to accept an extra risk when his level of health is higher, i.e. the "bad" of an additional risk weighs less with an increase in health. The term prudence (also third-order or downside risk aversion) was introduced by Kimball (1990).

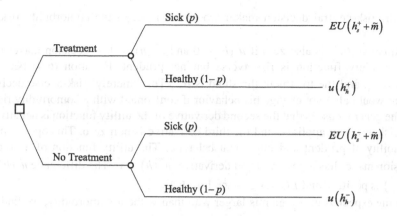

Fig. 6.1 Decision tree under diagnostic and comorbidity risks

In the following, we want to prove that $EG_P > g$ and derive the properties of the utility function that lead to prudent behavior. If $\widetilde{m}$ is a small risk, we can apply a Taylor expansion to approximate $EU(h_s + \widetilde{m})$:

$$EU(h_s + \widetilde{m}) \cong u(h_s) + u'(h_s) \cdot \underbrace{E[\widetilde{m}]}_{0} + \frac{1}{2}u''(h_s) \cdot \underbrace{\{E[\widetilde{m} - E[\widetilde{m}]]\}^2}_{\sigma_m^2}$$

$$\cong u(h_s) + \frac{\sigma_m^2}{2}u''(h_s). \tag{6.2}$$

Applying Eq. (6.2) to the difference in expected utilities between 'treatment' and 'no treatment', EG_P, yields

$$EG_P \cong u(h_s^+) - u(h_s^-) + \frac{\sigma_m^2}{2}\left(u''(h_s^+) - u''(h_s^-)\right)$$

$$\cong g + \frac{\sigma_m^2}{2}\left(u''(h_s^+) - u''(h_s^-)\right) \tag{6.3}$$

and thus

$$EG_P - g = \frac{\sigma_m^2}{2}\left(u''(h_s^+) - u''(h_s^-)\right). \tag{6.4}$$

Since $\sigma_m^2/2$ is positive, the sign of $(EG_P - g)$ is determined by the difference in the second derivatives of the utility function between 'treatment' and 'no treatment' $\left(u''(h_s^+) - u''(h_s^-)\right)$. The sign of this difference is determined by the third derivative of u.

If the decision maker would be risk-neutral, the second derivative of his utility function would be zero, and Eq. (6.4) could be written as $EG_P = g_N$. In this case, neither risk aversion nor prudence apply and the treatment threshold is p_N^{Rx}. Note that the risk-neutral decision maker would not react to the comorbidity risk, as $E[\tilde{m}] = 0$.

Equation (6.4) is also zero if $u''(h) < 0$ and $u'''(h) = 0$. A decision maker with such a utility function is risk-averse but not prudent. Equation (6.4) becomes $EG_P = g_A$, and the treatment threshold is p_A^{Rx}. This 'merely' risk-averse decision maker would also not change his behavior if confronted with a comorbidity risk.

The general case is that the second derivative of the utility function is negative— i.e., risk aversion applies—and the third derivative is non-zero. This opens up the possibility of prudent and imprudent behavior. The utility function of a prudent decision maker has a positive third derivative: $u'''(h) > 0$. The difference $u''\left(h_s^+\right) - u''\left(h_s^-\right)$ is positive and $EG_P > g$ —see Eq. (6.4).

If the expected utility gain is larger with than without comorbidity, we find

$$EG_P > g \Leftrightarrow p_P^{Rx} < p^{Rx} = \frac{1}{1 + g/l}, \tag{6.5}$$

The treatment threshold, then, is reduced by the presence of a comorbidity risk.[4] The order of treatment thresholds for the three types of decision makers is then

$$p_P^{Rx} < p_A^{Rx} < p_N^{Rx}. \tag{6.6}$$

Hence, the prudent physician treats his patients even more often and even earlier than a merely risk-averse physician. Faced with the uncontrollable comorbidity risk, he reacts by adjusting his strategy for the controllable diagnostic risk. He employs a risk-reducing strategy, using the 'treatment' option more often.

Figure 6.2 illustrates the utility function of a prudent decision maker. The upper part of the diagram shows his marginal utility as a function of health, which is positive but decreasing in health. Hence, marginal utility is smaller before than after treatment: $u'\left(h_s^+\right) < u'\left(h_s^-\right)$. The lower part of the diagram displays the second derivative of the utility function and indicates risk aversion. The second derivative has a positive slope; the third derivative of the utility function is thus positive. As can be gleaned from Fig. 6.2, the difference $u''\left(h_s^+\right) - u''\left(h_s^-\right)$ is positive, so that $EG_P > g$.

The convexity of the marginal utility curve illustrates what it means to say that a prudent decision maker fears a downside risk. The change in marginal utility from a small reduction in health is larger than the change in marginal utility from an increase in health. Hence, there is an asymmetry in the marginal valuation of downward and upward shifts in health. Compared to a merely risk-averse decision maker, the prudent one is even keener to prevent the bad outcome.

---

[4]Imprudent behavior, where $u'''(h) < 0$, is also possible; in this case, we have $p_P^{Rx} > p_A^{Rx}$. A further case is that the decision maker is risk-loving ($u'' > 0$) and, depending on the third derivative of his utility function, is also either prudent or imprudent.

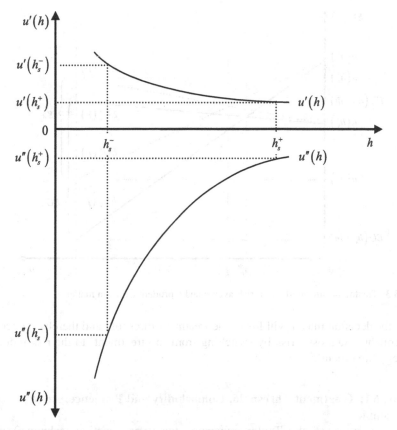

Fig. 6.2 Prudence and the third derivative of the utility function

Figure 6.3 displays the expected utility of a prudent decision maker in the situations with and without comorbidity risk. $EU_P(p)$ is reduced for both 'treatment' and 'no treatment'—note that there is no effect of comorbidity risk on expected utility for $p = 0$. The difference between the expected utility with and without comorbidity risk is increasing in the prevalence rate, reaching the maximum $EG_P - g_A$ at $p = 1$. At the same time, the treatment threshold decreases from p_A^{Rx} to p_P^{Rx}.

Comorbidity and prudence imply that the expected utility of not treating is discounted more strongly with an increasing a priori probability of illness than the expected utility of treating. As a consequence, 'treatment' becomes more attractive at low a priori probabilities and the treatment threshold decreases. The joint presence of exogenous and endogenous risks leads the prudent decision maker (unlike the merely risk-averse decision maker) to decrease the controllable risk even further. While risk aversion indicates a decision maker's preference regarding uncertainty, prudence gives information on how he weighs the endogenous risk against the exogenous risk. Prudent behavior reduces the controllable risk. In our

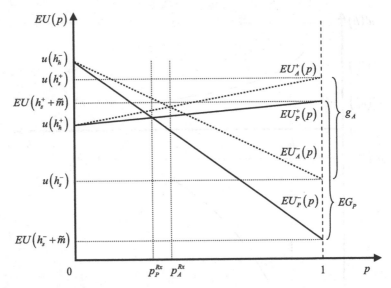

Fig. 6.3 Treatment thresholds for a risk-averse and a prudent decision maker

case, the decision maker will lower the treatment threshold and thereby reduce the controllable diagnostic risk by switching from 'no treatment' to the risk-reducing strategy 'treatment'.

Box 6.1: Treatment Threshold, Comorbidity and Prudence: An Example

So far, we used the Taylor expansion (an approximation technique) to calculate the treatment threshold for risk-averse and prudent decision makers. This requires the exogenous risk to be small. If we know the extent and probability of the risk, it is possible to calculate the treatment threshold directly. The following example is based on Eeckhoudt (2002), pp. 34.

Assume the following health states: $h_s^- = 4$; $h_s^+ = 49$; $h_h^- = 64$; $h_h^+ = 36$.

The decision maker is prudent and his utility function is given by $u(h) = \sqrt{h}$ (note that the second derivative is negative, while the third derivative is positive). Without the background risk, the treatment threshold is

$$p_A^{Rx} = \frac{\sqrt{64} - \sqrt{36}}{\sqrt{49} - \sqrt{4} + \sqrt{64} - \sqrt{36}} = \frac{2}{5 + 2}$$

$$= 0.286 \qquad \text{with } l_A = 2 \text{ and } g_A = 5.$$

Assume now that the decision maker faces a background risk $\tilde{m}$ which takes on the values +3 and −3 with equal probabilities. Since the exogenous

(continued)

> **Box 6.1** (continued)
> risk is only present if the patient is sick, we can recalculate the treatment
> threshold for a risk-averse and prudent decision maker as follows:
>
> $$p_P^{Rx} = \frac{\sqrt{64} - \sqrt{36}}{\left(0.5\left(\sqrt{49+3} + \sqrt{49-3}\right) - 0.5\left(\sqrt{4+3} + \sqrt{4-3}\right)\right) + \sqrt{64} - \sqrt{36}}$$
>
> $$= \frac{2}{5.17 + 2} = 0.279.$$
>
> While the disutility of treatment for the healthy is still $l_A = l_P = 2$, the
> expected utility gain from treatment for the sick increases from $g_A = 5$ to
> $EG_P = 5.17$. Comparing both situations, we can conclude that the back-
> ground risk reduces the treatment threshold, and therefore the point at
> which decision makers who are both risk-averse and prudent will switch
> from 'no treatment' to 'treatment'.

It follows that a mere observation of risk preference is not sufficient to explain a
physician's treatment decision if he is also confronted with comorbidity or a
varying severity of illness. We also need information on the decision maker's
prudence preference to explain his choices.

6.2 Prudence and Test and Treatment Decisions

6.2.1 The Perfect Test

In this section, we analyze how a perfect test affects a decision maker's expected
utility if he is confronted with a background risk. To this end, we compare his
decisions with and without the background risk. Index P marks the situation with
background risk, index A the situation without it. We choose A since the prudent
decision maker is also risk-averse, and without the background risk, only risk
aversion matters. The focus is, then, on the differential effect of prudence on
expected utility and, in turn, on the treatment decision.

The expected utility of the perfect test, as a function of the prevalence rate, for
the prudent individual in the situation with background risk (P) can be written as
follows:

$$EU_P^{pt}(p) = p \cdot EU\left(h_s^+ + \tilde{m}\right) + (1-p)u\left(h_h^-\right). \tag{6.7}$$

For the calculation of the expected utility gain from the test, we again differentiate
between the two probability intervals $\left[p < p_P^{Rx} \,;\, p \geq p_P^{Rx}\right]$, where p_P^{Rx} is the treatment threshold under comorbidity risk. The informational value of the perfect test

$VI_P^p(p)$ equals the difference in expected utility between the situations with and without the test. For $p < p_P^{Rx}$, we calculate

$$
\begin{aligned}
VI_P^p(p)\big|_{p<p_P^{Rx}} &= EU_P^{pt}(p) - EU_P^-(p) \\
&= p \cdot EU\big(h_s^+ + \tilde{m}\big) + (1-p)u\big(h_h^-\big) \\
&\quad - \big[p \cdot EU\big(h_s^- + \tilde{m}\big) + (1-p)u\big(h_h^-\big)\big] \\
&= p\big[EU\big(h_s^+ + \tilde{m}\big) - EU\big(h_s^- + \tilde{m}\big)\big].
\end{aligned}
$$

From Sect. 6.1 we know that $EU(h_s + \tilde{m}) \cong u(h_s) + (\sigma_m^2/2)u''(h_s)$ holds for a small risk $\tilde{m}$. Considering this equation, we obtain

$$
\begin{aligned}
VI_P^p(p)\big|_{p<p_P^{Rx}} &= p\Bigg[\underbrace{u\big(h_s^+\big) - u\big(h_s^-\big)}_{g_A} + \frac{\sigma_m^2}{2}\big[u''\big(h_s^+\big) - u''\big(h_s^-\big)\big]\Bigg] \\
&= p\Bigg[g_A + \frac{\sigma_m^2}{2}\big[u''\big(h_s^+\big) - u''\big(h_s^-\big)\big]\Bigg] = p \cdot EG_P.
\end{aligned}
\tag{6.8}
$$

The expected utility gain from the test is thus larger for $p < p_P^{Rx}$ than $p \cdot g_A$ if $u''' > 0$. The additional term $(\sigma_m^2/2)\big[u''\big(h_s^+\big) - u''\big(h_s^-\big)\big]$ reflects the expected utility gain from treatment due to prudence: The test identifies the sick and spares them the full manifestation of their comorbidity at the low health level which would materialize if they remained untreated.

For $p \geq p_P^{Rx}$, where the physician treats in the situation without a test, we have the familiar equation measuring the expected utility gain from preventing unnecessary treatment of the healthy

$$
VI_P^p(p)\big|_{p>p_P^{Rx}} = (1-p)l_A.
\tag{6.9}
$$

Combining Eqs. (6.8) and (6.9), we obtain the value of information of the test for a prudent decision maker facing a comorbidity risk as a function of the prevalence rate

$$
VI_P^p(p) = \begin{cases} p \cdot EG_P & \text{for} \quad 0 \leq p < p_P^{Rx}, \\ (1-p)l_A & \text{for} \quad p_P^{Rx} \leq p \leq 1, \end{cases}
$$

$$
\text{with } EG_P = \Bigg[g_A + \frac{\sigma_m^2}{2}\big[u''\big(h_s^+\big) - u''\big(h_s^-\big)\big]\Bigg].
\tag{6.10}
$$

Compared to the situation without comorbidity risk, this function is steeper for low a priori probabilities, as $EG_P > g_A$. Correspondingly, in the range of $p < p_P^{Rx}$ the test's informational value is larger for the prudent decision maker if a comorbidity risk is present. In the range where $p > p_P^{Rx}$, the curve and its slope remain unchanged, since a comorbidity risk only concerns the sick.

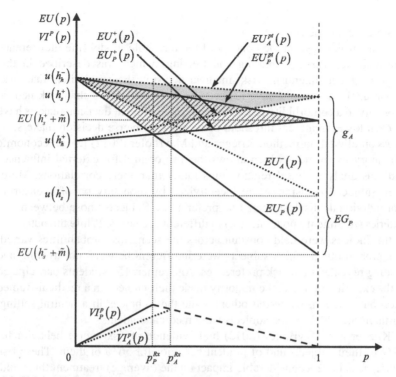

Fig. 6.4 Value of information of a perfect test: The effect of prudence

Figure 6.4 illustrates the effect that prudence has on the informational value of a perfect test. It displays $EU_A^{pt}(p)$ and $EU_P^{pt}(p)$ for the choices 'treatment' and 'no treatment' as well as the values of information $VI_A^p(p)$ and $VI_P^p(p)$ resulting from the difference between the two. It also reveals that the presence of a comorbidity risk reduces expected utility in both situations. The reduction, however, is larger for the 'no treatment' than the 'treatment' option, which is due to the impact of prudence.

Box 6.2: Patient Preferences and Treatment Thresholds—An Empirical Investigation

Several experiments have been implemented to evaluate whether individuals are risk-averse or prudent towards financial risks (for a discussion see Noussair et al. 2014). They confirm that individuals exhibit prudence as well as risk aversion.

However, the question is whether individuals behave similarly when it comes to non-financial risks, e.g., health risks. Krieger and Mayrhofer (2012) attempted to fill this gap by evaluating risk aversion and prudence in medical treatment decisions using an economic laboratory experiment. Their

(continued)

Box 6.2 (continued)

experiment is based on the concept of the threshold model (the indifference threshold between not treating and treating) which was described in this chapter. Under diagnostic risk, medical decision theory predicts that risk-averse decision makers have a lower treatment threshold than risk-neutral ones. Given a comorbidity risk in the sick state, prudent decision makers have an even lower treatment threshold than only risk-averse decision makers.

As an elicitation method Krieger and Mayrhofer (2012) use an economic laboratory experiment which allows them to control for external influences and thus analyze causal relationships rather than mere correlations. Moreover, subjects' decisions were incentivized by monetary payoffs, ensuring that individuals disclose their true preferences. Subjects chose between two lotteries (treatment / no treatment) in different scenarios. While the outcomes of the choices were held constant across the scenarios, probabilities varied. The probability at which subjects were indifferent between not treating and treating revealed their risk preferences. Altogether, 152 students participated in the experiment. Here, the majority made their choices in a medical-framed decision situation, while the others made their choices in a neutral setting. Furthermore, 20 % of the subjects were medical students.

Krieger and Mayrhofer (2012) find evidence of risk-averse behavior for 83 % of their subjects and of prudent behavior for 56 % of them. These risk preferences have a considerable impact on the (average) treatment threshold, reducing it by 41 % relative to the risk-neutral position. Risk aversion accounted for three quarters of this effect, and prudential behavior for one quarter. They found that the medical framing of the decision does not affect second-order risk preferences, but that it is associated with more frequent and stronger prudent behavior. Medical students, however, did not have divergent risk preferences.

In summary, Krieger and Mayrhofer (2012) revealed that risk aversion and prudence preferences also exist with regard to medical decisions. Thus, theoretical and empirical findings show the importance of integrating information on risk preferences for medical treatment recommendations and diagnostic technologies that is based on preference data. This implies that, for instance, clinical guidelines might need to be revisited and adjusted to account for risk preferences and comorbidity risks.

6.2.2 The Imperfect Test

If comorbidity is taken into account, the familiar decision tree for an imperfect test from Chap. 5 changes as illustrated in Fig. 6.5.

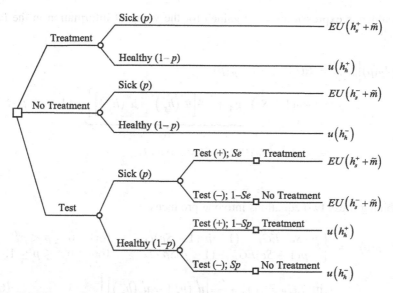

Fig. 6.5 Decision tree for an imperfect test under comorbidity risk

Given a comorbidity risk, the utility of the sick state changes from a certain to an uncertain value featuring the exogenous random variable $\tilde{m}$. By comparison, the utility in the healthy state remains constant and deterministic.

A prudent decision maker has the following expected value of information from an imperfect test:

$$EU_P^t(p) = p\left[Se \cdot EU\left(h_s^+ + \tilde{m}\right) + (1 - Se)EU\left(h_s^- + \tilde{m}\right)\right]$$
$$+(1 - p)\left[Sp \cdot u\left(h_h^-\right) + (1 - Sp)u\left(h_h^+\right)\right]. \tag{6.11}$$

The informational value of the test $VI_P(p)$ equals the difference in expected utility between the situations with and without a test. For $p < p_P^{Rx}$ and substituting

$$EU(h_s + \tilde{m}) \cong u(h_s) + \frac{\sigma_m^2}{2}u''(h_s)$$

we find

$$VI_P(p)\Big|_{p<p_P^{Rx}} = EU_P^t(p) - EU_P^-(p)$$

$$= p \cdot Se \underbrace{\left[g_A + \frac{\sigma_m^2}{2}\left[u''\left(h_s^+\right) - u''\left(h_s^-\right)\right]\right]}_{EG_P} -(1 - p)(1 - Sp)l_A$$

$$= p \cdot Se \cdot EG_P - (1 - p)(1 - Sp)l_A. \tag{6.12}$$

An analogous expression can be gained for the value of information in the range $p \geq p_P^{Rx}$:

$$VI_P(p)\big|_{p>p_P^{Rx}} = EU_P^t(p) - EU_P^+(p)$$

$$= -p(1 - Se) \underbrace{\left[g_A + \frac{\sigma_m^2}{2} \left[u''(h_s^+) - u''(h_s^-) \right] \right]}_{EG_P} + (1-p)Sp \cdot l_A$$

$$= -p(1 - Se)EG_P + (1-p)Sp \cdot l_A.$$

$$(6.13)$$

Combining these two equations into one produces

$$VI_P(p) = \begin{cases} p \cdot Se \cdot EG_P - (1-p)(1-Sp)l_A & \text{for} \quad 0 \leq p < p_P^{Rx}, \\ -p(1 - Se)EG_P + (1-p)Sp \cdot l_A & \text{for} \quad p_P^{Rx} \leq p \leq 1, \end{cases}$$

$$\text{with } EG_P = \left[g_A + \frac{\sigma_m^2}{2} \left[u''(h_s^+) - u''(h_s^-) \right] \right].$$

$$(6.14)$$

If we compare Eq. (6.14) with the test's value of information without the comorbidity risk, the difference $u''(h_s^+) - u''(h_s^-)$ is again decisive in determining whether or not the expected utility gain from the test increases under comorbidity risk. If the decision maker is prudent, the third derivative of u is positive, and thus $(u''(h_s^+) - u''(h_s^-)) > 0$. Hence, the expected utility gain from treatment for the sick $(EG_P > g_A)$ is larger with, than without, comorbidity risk. This result determines the impact of the background risk on the value of information—see Eq. (6.14). For $p < p_P^{Rx}$, as with the perfect test, the value of information increases if the background risk is present $(VI_P(p) > VI_A(p))$. In contrast to the perfect test, though, there is also an impact of the background risk at high prevalence levels: for $p \geq p_P^{Rx}$ the value of information decreases $(VI_P(p) < VI_A(p))$. The reason is that a false negative test outcome involves an expected utility loss due to the prudence motive which does not occur if all subjects undergo treatment.

These considerations have consequences for the test range, i.e., for the test and test-treatment thresholds. Without the comorbidity risk, the test threshold is[5]

$$p_A^t = \frac{1}{1 + LR^+(g_A/l_A)},$$

where $LR^+ = Se/(1 - Sp)$ is the positive likelihood ratio. If the comorbidity risk is present, we have

---

[5]The test and test-treatment thresholds can be found by setting the value of information in the two arms of Eq. (6.14) equal to zero and solving for p.

$$p_P^t = \frac{1}{1 + LR^+(EG_P/l_A)}$$

with $EG_P > g_A$, which in turn implies

$$p_P^t < p_A^t. \tag{6.15}$$

Accordingly, for the test-treatment threshold, with $LR^- = (1 - Se)/Sp$ as the negative likelihood ratio, we find: $p_A^{tRx} = \frac{1}{1+LR^-(g_A/l_A)}$ without and $p_P^{tRx} = \frac{1}{1+LR^-(EG_P/l_A)}$ with background risk.

Again, from $EG_P > g_A$ it follows that the test-treatment threshold decreases in the presence of the comorbidity risk:

$$p_P^{tRx} < p_A^{tRx}. \tag{6.16}$$

Similar to the effect of risk aversion on the test and test-treatment thresholds, we observe a leftward shift in the test-threshold range for a prudent decision maker facing comorbidity risk. This leads to more treatments, not only because of the leftward shift in the test-treatment threshold, but also because of the decision maker's earlier tests. Hence, prudence reinforces the decision maker's willingness to test and treat early.

For the perfect test, we have already established that the comorbidity risk increases the slope of the value of information curve at low rates of prevalence. This result also holds for the imperfect test:

$$\frac{\partial VI_P(p) - \partial VI_A(p)}{\partial p}\bigg|_{p<p_P^{Rx}} = Se[EG_P - g_A] > 0 \quad \text{for } u''' > 0. \tag{6.17}$$

For the upper range of a priori probabilities, $p \geq p_A^{Rx}$, we have

$$\frac{\partial VI_P(p) - \partial VI_A(p)}{\partial p}\bigg|_{p\geq p_A^{Rx}} = -(1 - Se)[EG_P - g_A] < 0 \quad \text{for } u''' > 0. \tag{6.18}$$

Hence, unlike the case of the perfect test, comorbidity risk affects the slope of the informational value curve at high rates of prevalence as well. The steeper curve can be explained by the increased utility loss from false-positive cases.

Figure 6.6 summarizes the impact of comorbidity risk on the test's informational value.

The treatment threshold decreases if comorbidity is present and the decision maker is prudent $(p_P^{Rx} < p_A^{Rx})$. The same result holds for the test threshold $(p_P^t < p_A^t)$ and the test-treatment threshold $(p_P^{tRx} < p_A^{tRx})$. At the same time, the utility gain increases more sharply in the lower prevalence interval $p < p_P^{Rx}$ and in the upper interval $p > p_A^{Rx}$. We conclude that the comorbidity risk reduces all

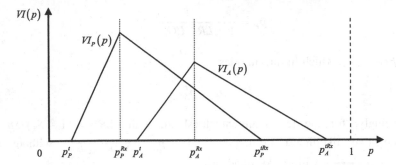

Fig. 6.6 Value of information of an imperfect test: The impact of comorbidity risk

thresholds. A prudent physician will thus test and treat more often than his colleagues who are either merely risk-averse or risk-neutral.

6.3 Prudence and the Therapeutic Risk

In Chap. 4, we analyzed the therapeutic risk and derived the success probability threshold where the physician is indifferent between treatment and no treatment. We then showed that risk aversion increases this threshold. The intuition for this result is that a risk-averse physician values the ratio between the utility gain from a successful treatment and the utility loss from a failed treatment (s/f) less than a risk-neutral physician. Now, one might expect that this ratio will become even less important when the physician is prudent. This, however, is not necessarily the case, as we will now show.

We start with the initial situation characterized in Chap. 4 where the physician knows for certain that the patient is sick and expects a probability of successful treatment equal to π. We now add a comorbidity risk. This background risk is independent of whether the patient undergoes treatment or not.

The expected utility from treatment is then

$$EU^+(\pi) = \pi \cdot EU\left(h_s^{+s} + \widetilde{m}\right) + (1 - \pi)EU\left(h_s^{+f} + \widetilde{m}\right). \qquad (6.19)$$

If $\widetilde{m}$ is a small risk, we can apply a Taylor expansion to approximate the expected utility of treatment:

$$EU^+(\pi) \cong \pi\left[u\left(h_s^{+s}\right) + \frac{\sigma_m^2}{2}u''\left(h_s^{+s}\right)\right] + (1 - \pi)\left[u\left(h_s^{+f}\right) + \frac{\sigma_m^2}{2}u''\left(h_s^{+f}\right)\right]. \qquad (6.20)$$

Similarly, the expected utility of 'no treatment'', if a comorbidity risk is present, can be approximated by

$$EU^-\left(h_s^- + \tilde{m}\right) \cong u(h_s^-) + \left(\sigma_m^2/2\right) \cdot u''\left(h_s^-\right). \qquad (6.21)$$

The difference in expected utilities between 'treatment' and 'no treatment' yields

$$EU^+(\pi) - EU^-(\pi) \cong \pi\left[u\left(h_s^{+s}\right) - u\left(h_s^-\right) + \frac{\sigma_m^2}{2}u''\left(h_s^{+s}\right) - \frac{\sigma_m^2}{2}\cdot u''\left(h_s^-\right)\right]$$

$$+ (1-\pi)\left[u\left(h_s^{+f}\right) - u\left(h_s^-\right) + \frac{\sigma_m^2}{2}u''\left(h_s^{+f}\right) - \frac{\sigma_m^2}{2}\cdot u''\left(h_s^-\right)\right]$$

$$\cong \pi\left[s + \frac{\sigma_m^2}{2}\left(u''\left(h_s^{+s}\right) - u''\left(h_s^-\right)\right)\right]$$

$$- (1-\pi)\left[f + \frac{\sigma_m^2}{2}\left(u''\left(h_s^-\right) - u''\left(h_s^{+f}\right)\right)\right]$$

$$\cong \pi ES_P - (1-\pi)EF_P,$$

$$(6.22)$$

where $ES_P = s + \left(\sigma_m^2/2\right) \cdot \left(u''\left(h_s^{+s}\right) - u''\left(h_s^-\right)\right)$ is the expected utility gain if the treatment is successful, and $EF_P = f + \left(\sigma_m^2/2\right) \cdot \left(u''\left(h_s^-\right) - u''\left(h_s^{+f}\right)\right)$ is the expected utility loss if treatment fails.

With a prudent decision maker, the third derivative of the utility function is positive. Then, as $h_s^{+s} > h_s^-$, we have $ES_P > s$ and, as $h_s^{+f} < h_s^-$, $EF_P > f$.

To find the success probability threshold π_P^{Rx}, we set the difference in Eq. (6.22) equal to zero and derive:

$$\pi_P^{Rx} = \frac{1}{1 + ES_P/EF_P}. \qquad (6.23)$$

The threshold from Chap. 4 is $\pi^{Rx} = 1/(1 + s/f)$. Thus, prudence increases the threshold provided that $ES_P/EF_P < s/f$. This will be the case if $u''\left(h_s^{+s}\right) - u''\left(h_s^-\right) > u''\left(h_s^-\right) - u''\left(h_s^{+f}\right)$. This condition requires concavity of the second derivative of the utility function. Hence, if $u''' > 0$ and $u^{iv} < 0$, we have $\pi_P^{Rx} > \pi^{Rx}$.

An individual with a utility function that has positive signs for uneven derivatives and negative signs for even derivatives is defined to be mixed risk-averse (Brocket and Golden 1987, and Caballé and Pomansky 1996). Such an individual would be more reluctant to undergo a risky treatment compared to an individual who is merely risk-averse.

6.4 Notes

Kimball (1990) introduced the notion of prudence in a paper on precautionary savings. Eeckhoudt and Kimball (1992) apply it to insurance demand in the presence of background risk. We draw heavily from Eeckhoudt (2002), who analyze the consequences of comorbidity risk for the treatment decision without diagnostic tests in Chap. 3.

Exercises

1. Assume the health states $h_s^- = 2; h_s^+ = 8; h_h^- = 20; h_h^+ = 16$, where '+' indicates 'treatment' and '−' indicates 'no treatment', and h and s respectively denote the healthy and the sick states. The decision maker has the following utility function: $u(h) = 20h - 0.5h^2$.

   (a) Calculate the treatment threshold.
   (b) Now assume a comorbidity risk $\tilde{m}$ under which the outcomes -1 and $+1$ occur with equal probability. Calculate the new threshold and comment.

2. Returning to the example in Box 6.1: Consider a perfect diagnostic test with $Se = Sp = 1$.

   (a) Calculate the value of information at the treatment thresholds (with and without comorbidity).
   (b) Plot the value of information against the prevalence for both situations and comment on the results.

   Now assume a diagnostic test with a sensitivity of 0.8 and a specificity of 0.7.

   (c) How do the treatment thresholds (with and without comorbidity) compare to (a)?
   (d) Calculate the test and test-treatment thresholds for situations with and without comorbidity.
   (e) Plot the value of information against the prevalence for both situations with and without comorbidity and comment.

3. Draw the expected utility diagram—analogous to Fig. 6.3—for a decision maker whose third derivative of the utility function is (a) zero and (b) negative. What can you say with respect to the treatment threshold with and without comorbidity?

References

Brocket, P. L., & Golden, L. L. (1987). A class of utility functions containing all the common utility functions. *Management Science, 33*(8), 955–964.

Caballé, J., & Pomansky, A. (1996). Mixed risk aversion. *Journal of Economic Theory, 71*(2), 485–513.

Eeckhoudt, L. (2002). *Risk and medical decision making*. Boston: Kluwer.

Eeckhoudt, L., & Kimball, M. (1992). Background risk, prudence and the demand for insurance. In G. Dionne (Ed.), *Contributions to insurance economics* (pp. 239–254). Boston: Kluwer.

Felder, S., & Mayrhofer, T. (2014). Risk preferences: Consequences for test and treatment thresholds and optimal cutoffs. *Medical Decision Making, 34*, 33–41.

Gollier, C., & Pratt, J. W. (1996). Risk vulnerability and the tempering effect of background risk. *Econometrica, 64*(5), 1109–1123.

Kimball, M. (1990). Precautionary saving in the small and in the large. *Econometrica, 58*(1), 53–73.

Krieger, M., & Mayrhofer, T. (2012). *Patient preferences and treatment thresholds under diagnostic risk—an economic laboratory experiment*. Ruhr Economic Papers No. 321.

Noussair, C. N., Trautmann, S. T., & van de Kuilen, G. (2014). Higher order risk attitudes, demographics, and financial decisions. *Review of Economic Studies, 81*(1), 325–355.

Chapter 7
Optimal Strategy for Multiple Diagnostic Tests

The spirit of decision analysis is divide and conquer.

Howard Raiffa[1]

So far, we have analyzed the use of a single diagnostic test and derived thresholds for the a priori probability of illness at which the test enters and exits the optimal choice set. In practice, decision makers often have a choice of several tests which they can apply individually or in combination. A physician can use a sequential testing strategy by applying one test first and another test second to confirm either positive or negative results from the first test. The alternative strategy is to use tests simultaneously. This is called parallel testing.

In this chapter, we analyze the situation where two tests (that are independent of each other) are available and can be combined in different ways. The optimal test strategy depends on the following four questions: First, is it better to use one test or two tests? Second, if two tests are performed, which positivity criterion should be applied for the composite test: conjunctive (positive if the results of both tests are positive, negative in all other cases) or disjunctive (negative if the results of both tests are negative, positive in all other cases)? Third, should the two tests be applied sequentially or simultaneously? Fourth, if tests are performed sequentially, in which order should they be used? This chapter provides answers to all these questions.

Section 7.1 analyzes the choice between two individual, dichotomous diagnostic tests. We derive an a priori probability of an illness at which point the decision maker is indifferent between the two tests and study the effect of both successive and parallel tests on the test and test-treatment thresholds. The optimal choice can be illustrated by means of level curves for the values of information provided by

---

[1]Raiffa, H.—*Decision Analysis: Introductory lectures on choices under uncertainty*—Addison-Wesley Publishing Company, Reading, Massachusetts—1968, p. 271.

© Springer-Verlag GmbH Germany 2017

S. Felder, T. Mayrhofer, *Medical Decision Making*,

DOI 10.1007/978-3-662-53432-8_7

each test in a 1×1 square which has sensitivity marked on the vertical axis and 1 minus specificity marked on the horizontal axis.

Section 7.2 deals with the combination of two tests in either a sequential or a parallel procedure. The main point made here is that the choice of the so called positivity criterion, determining how to deal with two possibly diverging outcomes, is crucial.

Section 7.3 shows the consequences of the composite test strategy on the test and test-treatment thresholds. Having multiple tests available, each with discriminatory power, increases the a priori probability interval within which testing is indicated.

Section 7.4 considers potential harm that tests may cause. It shows that sequential and parallel testing have different effects on the informational value of test strategies, as does the order in which sequential tests are applied. Section 7.5 shows that if harm from testing is considered, sequential tests always dominate parallel testing.

Section 7.6 closes with an incremental analysis of the use of multiple tests. We demonstrate that if the use of scarce medical resources provides a shadow value, the criterion of maximum informational value is not sufficient to warrant testing. Rather, considering the monetary costs of testing and treatment the corresponding additional monetized net utility must exceed the additional costs in order to justify the employment of a test strategy.

7.1 Choosing Among Two Tests

In medical practice, a physician often has the choice of several tests to diagnose a certain illness. The rational physician will compare the value of information that each test provides (perhaps taking into account the possible harm from testing) and choose the test with the better value. For the time being, we abstract from the cost of or the harm from testing and focus on the informational characteristics of the test.

For the expected value of information as a function of the a priori probability of an illness we have

$$VI(p) = \begin{cases} p \cdot Se \cdot g - (1-p)(1-Sp)l & \text{for} \quad 0 \leq p < p^{Rx}, \\ -p \cdot g(1-Se) + (1-p)Sp \cdot l & \text{for} \quad p^{Rx} \leq p \leq 1. \end{cases} \quad (5.8)$$

This indicates that the informational value increases if either the sensitivity or the specificity increases: $\partial VI(p)/\partial Se = p \cdot g > 0$ or $\partial VI(p)/\partial Sp = (1-p)l > 0$. Hence, a test that performs better with respect to one of these two measures and which, at the same time, does not perform worse with respect to the other measure compared to another test is dominant and should be preferred.

In general, a test is unlikely to be dominant over its alternatives, but will usually perform better regarding one measure and worse regarding the other; i.e., it will have a higher sensitivity and lower specificity, or vice versa. The relative performance of the alternative tests will then differ across the a priori probability of an illness range. The difference between the informational values of two tests is formulated in Eq. (5.8):

$$VI_1(p) - VI_2(p) = p(Se_1 - Se_2)g + (1-p)(Sp_1 - Sp_2)l. \qquad (7.1)$$

This enables us to derive the a priori probability of an illness at which the decision maker will be indifferent between two available tests:

$$p_{1;2}^t = \frac{1}{1 + \frac{Se_1 - Se_2}{Sp_2 - Sp_1} \cdot \frac{g}{l}} \qquad (7.2)$$

Not surprisingly, it is the tests' relative discriminatory power together with the gains g and losses l of treatment which determine the indifference point between the two tests.

Figure 7.1 compares the informational value of two tests, where test 1 has a higher specificity but lower sensitivity than test 2. Its higher specificity gives test 1 an advantage at low a priori probabilities. At higher probabilities the higher sensitivity of test 2 is weighted more heavily, rendering it the preferred choice. At $p = p_{1;2}^t$ the decision maker is indifferent as to which test to apply. Equation (7.2) reveals that only one indifference point exists; i.e., $VI_1(p)$ and $VI_2(p)$ intersect only once in the a priori probability interval.

There is an alternative way to present the choice between two tests, which will also be useful for the analysis of sequential tests. Figure 7.2 displays the two tests, T_1 and T_2, in a unity square with sensitivity on the vertical axis and $(1 - \text{specificity})$ on the horizontal axis. For each test i, the slope of the ray from the origin to T_i equals the positive likelihood ratio $LR_i^+ = Se_i/(1 - Sp_i)$, while the slope of the ray from the corner $(0,1)$ to T_i shows the negative likelihood ratio, $LR_i^- = (1 - Se_i)/S$ p_i. We note that test 1 has more discriminatory power for separating the sick and the healthy by means of a positive test outcome $(LR_1^+ > LR_2^+)$, whereas test 2 is better at separating the two sub-populations using a negative outcome $(LR_2^- < LR_1^-)$.

The relative discriminatory power of the two tests is given by the slope of the line joining T_1 and T_2:

$$\tan \alpha = \frac{Se_2 - Se_1}{(1 - Sp_2) - (1 - Sp_1)} = \frac{Se_1 - Se_2}{Sp_2 - Sp_1}. \qquad (7.3)$$

The angle α also determines the a priori probability of an illness at which the decision maker is indifferent between the two tests $p_{1;2}^t$; see Eq. (7.2). If $\alpha > 45°$, then $\tan \alpha > 1$, which in turn implies that $p_{1;2}^t$ is smaller than the treatment threshold $p^{Rx} = 1/(1 + g/l)$. Such a situation is displayed in Fig. 7.1. By contrast, if $\alpha < 45°$, the a priori probability of an illness at which two tests are equivalent lies beyond the treatment threshold: $p_{1;2}^t > p^{Rx}$. In order to find the preferred test, we add level curves for the value of information to the $(Se, 1 - Sp)$ square. They represent

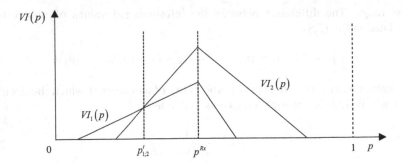

Fig. 7.1 Comparing the informational value of two tests

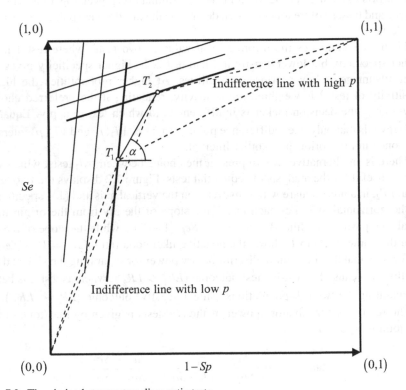

Fig. 7.2 The choice between two diagnostic tests

the geometric loci of sensitivities and specificities at which the informational value
of testing is constant. They could also be considered indifference curves, as the
physician is indifferent between the alternative tests, characterized by
corresponding sensitivities and specificities.

The level curves can be derived by setting the total differential of the value of information Eq. (5.8) equal to zero:

$$dVI = 0 = \frac{\partial VI}{\partial Se}dSe + \frac{\partial VI}{\partial(1 - Sp)}d(1 - Sp). \tag{7.4}$$

From Eq. (5.8), we obtain $\partial VI(p)/\partial Se = p \cdot g$ and $\partial VI(p)/\partial(1 - Sp) = -(1 - p)$ l. Inserting these expressions into Eq. (7.4) and transforming yields

$$\frac{dSe}{d(1 - Sp)} = \frac{(1 - p)l}{p \cdot g} = \frac{1}{\Omega \cdot (g/l)} > 0. \tag{7.5}$$

For given utility gains g and losses l and a given a priori probability of an illness, Eq. (7.5) provides the slope of the level curves for the value of information. The slope of these curves is positive, as $g, l > 0$. The further NW a level curve lies, the higher is the value of information. This orientation reflects the fact that the value of information is increasing in sensitivity and specificity. The maximum value of information would be achieved by a perfect test, which is situated at the (1,0) corner of the square.

The slope of the level curves for the value of information is decreasing in g and p, while increasing in l. At low a priori probabilities of an illness, the specificity of a test is more important, as the healthy should be detected and spared unnecessary treatment. At high a priori probabilities, the focus shifts towards the sensitivity of the test so as to ensure treatment of the sick. A high g gives more weight to the sensitivity, while a high l tends to favour tests with high specificity.

A comparison of Eqs. (7.5) and (7.3) determines the preferred test. Figure 7.2 displays two sets of level curves in a situation where one test is preferred over the other. The case with flat level curves represents a high a priori probability situation, while steep level curves indicate low probabilities.

The test which, in terms of the value of information level curves, lies closest to the corner (1,0) is the preferred test. In our example, test 1 dominates under low a priori probabilities (steep curves), and test 2 is preferred under high a priori probabilities (flat curves). A perfect test would always be preferred, irrespective of the a priori probabilities of illness and the g/l ratio.

Taking potential harm from testing into account does not fundamentally change the analysis of the preferred test. In particular, the technology set represented by points T_1 and T_2 remains constant. What does change is the slope of the indifference curves. Side effects of testing affect a patient's health status, which is the argument of his utility function. By contrast, the discriminatory power of the available tests makes up the restriction function for the decision maker's choice.

7.2 Combining Two Tests

If two tests are combined, a positivity criterion for the composite test must be defined. The criterion can be either conjunctive or disjunctive. A conjunctive positivity criterion implies that the outcome of the composite test is positive if both tests are positive, and negative in all other cases. A disjunctive positivity criterion implies that the outcome of a composite test is negative if both individual tests are negative, and positive in all other cases. Under the conjunctive positivity criterion, the decision maker treats the patient only if both tests are positive, while under the disjunctive positivity criterion he treats always except in the case of two negative results (see Table 7.1).

Given a sequential test strategy and a conjunctive positivity criterion, the second test is only performed if the first provides a positive result. Using the disjunctive positivity criterion in this case, the second test is only applied to patients with a negative result in the first test. The informational content of a composite test is independent of whether testing is parallel or sequential; this only matters if testing itself is harmful. Under parallel testing, patients are subject to harm from both tests, while the sequential test spares some patients harm from the second test.

Table 7.2 shows the sensitivity, the specificity and the likelihood ratio of the composite tests. Under the conjunctive positivity criterion, the composite test leads to a decrease in the sensitivity as compared to the individual tests. This is because some of the true positive cases in the one test become false negative cases in the other test. On the other hand, total specificity is increased by the composite test, since some false positive cases in one test turn into true negative cases in the other test.

Under the disjunctive positivity criterion, the combination of tests increases sensitivity and decreases specificity. The specificity falls as some of the true negative cases in one test will be false positive cases in the other test. Sensitivity

Table 7.1 Conjunctive and disjunctive composite tests

		Positivity criterion			
		Conjunctive		Disjunctive	
	Test 2	+	−	+	−
Test 1	+	Treatment	No treatment	Treatment	Treatment
	−	No treatment	No treatment	Treatment	No treatment

Table 7.2 Sensitivity, specificity and likelihood ratio of the composite test

	Positivity criterion	
	Conjunctive	Disjunctive
Sensitivity	$Se_1 \cdot Se_2$	$1 - (1 - Se_1) \cdot (1 - Se_2)$
Specificity	$1 - (1 - Sp_1) \cdot (1 - Sp_2)$	$Sp_1 \cdot Sp_2$
Likelihood ratio	$LR_1^+ \cdot LR_2^+$	$LR_1^- \cdot LR_2^-$

increases as compared to the individual test as the second test will detect additional true positive cases.

Combining tests increases the discriminatory power of separating the sick from the healthy as compared to the individual tests, given that both tests themselves provide more information than a mere randomized classification of patients, i.e., $Se_i + Sp_i > 1$, and thus $LR_i^+ > 1$ and $0 \leq LR_i^- < 1$ for $i = 1, 2$. Under the conjunctive positivity criterion the positive likelihood ratio increases $(LR_i^+ > 1$ for $i = 1, 2$ implies that $LR_1^+ \cdot LR_2^+ > LR_i^+)$, while under the disjunctive criterion the negative likelihood ratio decreases ($0 \leq LR_i^- < 1$ for $i = 1, 2$ implies that $LR_1^- \cdot LR_2^- < LR_i^-$).

Figure 7.3 plots the information from Table 7.2 in the $(Se, 1 - Sp)$ square. In addition to points T_1 and T_2, which indicate the discriminatory power of the individual tests, we now have points T_c and T_d for the combined test under the conjunctive and disjunctive positivity criteria. The slopes of the respective rays from the corners $(0,0)$ and $(1,1)$ to the four points measure the positive and negative likelihood ratios of the four test strategies. The composite tests have increased discriminatory power, as the positive likelihood ratio rises for the conjunctive

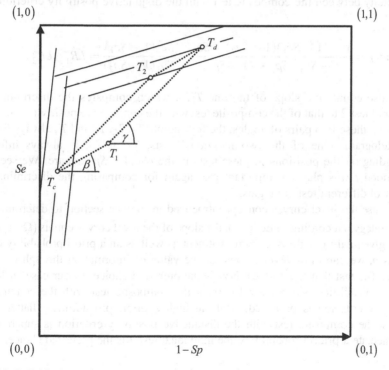

Fig. 7.3 Individual and composite tests in the $(Se, 1 - Sp)$ diagram

positivity criterion, and the negative likelihood ratio falls for the disjunctive positivity criterion compared to the individual tests (see Table 7.2). Hence, if multiple tests are available—each of which having discriminatory power—the combination of the tests enlarges the set of efficient test strategies (the efficient[2] set is $\{T_1, T_2\}$ without and $\{T_c, T_2, T_d\}$ with composite tests).

In Fig. 7.3 $\tan \beta$ yields the slope of the line $T_c T_1$, i.e., the ratio of the changes in sensitivity and specificity between the composite test with the conjunctive positivity criterion and test 1. We find

$$
\tan \beta = \frac{Se_1 - Se_1 \cdot Se_2}{(1 - Sp_1) - 1 - (1 - Sp_1)(1 - Sp_2)} = \frac{Se_1(1 - Se_2)}{(1 - Sp_1)Sp_2}
$$
$$
= LR_1^+ \cdot LR_2^-. \tag{7.6}
$$

Short inspection reveals that $\tan \beta$ also equals the slope of the line $T_2 T_d$, which compares the discriminatory power of the composite test with the disjunctive positivity criterion (with sensitivity equal to $1 - (1 - Se_1)(1 - Se_2)$ and specificity equal to $Sp_1 \cdot Sp_2$) and test 2.

$\tan \gamma$ is the slope of the line $T_1 T_c$, i.e., the ratio of the changes in sensitivity and specificity between the composite test with the disjunctive positivity criterion and test 1:

$$
\tan \gamma = \frac{1 - (1 - Se_1)(1 - Se_2) - Se_1}{1 - Sp_1 \cdot Sp_2 - (1 - Sp_1)} = \frac{Se_2(1 - Se_1)}{Sp_1(1 - Sp_2)} = LR_1^- \cdot LR_2^+. \tag{7.7}
$$

$\tan \gamma$ also equals the slope of the line $T_c T_2$, which compares the discriminatory power of test 2 to that of the composite test with the conjunctive positivity criterion.

Given these two pairs of angles, the four points T_1, T_2, T_c and T_d always form a parallelogram. One of the two individual tests, T_1 or T_2, is always inferior, depending on the positions of these tests in the $(Se, 1 - Sp)$ square. We see that likelihood ratios play an important role again for comparing the discriminatory power of different test strategies.

We use the level curves concept introduced in the last section to determine the best strategy. According to Eq. (7.5), the slope of the level curves equals $(\Omega \cdot g/l)^{-1}$. For a given gain g and loss l from treatment as well as an a priori probability of an illness p, we can draw level curves for the value of information through the four points. The test that lies furthest NW is the preferred choice. In our case, at low a priori probabilities (steeper level curves) the composite test with the conjunctive positivity criterion is preferred, while at high a priori probabilities (flatter level curves) the composite test with the disjunctive positivity criterion is superior. At intermediate a priori probabilities, the individual test 2 is the preferred choice.

---

[2]A test is (Pareto) efficient if there is no other test that is better than the other in terms of either sensitivity or specificity and that is at the same time not worse than the other.

7.3   Test and Test-Treatment Thresholds for Composite Tests

For the analysis of the test and test-treatment thresholds, we return to an explicit formulation of the value of information. As long as we do not consider the potential harm from or cost of a test, there is no need to differentiate between sequential and parallel procedures. The important point here is which positivity criterion is used.

Assume that the physician starts with test 1. Two options now arise, the expected utility of which we can calculate: The first is to apply test 2 to patients tested positive in test 1 (test c), and the second is to use test 2 for patients with negative results in test 1 (test d). Figures 7.4 and 7.5 present the respective decision trees for the two options.

For the expected utility of the two variants we find

$$
EU_c(p) = p\big[Se_1 \cdot Se_2 \cdot u(h_s^+) + (1 - Se_1 \cdot Se_2)u(h_s^-)\big]
$$
$$
+(1 - p)\big[(1 - Sp_1)(1 - Sp_2)u(h_h^+)
$$
$$
+(1 - (1 - Sp_1)(1 - Sp_2))u(h_h^-)\big] \tag{7.8}
$$

and

$$
EU_d(p) = p\big[(1 - Se_1)(1 - Se_2)u(h_s^-) + (1 - (1 - Se_1)(1 - Se_2))u(h_s^+)\big]
$$
$$
+(1 - p)\big[(1 - Sp_1 \cdot Sp_2)u(h_h^+) + Sp_1 \cdot Sp_2 \cdot u(h_h^-)\big]. \tag{7.9}
$$

Inspection of Eqs. (7.8) and (7.9) clarifies that the expected utility of both test c and test d is not affected by the sequence of their component tests. Hence, the important decision is not which test to use first, but rather along which branch to proceed in the second step. This is, of course, tantamount to choosing a positivity criterion.

To determine the informational value of the sequential tests, we subtract the expected utility of the respective reference case, $p \cdot u(h_s^-) + (1 - p)u(h_h^-)$ for $p < p^{Rx}$ and $p \cdot u(h_s^+) + (1 - p)u(h_h^+)$ for $p \geq p^{Rx}$, from the expected utility of the composite test to obtain

$$
VI_c(p) = \begin{cases} p \cdot Se_1 \cdot Se_2 \cdot g \\ -(1 - p)(1 - Sp_1)(1 - Sp_2)l & \text{for} \quad 0 \leq p < p^{Rx}, \\ \\ -p(1 - Se_1 \cdot Se_2)g \\ +(1 - p)(1 - (1 - Sp_1)(1 - Sp_2))l & \text{for} \quad p^{Rx} \leq p \leq 1. \end{cases} \tag{7.10}
$$

and

$$
VI_d(p) = \begin{cases} p(1 - (1 - Se_1)(1 - Se_2))g \\ -(1 - p)(1 - Sp_1 \cdot Sp_2)l & \text{for} \quad 0 \leq p < p^{Rx}, \\ \\ -p(1 - Se_1)(1 - Se_2)g \\ +(1 - p)Sp_1 \cdot Sp_2 \cdot l & \text{for} \quad p^{Rx} \leq p \leq 1. \end{cases} \tag{7.11}
$$

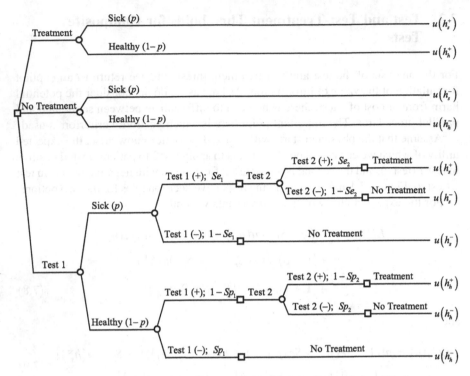

Fig. 7.4 Decision tree for a sequential test (test 2 applied if the first result is positive)

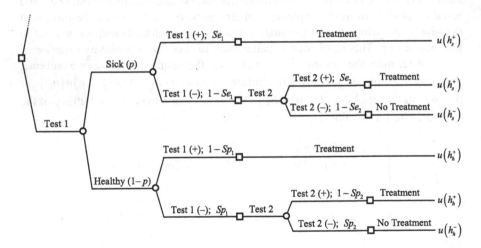

Fig. 7.5 Decision tree for a sequential test (test 2 applied if the first result is negative)

Let us first consider the option with the conjunctive positivity criterion. The lower sensitivity has a negative effect on the value of information: The probability of true positive test results decreases in the lower a priori probability of illness range ($p < p^{Rx}$), and the probability of false negative results increases in the upper a priori probability range ($p \geq p^{Rx}$) as compared to the individual tests. The increased specificity raises the value of information, either because fewer false positive cases occur (than in the reference case 'no treatment') or because of more correct negative results (compared to the reference case 'treatment').

Under the disjunctive positivity criterion, sequential testing reduces total specificity and increases total sensitivity in comparison to the individual tests, with corresponding effects on the value of information: The probability of true positive test results increases in the lower a priori probability range, and the probability of false negative cases decreases in the upper a priori probability range. Compared to the individual tests, this leads to a higher value of information. However, the lower specificity yields a higher probability of false positive cases in the lower a priori probability of illness range ($p < p^{Rx}$) and a lower probability of true negative cases in the upper a priori probability range ($p \geq p^{Rx}$), leading to a lower value of information.

To determine the optimal test strategy, the decision maker must make a choice between either performing a single test or using a composite test—and given he chooses the latter, he must also choose between applying the conjunctive or the disjunctive positivity criterion. This choice will depend on the a priori probability of illness, the relative discriminatory power of the tests, as well as the ratio g/l.

Using Eqs. (7.10) and (7.11), we can calculate the a priori probability of illness at which the decision maker is indifferent between using the composite test (conjunctive or disjunctive) and the individual test (1 or 2)

$$p^t_{1;c} = \frac{1}{1 + LR^+_1 \cdot LR^-_2 \cdot g/l}, \quad p^t_{2;c} = \frac{1}{1 + LR^+_2 \cdot LR^-_1 \cdot g/l}, \quad (7.12)$$

$$p^t_{1;d} = \frac{1}{1 + LR^-_1 \cdot LR^+_2 \cdot g/l}, \quad p^t_{2;d} = \frac{1}{1 + LR^-_2 \cdot LR^+_1 \cdot g/l}. \quad (7.13)$$

The two equations reveal that there are, not four, but only two indifference points in the a priori probability interval: $p^t_{1;c} = p^t_{2;d}$ and $p^t_{1;d} = p^t_{2;c}$. This reflects the fact that the four points in Fig. 7.3 form a parallelogram. The indifference points are larger or smaller than the treatment threshold ($p^{Rx} = 1/(1 + g/l)$) depending on whether the product of the two likelihood ratios in the denominator of the equations is larger or smaller than one. In terms of Fig. 7.3, this condition refers to the size of the angles β and γ. If an angle is larger (smaller) than 45°, its tangent is greater (smaller) than one, which in turn implies that the corresponding indifferent a priori probability of illness is smaller (larger) than the treatment threshold p^{Rx}. In this case, there is always only one a priori probability at which the decision maker is indifferent between two tests. It follows that the two informational value curves only intersect once, a property we have already derived for the comparison of two individual tests.

Box 7.1: An Example of Sequential Testing

Assume two tests are available to the physician. The first has a sensitivity of 70 % and a specificity of 60 %. The sensitivity of the second test is 80 % and the specificity is 90 %. Furthermore, assume that the population to be tested contains 1000 individuals, 25 % of which are sick. Since test 2 is more costly than test 1, the physician will use test 1 for the whole population and test 2 only for a subset of individuals. Assume that he will apply the conjunctive positivity criterion and perform test 2 only on patients with a positive outcome in the first test.

We can present the results of the first test in a 2 × 2 table (see Chap. 2):

		True State		
		Sick	Healthy	Total
Result of test 1	Positive	175	300	475
	Negative	75	450	525
	Total	250	750	1000

In total, 475 people received a positive result in test 1. These individuals are tested again for clarification:

		True State		
		Sick	Healthy	Total
Result of test 2	Positive	140	30	170
	Negative	35	270	305
	Total	175	300	475

The total sensitivity is calculated based on the number of individuals who received correct positive results in both tests:

$$\frac{140}{250} = 0.56 \quad \text{or} \quad Se_1 \cdot Se_2 = 0.7 \cdot 0.8 = 0.56.$$

The total specificity consists of the healthy individuals with a negative result in both test 1 (450) and test 2 (270) divided by the total number of healthy persons (750). The total specificity is therefore:

$$\frac{450 + 270}{750} = 0.96 \quad \text{or} \quad Sp_1 + (1 - Sp_1)Sp_2 = 0.6 + (1 - 0.6) \cdot 0.9 = 0.96.$$

(continued)

Box 7.1 (continued)

The total specificity is thus higher than the specificities of the individual tests, while the total sensitivity is lower than the sensitivities of the individual tests. Hence, the composite test under the conjunctive positivity criterion should be used if the a priori probability of an illness is low and many false positive test results are expected (e.g., in the case of screening).

Let us now analyze the effect of composite testing on the a priori probability of illness thresholds. Under the conjunctive positivity criterion, the test threshold can be calculated based on Eq. (7.10):

$$p_c^t = \frac{1}{1 + LR_c^+ \cdot g/l} \quad \text{with} \quad LR_c^+ = LR_1^+ \cdot LR_2^+. \tag{7.14}$$

Provided that both tests have discriminatory power $(LR_1^+, LR_2^+ > 1)$, $p_c^t < p_1^t, p_2^t$, i.e., the test threshold for the composite test with the conjunctive positivity criterion is lower than for each individual test.

For the disjunctive positivity criterion at low a priori probabilities, Eq. (7.11) leads to

$$p_d^t = \frac{1}{1 + LR_d^+ \cdot g/l} \quad \text{with} \quad LR_d^+ = \frac{1 - (1 - Se_1)(1 - Se_2)}{1 - Sp_1 \cdot Sp_2}. \tag{7.15}$$

It can be shown that $LR_c^+ > LR_d^+ > 1$ [3,4] which implies that $p_c^t < p_d^t < p^{Rx}$. Applying the conjunctive positivity criterion at low a priori probabilities thus also implies a higher informational value than using the disjunctive positivity criterion.

Interestingly, it holds that $p_d^t > p_i^t$ if $LR_i^+ > LR_j^+ \cdot LR_i^-$ for $i, j = 1, 2$ with $i \neq j$. In terms of Fig. 7.3, the slope of the line $T_i T_d$ can be compared to that of LR_i^+ for $i = 1, 2$, i.e., $\tan \gamma$ and $\tan \beta$ with LR_i^+, respectively. In this example, the following inequalities hold: $\tan \gamma < LR_1^+$ and $\tan \beta < LR_2^+$. If test 2 were to dominate test 1 $(Se_2 > Se_1 \text{ and } Sp_2 > Sp_1)$, the inequality would be violated for test 1, which in turn would imply that $p_d^t < p_1^t$.

---

[3] $LR_c^+ - LR_d^+ > 0$ if $Se_1 \cdot Se_2(1 - Sp_1 \cdot Sp_2) - (Se_1 + Se_2 - Se_1 \cdot Se_2)(1 - Sp_1)(1 - Sp_2) > 0$. Transformation leads to $Se_1 \cdot Se_2(1 - Sp_1 + 1 - Sp_2) - (Se_1 + Se_2)(1 - Sp_1)(1 - Sp_2) > 0$. The next step results in $Se_1(1 - Sp_1)(Se_2 + Sp_2 - 1) + Se_2(1 - Sp_2)(Se_1 + Sp_1 - 1) > 0$, which holds true for tests with discriminatory power.

[4] Divide the numerator and denominator of LR_d^+ by the product $Sp_1 \cdot Sp_2$ to obtain $LR_d^+ = (1/Sp_1 \cdot Sp_2 - LR_1^- \cdot LR_2^-)/(1/Sp_1 \cdot Sp_2 - 1)$. As the negative likelihood ratios are smaller than one, the numerator exceeds the denominator, and hence $LR_d^+ > 1$.

Under the disjunctive positivity criterion, the test-treatment threshold—see Eq. (7.11)—becomes

$$p_d^{tRx} = \frac{1}{1 + LR_d^- \cdot g/l} \quad \text{with } LR_d^- = LR_1^- \cdot LR_2^-. \tag{7.16}$$

If both tests have discriminatory power ($LR_1^-, LR_2^- < 1$), $p_d^{tRx} > p_1^{tRx}, p_2^{tRx}$, i.e., the test-treatment threshold of the composite test increases compared to the individual tests.

For the conjunctive positivity criterion at high a priori probabilities, we finally obtain, based on Eq. (7.10), the following test-treatment threshold:

$$p_c^{tRx} = \frac{1}{1 + LR_c^- \cdot g/l} \quad \text{with } LR_c^- = \frac{1 - Se_1 \cdot Se_2}{1 - (1 - Sp_1)(1 - Sp_2)}. \tag{7.17}$$

Here $LR_d^- < LR_c^- < 1$, and thus $p_d^{tRx} > p_c^{tRx} > p^{Rx}$. At high a priori probabilities of illness, the disjunctive positivity criterion is the first choice, as it has the highest sensitivity and thus provides the higher informational value.

The inequality $LR_i^+ > LR_j^+ \cdot LR_i^-$ again determines whether $p_c^{tRx} < p_i^{tRx}$ for $i, j = 1, 2$, $i \neq j$. In the situation displayed in Fig. 7.3, using the sequential test with the positivity criterion at high a priori probabilities does not raise the test-treatment threshold.

Under regular conditions, we thus have the following order of thresholds:

$$p_c^t < p_1^t, p_2^t < p_d^t < p^{Rx} < p_c^{tRx} < p_1^{tRx}, p_2^{tRx} < p_d^{tRx}.$$

We can conclude that an optimal combination of tests extends the a priori of probability range within which testing is indicated. Optimal sequencing of the tests depends on the discriminatory power of the individual tests, as well as on the gains from treatment for the sick and the loss from treatment to the healthy.

For illustration, Fig. 7.6 presents the value of information for two tests (used individually and in combination) with the following characteristics: $Se_1 = 0.7$; $Sp_1 = 0.6$; $Se_2 = 0.8$; $Sp_2 = 0.8$; $g = 4$; $l = 1$. The treatment threshold in this example is 0.2. Test 2 is preferred to test 1 over the whole a priori probability of illness range. Hence, test 1 would never be used on its own. Under composite testing, using only test 2 remains the dominant strategy in the middle range. However, at the edges of the a priori probability range combined testing is advantageous. At lower a priori probabilities of an illness, the gain from composite testing exceeds that from independently administered tests. The decision maker would thus use test 1 on the positive cases from test 2. This strategy increases total specificity; hence, more healthy individuals will be spared unnecessary treatment.

In our example, combined testing primarily shifts the test range to higher a priori probabilities: The test-treatment threshold increases from 0.5 to 0.67, and administering test 2 to test 1-negative cases is indicated above an a priori probability of

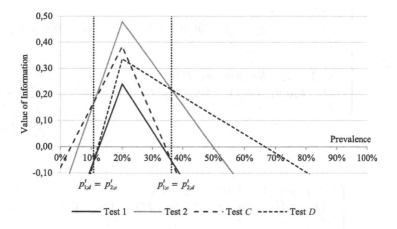

Fig. 7.6 Informational value of a sequential test

0.36. This combination increases total sensitivity: More true positive cases are detected, which is more relevant at higher a priori probabilities.

Figure 7.6 also displays the a priori probabilities at which a decision maker is indifferent between a composite test and an individual test. For comparisons involving test 1, the informational value is negative at the a priori probabilities marking indifference, again due to the relatively poor performance of test 1. This also explains the lower test threshold of test D and the higher test-treatment threshold of test C as compared to test 1.

In Chaps. 5 and 6, we analysed the consequences of risk aversion and higher-order risk preferences for test and test-treatment thresholds. The derived results also apply for the thresholds of composite tests, since they are, like the thresholds of single tests, determined by the ratio between the utility gain in the sick and the utility loss of treatment in the healthy state, g/l. Risk aversion shifts both the test and the test-treatment thresholds of composite tests to the left, and prudence implies an even larger leftward shift of the thresholds.

7.4   The Optimal Sequence of and Potential Harm from Testing

Expanding our analysis to take into account the harm from testing, we assume for simplicity that complications due to testing are independent of the patient's health state: $l_j^i = l_t$ for $i = +, - \; ; j = h, s$. We can derive the informational value of the sequential test from Eqs. (7.10) and (7.11) when the decision maker starts with test 1. Depending on the decision maker's choice of the positivity criterion, we obtain:

$$VI_{1;c}(p) = \begin{cases} p \cdot Se_1(Se_2 \cdot g - l^{t_2}) \\ -(1-p)(1-Sp_1)((1-Sp_2)l + l^{t_2}) & \text{for} \quad 0 \leq p < p^{Rx}, \\ -l^{t_1} \\ \\ -p((1-Se_1 \cdot Se_2)g + Se_1 \cdot l^{t_2}) \\ +(1-p)(Sp_1 \cdot l + (1-Sp_1)(Sp_2 \cdot l - l^{t_2})) & \text{for} \quad p^{Rx} \leq p \leq 1. \\ -l^{t_1} \end{cases}$$

$$(7.18)$$

or

$$VI_{1;d}(p) = \begin{cases} p(Se_1 \cdot g + (1-Se_1)(Se_2 \cdot g - l^{t_2})) \\ -(1-p)((1-Sp_1 \cdot Sp_2)l + Sp_1 \cdot l^{t_2}) & \text{for} \quad 0 \leq p < p^{Rx}, \\ -l^{t_1} \\ \\ -p(1-Se_1)((1-Se_2)g + l^{t_2}) \\ +(1-p)Sp_1(Sp_2 \cdot l - l^{t_2}) & \text{for} \quad p^{Rx} \leq p \leq 1. \\ -l^{t_1} \end{cases}$$

$$(7.19)$$

The first test applies to all patients, while the second test is only used on a subset of patients. Thus, if testing involves harm to the patient, it matters whether the decision maker starts with test 1 or test 2. Ceteris paribus, using the more harmful test first is disadvantageous; hence, we expect the decision maker to begin with the less harmful test (of course this also depends on the test accuracies).

Equations (7.18) and (7.19) reveal that accounting for possible harm from testing affects the optimal order of the sequential test. Comparing the informational value of the sequence variants $VI_{1;c}(p)$ and $VI_{2;c}(p)$ under the conjunctive positivity criterion, we derive the following relationship:

$$VI_{1;c}(p) \underset{<}{\overset{>}{=}} VI_{2;c}(p)$$

$$\Leftrightarrow -l^{t_1} + (p(1-Se_1) + (1-p)Sp_1)l^{t_2} \underset{>}{\overset{<}{=}} -l^{t_2} + (p(1-Se_2) + (1-p)Sp_2)l^{t_1}.$$

$$(7.20)$$

The expressions on the second line compare the expected total harm of the two tests. It includes the certain harm by the use of a particular test i (i.e., $-l^{t_i}$) minus the harm that the patient is spared if the test result is negative, the probability being equal to $p(1-Se_i) + (1-p)Sp_i$. This later reflects the benefits of using this particular test first, since a patient with a negative result will not be subjected to further testing. The difference can be interpreted as the expected net harm of using a particular test first. The lower this difference in absolute terms, due either to a low harm involved using the test or a high probability of a negative outcome, the more likely the test will be used first.

For the sequential test under the disjunctive positivity criterion, we find, accordingly,

$$VI_{1;d}(p) \gtrless VI_{2;d}(p)$$

$$\Leftrightarrow -l^{t_1} + (p \cdot Se_1 + (1-p)(1-Sp_1))l^{t_2} \lessgtr -l^{t_2} + (p \cdot Se_2 + (1-p)(1-Sp_2))l^{t_1}.$$

$$(7.21)$$

This comparison is similar to the one above, except that with the disjunctive criterion the probability of a positive test outcome is decisive, i.e., the probability that the patient will not be subject to the second test, but will instead receive treatment immediately. If a test has a high probability of a negative outcome or the subsequent test is highly harmful, the more likely this test will be used.

It follows from these comparisons that a harmless test should always be used first, provided the informational value of the composite test is positive. Note also that conditions (7.20) and (7.21) hold irrespective of whether the reference case is 'treatment' or 'no treatment' in the situation without testing. Nevertheless, the decision whether to use the second test for positive or negative first results can depend on whether a patient's expected probability of illness is above or below the treatment threshold.

Figures 7.7 and 7.8 take up the example of Fig. 7.6 ($Se_1 = 0.7$; $Sp_1 = 0.6$; $Se_2 = 0.8$; $Sp_2 = 0.8$; $g = 4$; $l = 1$), but assume that test 2 is harmful, while test 1 inflicts no harm ($l^{t_1} = 0$ and $l^{t_2} = 0.4$). Consider first the sequential test starting with the harmless test 1 (see Fig. 7.7). Test 2 is no longer the preferred strategy in the intermediate a priori probability range. In fact, exclusive use of test 2 is always

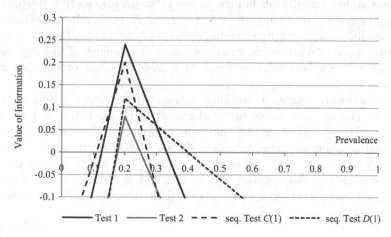

Fig. 7.7 Informational value of a sequential test with a harmful test 2 (starting with test 1)

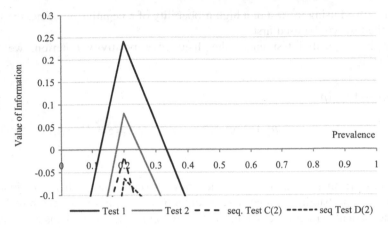

Fig. 7.8 Informational value of a sequential test with a harmful test 2 (starting with test 2)

dominated by either exclusive use of test 1 or by a sequential test. At low a priori probabilities test 2 can be used on patients with a positive first result.

Only at high a priori probabilities should test 2 be used on patients with a negative result in test 1. The increase in total sensitivity, i.e., in the number of true positive cases, justifies the harm incurred by test 2.

The alternative order, i.e., starting with test 2 and continuing with test 1, produces a negative value of information over the whole a priori probability range, irrespective of the positivity criterion applied. As a consequence, a rational decision maker would not perform this test strategy.

Box 7.2: Screening Programs: An Application of Sequential Tests

Preventive screening is by nature carried out under conditions of low prevalence. At low a priori probabilities the loss to healthy patients from treatment weighs more heavily. In this range, decision makers should tolerate decreased sensitivity, i.e., accept a higher number of false negative cases. The advantage of the sequential test is its increased specificity. The number of true negative results will rise and more patients be spared the harm of unnecessary treatment.

An optimally structured screening program will also consider the harm of testing, arising for example in the diagnosis of breast, bowel or prostate cancer. The physician has the choice of non-invasive diagnostics (breast: palpitation, mammography; prostate: palpitation, PSA-test; bowel: stool test) and invasive test methods (breast and prostate: biopsy; bowel: colonoscopy). As invasive diagnostics involve a risk to the patient, they are not used first, but performed only if non-invasive diagnostics produces a positive test result.

(continued)

> **Box 7.2** (continued)
>
> Still, not testing might be the preferred option. One candidate for a 'no test' strategy is prostate cancer, the second leading cause of cancer deaths among men. Prostate cancer is often dormant and the patients elderly. Treatment can be invasive (radical prostatectomy) and produce permanent complications such as impotence and incontinence. Finally, biopsy involves short-term morbidity and screening is costly. Krahn et al. (1994) concluded that screening asymptotic men for prostate cancer is not cost-effective. It may result in poorer health outcomes and will raise costs dramatically.

Note that in the present model risk preferences have no effect on the optimal sequence of tests. This observation, however, is due to the assumption that the harms of the tests do not depend on the actual health state. If an invasive test were more harmful in the sick than in the healthy state and individual tests differed in their invasiveness, risk preferences would clearly have an effect on the sequence of using the tests.

7.5 Parallel or Sequential Testing?

If—as the above analysis has shown—composite tests are to be preferred to individual tests and a positivity criterion has been chosen, it remains to be clarified whether two tests should be applied together (parallel) or one after the other (sequentially). The sequential procedure always leads to less harm on average, because the second test is not necessarily applied. A sequential test therefore dominates parallel testing.

This is easy to prove by comparing the informational value of the two procedures. Let us just consider the parallel test under the conjunctive positivity criterion. This test strategy implies the following informational value:

$$
VI_{1,2;c}(p) = \begin{cases} p \cdot Se_1 \cdot Se_2 \cdot g \\ -(1-p)(1-Sp_1)(1-Sp_2)l & \text{for} \quad 0 \le p < p^{Rx}, \\ -l^{t_1} - l^{t_2} \\ \\ -p(1 - Se_1 \cdot Se_2)g \\ +(1-p)(Sp_1 + (1-Sp_1)Sp_2)l & \text{for} \quad p^{Rx} \le p \le 1. \\ -l^{t_1} - l^{t_2} \end{cases}
\tag{7.22}
$$

Comparison with Eq. (7.18) reveals that $VI_{2;c}(p) > VI_{1,2;c}(p)$. This inequality holds for all possible test strategies. If testing is harmful or costly in monetary terms, the optimally ordered sequential test dominates parallel testing.

There are other circumstances in the composite use of tests which may affect the choice between a parallel and sequential procedure. Sequential testing is more time-consuming, since the result of the first test must be known before the second test can be performed. This may involve additional costs and risks, due to, for instance, longer waiting times or length of stay in the emergency department/hospital. Such costs should also be included when considering the different test strategies and may tend to favor parallel testing (see Ament and Hasman 1993).

7.6   The Cost of Treatment and Testing and Composite Tests

Following Chap. 5, we can use the concept of the incremental net benefit to include the cost of test i, c^{t_i}, and the cost of treatment, c^{Rx}. For the sequential test, starting with test 1 and proceeding with test 2, if test 1 is positive (i.e., using the conjunctive criterion), we obtain:

$$INB_{1;c}(p)$$
$$= \begin{cases} -c^{t_1} + p \cdot Se_1\left(Se_2 \cdot \lambda \cdot q_g - c^{t_2} - c^{Rx}\right) \\ -(1-p)(1-Sp_1)((1-Sp_2)\lambda \cdot q_l + c^{t_2} + c^{Rx}) & \text{for } 0 \le p < p^{Rx}, \\ \\ -c^{t_1} - p\left((1-Se_1 \cdot Se_2)\left(\lambda \cdot q_g - c^{Rx}\right) + Se_1 \cdot c^{t_2}\right) \\ +(1-p)(Sp_1(\lambda \cdot q_l + c^{Rx}) + (1-Sp_1)(Sp_2(\lambda \cdot q_l + c^{Rx}) - c^{t_2})) & \text{for } p^{Rx} \le p \le 1. \end{cases}$$
$$(7.23)$$

This equation is similar to Eq. (7.18), except that—besides applying QALYs—we replaced the harm from testing with its monetary cost and considered the cost of treatment as well.

When comparing two tests to decide which one to use first, we find:

$$INB_{1;c}(p) \overset{\ge}{\underset{<}{\,}} INB_{2;c}(p) \Leftrightarrow -c^{t_1} + (p(1-Se_1) + (1-p)Sp_1)(c^{t_2} + c^{Rx}) \overset{\le}{\underset{>}{\,}}$$
$$- c^{t_2} + (p(1-Se_2) + (1-p)Sp_2)(c^{t_1} + c^{Rx}). \quad (7.24)$$

The comparison thus considers the expected net cost of the test sequence. There is the direct cost of the first test involved in the sequence as well as the expected cost savings if the outcome is negative, since then the second test will not be applied.

For the incremental net benefit when test 1 and test 2 are combined with the disjunctive criterion, starting with test 1, it holds that:

$$INB_{1;d}(p) = \begin{cases} -c^{t_1} + p\left(Se_1\left(\lambda \cdot q_g - c^{Rx}\right) + (1 - Se_1)\left(Se_2\left(\lambda \cdot q_g - c^{Rx}\right) - c^{t_2}\right)\right) \\ \quad -(1-p)((1 - Sp_1 \cdot Sp_2)(\lambda \cdot q_l + c^{Rx}) + Sp_1 \cdot c^{t_2}) & \text{for } 0 \le p < p^{Rx}, \\[2ex] -c^{t_1} - p(1 - Se_1)\left((1 - Se_2)\left(\lambda \cdot q_g - c^{Rx}\right) + c^{t_2}\right) \\ \quad +(1-p)Sp_1(Sp_2(\lambda \cdot q_l + c^{Rx}) - c^{t_2}) & \text{for } p^{Rx} \le p \le 1. \end{cases}$$

$$(7.25)$$

When comparing the two possible sequences of the tests applying the disjunctive criterion, we obtain:

$$INB_{1;d}(p) \overset{>}{\underset{<}{\gtrless}} INB_{2;d}(p) \Leftrightarrow -c^{t_1} + (p \cdot Se_1 + (1 - p)(1 - Sp_1))\left(c^{t_2} + c^{Rx}\right) \overset{\le}{\underset{>}{\lessgtr}}$$
$$-c^{t_2} + (p \cdot Se_2 + (1 - p)(1 - Sp_2))(c^{t_1} + c^{Rx}).$$

$$(7.26)$$

Again, the expected cost of a particular test sequence is decisive. With the disjunctive criterion, the probability of a positive outcome of the first test used in the sequence is important since a positive test result implies that the second test will not be applied. The higher this probability is, the higher are the expected cost savings.

The inequalities Eqs. (7.24) and (7.26) reveal that risk aversion and higher-order risk preferences do not affect the sequencing of tests when we consider the costs of testing and treatment. This is different to the situation with potential harm of tests, since only the latter affects a patient's health status.

The *INB* analysis with several test options has some subtleties, which we want to address shortly. Principally, a test can be applied, provided that its incremental net benefit is positive. However, this is a necessary, but not a sufficient condition. If several tests are available, the reference cases "no treatment" and "treatment" used so far become irrelevant, and we have to make the direct comparison between the tests.

Accordingly, when comparing two simple tests, test i is preferred to test j only if

$$INB_i^j(p) = INB_j(p) - INB_i(p)$$
$$= p \cdot \Delta Se\left[\lambda \cdot q_g - c^{Rx}\right] + (1 - p)\Delta Sp[\lambda \cdot q_l + c^{Rx}] - \Delta c^t > 0, \qquad (7.27)$$

where we used the definition of a test's incremental net benefit (5.40), and Δ denotes the change in the respective parameter between test i and test j. This equation compares the utility in monetary terms with the costs between the two tests. A higher sensitivity leads to a benefit in the sick states, but comes with higher expected treatment costs. By comparison, a higher specificity results in benefits in the healthy state and reduces the expected treatment cost. Note that the inclusion of the treatment cost renders a test with a high specificity more attractive, since such a test reduces the expected treatment cost.

From Eq. (7.27), we see that a positive incremental net benefit of test j compared to the reference treatment case, $INB_j(p) > 0$, does not necessarily imply that its incremental net benefit compared to test i is also positive, $INB_i^j(p) > 0$.

Figure 7.9 displays the INB between two tests, starting with the INB of the two tests presented in Fig. 7.1, but including cost of testing and treatment as well. p_m^{t1} and p_m^{t2} denote the respective test thresholds. Test 1 with its higher specificity is used at lower a priori probabilities (despite its possibly higher cost) than test 2. At $p = p_m^{t2}$, the incremental net benefit of test 2 becomes non-negative. But it will not be used, as test 1 still has a higher incremental net benefit. At $p = p_m^{t12}$, the INB of the two tests are equal. If the a priori probability increases further, test 2 is the preferred test.

$INB_1^2(p)$ is linearly increasing in p. It changes its sign from negative to positive at $p = p_m^{t12}$. The figure also clarifies that we need both $INB_2(p) > 0$ and $INB_1^2(p) > 0$ in order to accept the use of test 2.

It is interesting to note that this marginal analysis is similar to the incremental-cost-effectiveness ratio (ICER) of a medical intervention applied in health technology assessments. If we set Eq. (7.27) equal to zero, the ICER is equal to the marginal willingness to pay for a QALY:

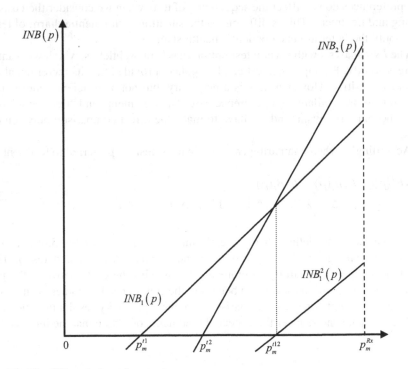

Fig. 7.9 The INB analysis with several tests

$$ICER_i^j\left(p_m^{t12}\right) = \frac{\Delta c^t + \left[p_m^{t12} \cdot \Delta Se - \left(1 - p_m^{t12}\right)\Delta Sp\right]c^{Rx}}{p_m^{t12} \cdot \Delta Se \cdot q_g + \left(1 - p_m^{t12}\right)\Delta Sp \cdot q_l} = \lambda, \tag{7.28}$$

The numerator of the ICER includes the change in the cost of testing and the change in the expected cost of treatment. The nominator compares the QALY change between the two tests. At the a priori probability of illness where the two tests have the same incremental net benefit, the ICER is equal to λ. We finish by noting that this equality also holds at all thresholds that include the cost of testing and treatment.

7.7 Notes

Hershey et al. (1986) were the first to introduce a clinical decision analysis of two tests, while Ament and Hasman (1993) provide a thorough analysis of this case. For the incremental cost-effectiveness, including the concept of the shadow price of a budget, refer to Weinstein et al. (1980) and Drummond et al. (1987).

Exercises

1. Assume there is a specific treatment for an illness from which a sick patient will benefit with 0.4 QALYs. But the patient might not actually suffer from the diagnosed illness and therefore experience a loss of 0.1 QALYs from unnecessary treatment. A diagnostic test available to the physician has $Se = 0.6$ and $Sp = 1$. Assume that the harm is equivalent to an additional QALY loss equal to $l^t = 0.01$ for both the sick and the healthy. Equation (5.8), then, changes to

$$VI(p) = \begin{cases} p \cdot Se \cdot g - (1 - p)(1 - Sp)l - l^t & \text{for} \quad 0 \leq p < p^{Rx}, \\ -p \cdot g(1 - Se) + (1 - p)Sp \cdot l - l^t & \text{for} \quad p^{Rx} \leq p \leq 1. \end{cases}$$

(a) Calculate the treatment threshold, the test and test-treatment thresholds, as well as the value of information for the situation in which a non-harmful test is available.

(b) Display the situation in a graph.

(c) How is the treatment decision affected if a test is harmful?

A second test now becomes available. It has the same specificity but a higher sensitivity than the first test ($Sp = 1$ and $Se = 0.8$). The QALY loss for the second test is 0.02, which is higher than that of the first test.

(d) What is the minimum a priori probability of an illness at which the physician will prefer the second test?

(e) Calculate the overall sensitivity and specificity if the physician tests sequentially, starting with the first test and proceeding with the second test for patients who received a positive first result.

(f) How will the physician's choice change if the QALY loss of the second test increases to 0.05?

2. Figure 7.3 reveals that one of the two individual tests is always inferior. Prove the following general proposition: If $VI_i(p) > VI_c(p)$ or $VI_i(p) > VI_d(p)$, then $VI_j(p) < VI_i(p)$, $i \neq j$.

3. Demonstrate the following two inequalities: $p_d^{tRx} > p_c^{tRx} > p^{Rx}$. You may follow the approach used in footnotes 2 and 4.

4. Assume two tests with the following properties: $Se_1 = 0.6$, $Sp_1 = 0.9$ and $Se_2 = 0.7$, $Sp_2 = 0.8$. Furthermore, the utility gain for sick patients will be 4 QALYs and the utility loss to healthy patients 1 QALY.

(a) Calculate the overall sensitivity and specificity of the composite test (for both the conjunctive and the disjunctive positivity criterion).

(b) Calculate the positive and negative likelihood ratios of the two single tests, as well as the likelihood ratios of the composite test with conjunctive and disjunctive positivity criteria.

(c) Draw Fig. 7.3 for the given test properties.

(d) Which test strategy will be preferred at the a priori probabilities of 0.1, 0.5 and 0.9?

(e) Draw level curves of informational value for these a priori probabilities.

(f) In which prevalence range is which alternative dominant?

(g) Draw Fig. 7.6 for the given test properties.

5. Hull et al. (1981) analyzed diagnostic strategies for deep vein thrombosis (DVT). The table below shows the outcomes and costs generated by two alternative strategies: impedance plethysmography (IPG) alone versus IPG plus outpatient venography if IPG is negative.

Program	Test result	Presence of DVT		Costs (US$)
		yes	no	
IPG alone	+	142	5	321,488
	−	59	272	
IPG plus venography	+	201	5	603,552
if IPG is negative	−	0	272	

Perone et al. (2001) report the following (3-month) quality-adjusted expected survival probabilities for a 50-year-old patient with a life expectancy of 29 years: 99.518 % (with DVT and treatment), 97.5 % (with DVT and no treatment), 99.768 % (without DVT and treatment) and 100 % (without DVT and no treatment).

(a) Calculate the a priori probability of DVT, the sensitivity and specificity of the individual and the combined test.

(b) Calculate the QALY values for each scenario, as well as the utility gain and loss from treatment and the treatment threshold. For the given a priori probability, which is the best strategy without a test?

(c) Calculate the test and test-treatment thresholds for each individual test as well as the composite test. For the given a priori probability, which is the best strategy when tests are available?

(d) Assume that treatment of a patient costs 2755 US$ and that the shadow value of the budget constraint is 50,000 US$ per additional QALY. Which is the best strategy?

References

Ament, A., & Hasman, A. (1993). Optimal test strategy in the case of two tests and one disease. *International Journal of Bio-Medical Computing, 33*(3–4), 179–197.

Drummond, M. F., O'Brien, B., Stoddart, G. L., & Torrance, G. W. (1987). *Methods for the economic evaluation of health care programmes*. Oxford: Oxford University Press.

Hershey, J. C., Cebul, R. D., & Williams, S. V. (1986). Clinical guidelines for using two dichotomous tests. *Medical Decision Making, 6*(2), 68–78.

Hull, R., Hirsh, J., Sackett, D. L., & Stoddart, G. L. (1981). Cost-effectiveness of clinical diagnosis, venography and non-invasive testing in patients with symptomatic deep-vein thrombosis. *New England Journal of Medicine, 304*, 1561–1567.

Krahn, M. D., Mahoney, J. E., Eckman, M. H., Trachtenberg, J., Pauker, S. G., & Detsky, A. S. (1994). Screening for prostate cancer: A decision analytic view. *JAMA, 272*(10), 773–780.

Perone, N., Bounameaux, H., & Perrier, A. (2001). Comparison of four strategies for diagnosing deep vein thrombosis: A cost-effectiveness analysis. *The American Journal of Medicine, 110* (1), 33–40.

Weinstein, M. C., Fineberg, H. V., Elstein, A. S., Frazier, H. S., Neuhauser, D., Neutra, R. R., et al. (1980). *Clinical decision analysis*. Philadelphia: W.B. Saunders.

Chapter 8
The Optimal Cutoff Value of a Diagnostic Test

> Also ist allein im wirklichen Handeln der Wille selbst thätig.
>
> Arthur Schopenhauer[1]

The last chapter revealed the necessity of defining a positivity criterion when choosing the optimal diagnostic test and treatment strategy if multiple tests are available. The importance of the positivity criterion is even more evident if an individual test is based on a measurement variable, a so-called marker. The blood sugar level, for instance, provides information on the probability that a patient suffers from diabetes. Having measured a patient's blood sugar, the physician must decide how to interpret the observation in terms of the patient's health state. This is tantamount to choosing a cutoff value and, depending on the observed blood sugar level, deciding whether the outcome is positive or negative.

Section 8.1 analyzes the relationship between the cutoff value and the endogenous test characteristics, sensitivity and specificity, and derives the Receiver Operating Characteristic curve (ROC curve).

Section 8.2 characterizes the choice of the optimal cutoff value. In choosing a cutoff value, the decision maker considers the endogenous sensitivity and specificity of the test and the respective utility gains and losses of treatment for the sick and the healthy. The choice of the optimal cutoff value can be illustrated by combining the ROC curve with the level curves for a test's informational value which we derived in Chap. 7.

Section 8.3 studies the implications of choosing the optimal cutoff value for the test and test-treatment thresholds. We show that the a priori probability of illness range within which testing should be preferred widens if the chosen cutoff value maximizes the test's informational value.

Section 8.4 deals with multiple tests, one component of which is based on different measurement values indicating the ex posteriori probability of the illness. We show how the ROC curve can be calculated under these circumstances. With

---

[1]'Thus the will is revealed only in the act.'—Schopenhauer, A.—*Die Welt als Wille und Vorstellung*—Brockhaus Verlag, Leipzig—1859, p. 281.

© Springer-Verlag GmbH Germany 2017
S. Felder, T. Mayrhofer, *Medical Decision Making*,
DOI 10.1007/978-3-662-53432-8_8

multiple markers it is no longer feasible to determine optimal cutoff values at the level of the individual markers. Instead, based on the observed marker values, it is possible to calculate the sensitivity and specificity, and thus the discriminatory power, of the test as a whole. This information is the basis for determining the test outcome. We show that comparing the implied discriminatory power of the observations with the optimal discriminatory power on the ROC curve leads to a conclusion regarding the test outcome. The analysis is similar to the choice between multiple diagnostic tests discussed in the last chapter. We present the theory with the example of the triple test, which is used in prenatal diagnostics to detect chromosomal disorders of the fetus.

8.1   Endogenous Test Characteristics

Given a continuous measurement variable, the test characteristics, sensitivity and specificity become endogenous. Figure 8.1 illustrates this, showing the density function of a marker t for healthy patients $f_h(t)$ and for sick patients $f_s(t)$ (upper part of the graph). The cumulative distribution functions $F_h(t)$ and $F_s(t)$ (bottom part of the graph) correspond to the density functions and indicate the shares of healthy and sick individuals with a measurement value of t or less. A higher value of t indicates an increased probability of the illness; accordingly, Fig. 8.1 shows a higher mean marker value for the sick individuals than for the healthy individuals ($\mu_s > \mu_h$). We assume that the cumulative distribution functions do not intersect, hence $F_h(t) \geq F_s(t)$.

The value x in Fig. 8.1 denotes one possible cutoff value of the test: The test result is positive for measurement values $t \geq x$ and negative for values $t < x$. The sensitivity of the test with a general cutoff value x is then defined as follows:

$$Se(x) = \int_x^\infty f_s(t)dt = 1 - F_s(x), \qquad (8.1)$$

where t is the marker variable. The integral $\int_x^\infty f_s(t)dt$ represents the area below the density function $f_s(t)$ to the right of a possible cutoff value x. This is the sensitivity, i.e., the probability that a sick patient is correctly detected by the test (true positive rate). This probability can also be represented by the cumulative distribution function $F_s(x)$ with a maximal value of one, $F_s(x = \infty) = 1$. The difference $1 - F_s(x)$ is the cumulative share of all sick patients minus the cumulative share of the sick with a negative test outcome ($F_s(x)$; false-negative rate). In Fig. 8.1, given the cutoff value x, the sensitivity of the test is 0.8, as $F_s(x) = 0.2$.

For the specificity, considering the density function of the marker for the healthy leads to

$$Sp(x) = \int_{-\infty}^x f_h(t)dt = F_h(x). \qquad (8.2)$$

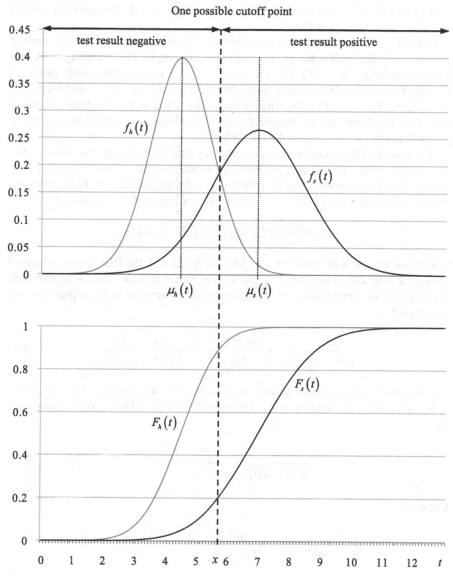

Fig. 8.1 Density and cumulative distribution functions of a measurement variable for the sick and the healthy

The integral $\int_{-\infty}^{x} f_h(t)dt$ represents the area below the density function $f_h(t)$ to the left of x. This corresponds to the share of all healthy patients with a negative test result because their measurement value is smaller than the cutoff value x—or, alternatively, to the share of healthy patients who are correctly identified by the test. Likewise, we can calculate the specificity using the cumulative distribution function for the healthy, $F_h(x)$. The specificity is the value of the cumulative distribution function at the cutoff value x, $F_h(x)$. In Fig. 8.1, the specificity of the test with cutoff value x is 0.9.

Equations (8.1) and (8.2) reveal that sensitivity and specificity move in opposite directions. If the cutoff value x of the test shifts to the right, the specificity of the test increases $(dSp(x)/dx = dF_h(x)/dx = f_h(x) > 0)$ and more healthy individuals are classified correctly. At the same time, the test's sensitivity decreases $(dSe(x)/dx = -dF_s(x)/dx = -f_s(x) < 0)$, which implies that fewer sick individuals are classified correctly. Note that the density functions themselves give the changes in the probabilities from a change in the cutoff value.

The choice of the cutoff value thus involves a trade-off between sensitivity and specificity, or the share of true positive cases and the share of true negative cases. This trade-off is represented by the ROC curve. Mathematically, the ROC curve is a graph representing a tuple of $(Se, 1 - Sp)$ for each value of the marker x:

$$graph(ROC(x)) = \{(Se(x), 1 - Sp(x))\}.$$

Given that the test is informative, i.e., $Se(x) + Sp(x) > 1$, the ROC curve is located above the diagonal in the $(Se, 1 - Sp)$ square. Since the functions Se and Sp both depend on x, we can calculate the slope of the ROC curve using the expressions we just derived:

$$\frac{dSe}{d(1 - Sp)} = \frac{dSe/dx}{d(1 - Sp)/dx} = \frac{-f_s(x)}{-f_h(x)} = \frac{f_s(x)}{f_h(x)}. \qquad (8.3)$$

An ideal ROC curve is entirely concave from below, implying that the slope of the curve is monotone in a change in x. The curvature of the ROC curve is determined by

$$\frac{dSe^2}{d^2(1 - Sp)} = -\frac{f_s'f_h - f_h'f_s}{(f_h)^2}. \qquad (8.4)$$

Concavity,

$$\frac{dSe^2}{d^2(1 - Sp)} < 0,$$

is given if $f_s'/f_s > f_h'/f_h$. For a normally distributed density function this condition can be shown to imply $(\mu_s - x)/\sigma_s > (\mu_h - x)/\sigma_h$ for all x, where μ and σ are the means and the standard deviations of the two distributions. Thus, the standardized distribution of the measurement variable among sick patients should be greater than the standardized distribution of the variable among healthy patients, provided the marker is positively correlated with the presence of the illness.

8.2 The Optimal Cutoff Value

The choice of the optimal cutoff value is basically equivalent to the choice between different tests that are each defined by a particular cutoff value. The optimal test maximizes expected utility given the exogenous parameters, a priori probability of illness p, and the utility consequences of treatment for the sick g and the healthy l. We can write the value of information as a function of the general cutoff value x:

$$VI(x) = \begin{cases} p \cdot Se(x)g - (1-p)(1-Sp(x))l & \text{for} \quad 0 \le p < p^{Rx}, \\ -p \cdot g(1 - Se(x)) + (1-p)Sp(x)l & \text{for} \quad p^{Rx} \le p \le 1. \end{cases} \tag{8.5}$$

The optimal cutoff value maximizes the test's value of information. Hence, we calculate the first derivative with respect to x and set it equal to zero:

$$\frac{\partial VI(x)}{\partial x} = p\frac{\partial Se(x)}{\partial x}g + (1-p)\frac{\partial Sp(x)}{\partial x}l = 0.$$

Taking into account Eqs. (8.1) and (8.2), we find

$$(1-p)f_h(x^*)l = p \cdot f_s(x^*)g. \tag{8.6}$$

The optimal cutoff value x^* equates the expected marginal benefit and the expected marginal cost of an infinitesimal increase in the cutoff value. The expected marginal benefit is given on the left-hand side of Eq. (8.6): $1 - p$ is the probability that an individual is healthy, $f_h(x^*)$ equals the increase in the probability that the test correctly identifies a healthy individual, and l is the utility that a healthy individual gains from not being treated. The product of the three terms, then, is the total expected utility gain from a marginal increase in the cutoff value x. The expected marginal cost is stated on the right-hand side of Eq. (8.6): $-f_s(x^*)$ equals the decrease in the probability that the test does not detect a sick individual if x increases, and $-g$ is the utility loss of a sick individual who remains untreated. The product of the two terms multiplied by the a priori probability of illness is the expected utility loss of a marginal increase in x. The value of information is maximized if the cutoff value is chosen such that expected marginal cost equals expected marginal benefit.

Rewriting Eq. (8.6) yields

$$\frac{f_s(x^*)}{f_h(x^*)} = \frac{(1-p)l}{p \cdot g} = \frac{1}{\Omega \cdot g/l}. \tag{8.7}$$

This is the same equation we derived in the last chapter for the slope of the level curve for a test's informational value in the $(Se, 1 - Sp)$ square:

$$\frac{dSe}{d(1-Sp)} = \frac{1}{\Omega \cdot g/l}. \tag{8.8}$$

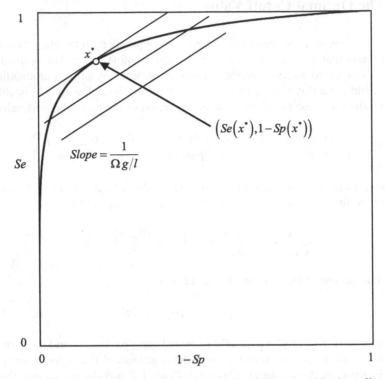

Fig. 8.2 ROC curve and level curves of the value of information—the optimal cutoff value

Equation (8.8) thus characterizes the optimal cutoff value on the ROC curve. At the highest possible informational value, the corresponding level curve is tangential to the ROC curve—see Eq. (8.3). Figure 8.2 displays the ROC curve corresponding to the density functions displayed in Fig. 8.1, as well as the optimal cutoff value given the values of the exogenous parameters.

According to Eq. (8.8), the optimal cutoff value depends on the a priori probability of illness p and the utility consequences of treatment for a sick (g) and a healthy individual (l). An increase in the prevalence rate or in the utility gain from treatment for the sick flattens the slope of the level curves of informational value, while an increase in the utility loss from treatment for the healthy steepens it.

Box 8.1: Alternative Optima on the ROC Curve?

In clinical epidemiology, reference is often made to optima on the ROC curve other than the one that maximizes the informational value of the test. One is the Euclidian point E which minimizes the Euclidian distance between the ROC curve and the corner $(1,0)$. This is tantamount to minimizing the sum of the squared errors of the decision (type I and type II errors):

(continued)

Box 8.1 (continued)

$$\sqrt{[1 - Se(x)]^2 + [1 - Sp(x)]^2}.$$

In this case, the level curves for the value of information are concentric circles around the corner (1,0). The Euclidian norm does not consider the prevalence of the sickness, or the respective utility consequences of treatment for the sick and the healthy.

A further decision rule minimizes the sum of the two errors: $1 - Se(x) + 1 - Sp(x)$. This corresponds to the Manhattan norm (also called the Manhattan distance or city block distance): Starting from the corner (1,0), the shortest distance to the ROC-curve (point M) is chosen in the manner of a taxi driver who is forced to driving around blocks rather than diagonally through them. An equivalent method that yields the same result is the Youden index (Youden 1950) which refers to the maximization of the sum of sensitivity and specificity (sometimes also referred to as Youden's J statistic: $J = Se + Sp - 1$). The level curves for the value of information in case of the Manhattan norm are lines with a slope of one. Like the Euclidian norm, the Manhattan norm does not consider exogenous factors beyond those of the diagnostic technology in the choice of the optimal cutoff value. Sometimes an extension of the Manhattan norm is used which weights type I and type II errors with their relative probabilities: $p(1 - Se(x)) + (1 - p)(1 - Sp(x))$. Either way, neither the original Manhattan norm nor the weighted Manhattan norm (point M') do consider the utility and disutility of treatment. Hence, it is also not consistent with expected utility maximization and should not warrant special attention.

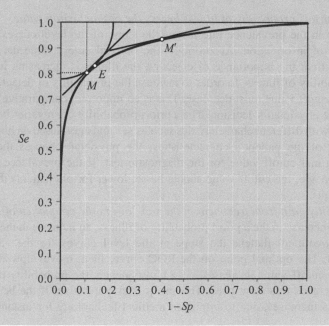

(continued)

Box 8.1 (continued)

There exists disease-specific cutoff rules that—indirectly—include utility weighting. One such case is the measurement of cardiac troponin (a blood test which is applied to patients who present chest-pain symptoms in the emergency department) to test for acute coronary syndrome especially myocardial infarction. The threshold for a positive (elevated) troponin result is usually set at the 99th percentile of the healthy population (Thygesen et al. 2012). This high rule-in threshold ensures a relatively low rate of false-positive patients who would otherwise end up directly in the catheterization laboratory undergoing an invasive coronary angiography (of course, other diagnostic tests are applied to patients with negative test outcomes to ensure that acute coronary syndrome is ruled out).

The effect of changes in the exogenous parameters of the optimal cutoff value can be described by the effects of changes in the cutoff value on the sensitivity and specificity and thus on the slope of the level curves for the value of information. In Fig. 8.1, for example, an increase in x lowers the sensitivity and increases the specificity of the test. This implies a shift backwards along the ROC curve and—due to the concavity of the ROC curve—an increase in the slope of the level curves for the values of information. The cutoff value and the slope of the level curves are thus positively correlated—provided that the marker is positively correlated with the existence of the sickness. Given the effects of a change in the cutoff value on sensitivity and specificity, we can consider the relationship between the cutoff value and changes in the exogenous factors p, g and l via their effects on the slope of the level curves—see Eq. (8.8).

We derive the following general rules regarding the choice of the cutoff value:

1. *A higher a priori probability of illness lowers the optimal cutoff value.*
   An increase in the prevalence rate lowers the slope of the level curves of the test's value of information. Accordingly, the optimal cutoff value decreases. This is intuitive: the importance of detecting the illness is increasing in the a priori probability of illness. In order to increase the probability of detecting the illness, the cutoff value must decrease. This is an important comparative statics result for the physician's decision. The a priori probability often varies between individuals with different characteristics such as sex and age. Based on his initial observation of the patient's characteristics, the physician chooses the individually optimal cutoff value for the diagnostic test. If the prevalence rate is increasing in age, the cutoff value should be set lower for old patients than for young patients.

2. *A higher utility gain from treatment of the sick lowers the optimal cutoff value.*
   As with an increase in the a priori probability of illness, an increase in the utility gain from treatment flattens the slope of the level curves for the value of information. The optimal point on the ROC curve, then, moves upwards and the optimal cutoff value decreases. As a consequence, the probability that the patient undergoes treatment rises. This result is also intuitive: If the benefit to sick patients increases, due to improved medical technology for instance, the

hurdle for access to treatment should be lowered. Similarly, improvements in terms of reduced side effects or lower costs should also result in a lower cutoff value.

3. *An increase in the utility loss from treatment for the healthy raises the optimal cutoff value.*

   By contrast, if the utility loss from treatment experienced by a healthy individual increases, so will the optimal cutoff value. This results in fewer treatments. The potential harm from testing, if it affects sick and healthy individuals alike, will also increase the optimal cutoff value, as it lowers the g/l ratio.

4. *The cost of testing does not affect the optimal cutoff value, while an increase in the cost of treatment increases it.*

   Once the decision has been taken to apply the test, the corresponding costs are bygones and will thus not affect the optimal cutoff value.[2] By contrast, an increase in the cost of treatment will increase the optimal cutoff value.

5. *Risk aversion lowers the optimal cutoff value* (see Felder and Mayrhofer 2014).

   In Chap. 5, we compared risk-neutral and risk-averse decision makers and showed that $g_A > g_N$ and $l_A < l_N$. Due to the diminishing marginal utility of health, the risk-averse decision maker values the utility gain from treatment of the sick (utility loss from treatment for the healthy) more (less) than the risk-neutral decision maker. He will be willing to give up more specificity to gain sensitivity than the risk-neutral decision maker. It follows that the risk-averse decision maker will choose a lower cutoff value.

6. *Prudence lowers the optimal cutoff value.*

   In Chap. 6, we showed that prudence intensifies the effects of risk aversion. If we add prudence to the model, the first order condition (8.6) for the optimal cutoff value becomes

$$p \cdot f_s(x^*)EG_P = (1-p)f_h(x^*)l, \tag{8.9}$$

where

$$EG_P = \left[g + \frac{\sigma_m^2}{2} \left[u''(h_s^+) - u''(h_s^-) \right] \right].$$

If comorbidity risk is present and the decision maker is risk-prudent, the marginal costs of an increase in the cutoff value rises. The rationale is that the marginal value of health in the sick state with background risk is higher for a prudent decision maker than for a merely risk-averse one. The prudent decision maker takes the comorbidity risk into account and lowers the cutoff value even further.

---

[2]The cost of testing does, however, play a role for the optimal cutoff value in sequential tests. The choice of the cutoff value for the first test must consider the cost of the second test, since it influences the probability that the patient will be subject to the second test.

8.3   Test and Test-Treatment Thresholds and the Optimal Cutoff Value

Choosing a cutoff value also has consequences for the thresholds of the a priori probability of illness. For a priori probabilities below the test threshold, the informational value of the test is negative,[3] as the expected utility gain from testing the sick is smaller than the expected utility loss from testing the healthy. If a test can be improved by increasing the cutoff value, the likelihood of a false-positive test result will be reduced, in turn allowing the decision maker to lower the test threshold. Similar arguments apply for the test-treatment threshold, the minimal prevalence rate at which treatment should be administered immediately without testing. Here, the lack of utility gain for patients with false-positive test results governs the decision. Reducing the cutoff value increases the expected utility of testing, so that the test-treatment threshold rises.

Let us analyze these relationships more formally. In general terms, it must hold that

$$VI(x^*) \geq VI(x). \tag{8.10}$$

In other words, the expected utility of an optimally chosen cutoff value must be at least as high as the expected utility of an arbitrarily determined cutoff value.

This must also hold at the test threshold p^t. This threshold is defined by $VI(p^t) = 0$. Moreover, the informational value line has a positive slope around p^t: $\partial VI(p^t)/\partial p > 0$. Writing the test threshold as a function of the cutoff value, we then obtain

$$p^t(x^*) \leq p^t(x). \tag{8.11}$$

In the extreme case, the test threshold can even disappear if the cutoff value is optimally set. As an illustration, consider $p = 0$ where $VI(x) = -(1 - Sp(x))l$ is negative if specificity is below one. However, if the cutoff value is raised to the point where no more false-positive cases occur—i.e., where specificity is one—the value of information is non-negative and the test threshold is $p^t = 0$.

Similarly, $VI(p^{tRx}) = 0$ defines the test-treatment threshold p^{tRx}. The informational value line has a negative slope around p^{tRx}: $\partial VI(p^{tRx})/\partial p < 0$. Finally, the test-treatment threshold can be written as a function of the cutoff value:

$$p^{tRx}(x^*) \geq p^{tRx}(x). \tag{8.12}$$

Here, again, it should be possible to increase the test-treatment threshold such that $p^{tRx} = 1$ results in the extreme. The value of information is usually negative at $p = 1, VI(x) = -(1 - Se(x))g. VI(x^*) \geq 0$ can be achieved if the cutoff value is set

---

[3]Strictly speaking, the difference between the expected utility of testing and the expected utility of 'no treatment' is negative and the value of information is zero, as the decision maker would not employ the test in this prevalence range. For simplicity, we abstract from this complication again.

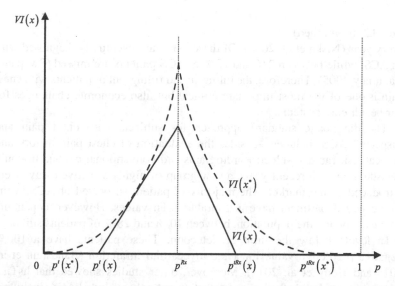

Fig. 8.3 Value of information—arbitrarily vs. optimally chosen cutoff values

so low such that no false-negative test results occur. Thus, test and test-treatment thresholds disappear and testing is indicated over the whole prevalence range if the test is optimally designed. Accordingly, the value of information is strictly positive over the whole prevalence range except at the boundaries. Only if the test is harmful or costly will some prevalence ranges exist in which testing is not indicated.

Figure 8.3 illustrates this. $VI(x)$ is the value of information curve for a given cutoff value x, and thus for a fixed sensitivity and specificity. The curve is linear in the prevalence rate with two arms that are separated by the treatment threshold p^{Rx}, as we know from Chap. 5. If the cutoff value can be chosen, sensitivity and specificity become endogenous. As a consequence, the value of information increases over the whole prevalence range, except for one rate at which the fixed cutoff value is optimal (i.e., $x = x^*$). The value of information curve is then no longer linear in the a priori probability of illness.

Figure 8.3 gives an example of the possible curvature of the maximized informational value curve $VI(x^*)$, where testing actually applies over the whole testing range.

Box 8.2: Using Multiple Cutoff Values as Rule-In and Rule-Out Criteria
In clinical practice, sometimes multiple cutoff values are used for one marker. Let us go back to the troponin example that we presented in Box 8.1. To recap, patients that present chest pain symptoms at the emergency department are suspected of having an acute coronary syndrome (ACS). In the United States, chest pain is the leading cause of emergency department visits for patients over 15 years of age, resulting in more than 6 million patient visits

(continued)

Box 8.2 (continued)

every year (Niska et al. 2010). Of these, 33 % are eventually diagnosed with an ACS, while between 2 % and 10 % of ACS patients are missed (Swap and Nagurney 2005). Therefore, the ruling-in and ruling-out of patients with chest pain is one of the most important clinical but also economic challenges for our health care systems.

The diagnostic standard approach for subjects with chest pain and suspected ACS includes—besides the evaluation of chest pain history and clinical risk factors—electrocardiograms and conventional cardiac troponin measurements. In recent years, a new group of highly sensitive assays were introduced to the market. The majority of patient suspected of ACS in the emergency department have measurable hsTn values. However, depending on the assay and the population, between 10 % and 28 % of patients still have hsTn levels below the limit of detection. These patients have a 100 % negative predictive value for acute myocardial infarction (Bandstein et al. 2014 and Body et al. 2011). Moreover, other studies showed that hsTn I concentrations below the limit of detection not only excluded ACS (including unstable angina pectoris) but also significant coronary stenosis in those undergoing subsequent coronary computed tomography angiography (coronary CTA) (Januzzi et al. 2015).

Therefore, multiple cutoff values in highly sensitive troponin assays (which translates into multiple tests from the same marker) can be used to rule-in (hsTn >99th percentile) or rule-out (hsTn < limit of detection) patients with chest pain with suspected ACS. Ferencik et al. (2015) showed that patients with hsTn I levels above the limit of detection but below the 99th percentile had an intermediate risk of ACS with an event rate of 9 %. In this group, the subsequent use of Coronary CTA could reclassify the risk of ACS. None of the patients at intermediate risk who showed no evidence of significant stenosis or high-risk plaque (Puchner et al. 2014) in the coronary CTA (54 %) had ACS (NPV = 100 %). On the other hand, intermediate risk patients with significant stenosis and high-risk plaque had an ACS event rate of 69 %. In summary, the majority of patients with chest pain could possibly be discharged 2 h after presenting their case at an emergency department using a combined approach of highly sensitive troponin as well as a coronary CTA. Such a procedure would therefore lead to less additional testing and thereby decrease radiation exposure and reduce health care costs.

Interestingly, hsTn assays are now widely used in Europe and recommended by the European Society of Cardiology (Roffi et al. 2016). In contrast, American guidelines still recommend the use of conventional troponin assays (Anderson et al. 2011) due to the lack of U.S. Food and Drug Administration approval for hsTn assays in the United States.

8.4 Multiple Tests with Endogenous Sensitivity and Specificity: Triple-Test and Amniocentesis

In Chap. 7, we analyzed the optimal strategy for using multiple tests with given sensitivity and specificity. In this section, we extend this analysis and include tests based on multiple markers. We use the example of the triple test. The triple test is designed to detect chromosome anomalies in unborn babies. It is based on three biochemical markers in the mother's blood. Each of these markers is normally distributed and differs between women with affected and unaffected fetuses. More-over, the distributions of the markers are correlated with each other. Under these circumstances, it is not meaningful to set cutoff values for the individual markers to determine the test outcome. One observation of all three markers, however, permits the calculation of conditional probabilities, sensitivity and specificity, which in turn can be used to determine the test outcome.

Let us consider the indication for applying the triple test in more detail. The prevalence of fetal chromosomal disorders is low overall, but increases sharply with the age of the pregnant women. The fetus of a 35-year-old has a 3.6 times higher probability of being affected than that of a 25-year-old. In the past, a 35-year-old would often undergo amniocentesis, a test of the amniotic fluid gained by punctur-ing the amnion. Amniocentesis is an almost perfect test, but is harmful in the sense that it leads to procedure-related miscarriage of affected and unaffected fetuses alike in about one in sixty cases. Amniocentesis is usually not performed on younger women, due both to the low prevalence rate of fetal malformation and the potential harm from the procedure. In terms of the threshold analysis, a young woman's probability of bearing an abnormal fetus was considered to be below the test threshold. In the mid-1990s a non-invasive triple test became available which can be used before amniocentesis to specify the probability of a chromosomal dis-order. The triple test has significantly less discriminatory power than the amnio-centesis (sensitivity of 0.69 and specificity of 0.95 on average), but it does not carry the threat of a spontaneous abortion.

When applying the triple test, the positivity criterion has to be determined. The decision maker faces the usual trade-off between high sensitivity and low specific-ity, and vice versa. We characterize his choice in three steps. First, we show how the ROC curve can be computed from the known distributions of the three biochemical markers. Second, we present the properties of the optimal choice along the ROC curve. Finally, we deal with the determination of the positivity criterion.

8.4.1 The ROC Curve of the Triple Test

The triple test is based on three biochemical markers, AFP (α − fetoprotein), uE$_3$ (unconjugated oestriol) and HCG (human chorionic gonadotropine). Observing one value for each marker produces a triple (X, Y, Z) where $X = $ AFP, $Y = $ uE$_3$ and $Z = $ HCG. This can be used to calculate sensitivity and specificity. Formally, *Se* and Sp as a function of (X, Y, Z) are defined as follows (note that HCG has the opposite orientation of AFP and uE$_3$):

$$Se(X, Y, Z) = \text{Prob}(x \leq X, y \leq Y, z \geq Z)$$
$$= \int_{Z}^{\infty} \int_{-\infty}^{Y} \int_{-\infty}^{X} f_s(x, y, z)dxdydz \qquad (8.13)$$

and

$$1 - Sp(X, Y, Z) = \text{Prob}(x \leq X, y \leq Y, z \geq Z)$$
$$= \int_{Z}^{\infty} \int_{-\infty}^{Y} \int_{-\infty}^{X} f_h(x, y, z)dxdydz, \qquad (8.14)$$

where $f_s(x, y, z)$ and $f_h(x, y, z)$ are the respective trivariate densities of sick and healthy fetuses. The distributions are not orthogonal, which is a major challenge for the computation of the cumulative distribution functions. $(Se, 1 - Sp)$ pairs can be calculated for each triple (X, Y, Z) drawn from the distributions of the markers by employing an econometric algorithm. Figure 8.4 presents the results of these calculations. It is evident that most $(Se, 1 - Sp)$ pairs are dominated by other pairs that are better in terms of either sensitivity or specificity, but which are not worse the other. The ROC curve is the outer envelope, representing all $(Se, 1 - Sp)$ pairs that are not dominated.

Based on the calculation of the efficient $(Se, 1 - Sp)$ pairs, Felder et al. (2003) estimated the ROC curve of the triple test to be logarithmic in form: $Se = 1$

Fig. 8.4 Conditional probabilities Se and $(1 - Sp)$ for 55,000 triple pairs[4]

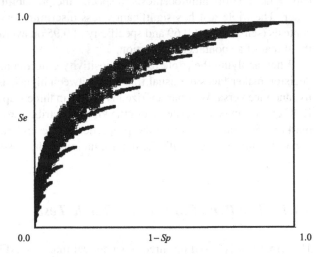

[4]Felder et al. (2003), © 2003 by SAGE, reprinted by permission of SAGE Publications.

$+0.1827 \cdot \ln(1 - Sp)$. We use this equation below to find the optimal cutoff value along the ROC curve depending on the exogenous parameters.

8.4.2 The Value of Information and Optimal Use of the Triple Test with Amniocentesis

The triple test is performed before amniocentesis. The combination of the two results in a sequential test with a conjunctive positivity criterion. If the outcome of the triple test is negative, testing stops. If the outcome is positive, the woman undergoes amniocentesis. We assume here that the fetus will be aborted if the outcome of amniocentesis is positive.[5] From Chap. 7, we know that the expected additional utility from sequential testing (under a conjunctive positivity criterion) compared to 'no testing' amounts to

$$
VI_c^1(p) = \begin{cases}
\begin{array}{l} p \cdot Se_1(Se_2 \cdot g - l^{t_2}) \\ \quad -(1-p)(1-Sp_1)((1-Sp_2)l + l^{t_2}) \\ \quad -l^{t_1} \end{array} & \text{for} \quad 0 \le p < p^{Rx}, \\[2em]
\begin{array}{l} -p((1 - Se_1 \cdot Se_2)g + Se_1 \cdot l^{t_2}) \\ \quad +(1-p)(Sp_1 \cdot l + (1-Sp_1)(Sp_2 \cdot l - l^{t_2})) \\ \quad -l^{t_1} \end{array} & \text{for} \quad p^{Rx} \le p \le 1.
\end{cases}
$$

$$(7.18)$$

We assume that amniocentesis is a perfect test ($Se_2 = Sp_2 = 1$), which simplifies Eq. (7.18) to

$$
VI_c^1(p) = \begin{cases}
\begin{array}{l} p \cdot Se_1(g - l^{t_2}) \\ \quad -(1-p)(1-Sp_1)l^{t_2} \\ \quad -l^{t_1} \end{array} & \text{for} \quad 0 \le p < p^{Rx}, \\[2em]
\begin{array}{l} -p((1 - Se_1)g + Se_1 l^{t_2}) \\ \quad +(1-p)(l - (1-Sp_1)l^{t_2}) \\ \quad -l^{t_1} \end{array} & \text{for} \quad p^{Rx} \le p \le 1.
\end{cases}
$$

$$(8.15)$$

g denotes the utility gain from detecting an unborn with a chromosomal anomaly. $l^{t_1} \equiv l^{t_{TT}}$ are the intangible costs[6] to a pregnant women of a false-positive triple test

---

[5]Mansfield et al. (1999) report termination rates after terminal diagnosis for five diagnoses in a systematic literature review. They were highest following a prenatal diagnosis for Down's syndrome (92 %) and for Klinefelter syndrome (58 %). The inclusion of alternative 'treatment' options would extend our analysis, as the harm from amniocentesis is then relevant both in the case of positive and negative test outcomes.

[6]Intangible costs include pain and anguish, or more generally the loss of quality of life due to an illness.

before receiving the negative result of amniocentesis. The probability that this occurs is equal to $(1 - p)(1 - Sp_1)$. $l'^2 \equiv l'^M$ is the utility loss from a spontaneous abortion of a healthy fetus. The probability of a procedure-related miscarriage during or after amniocentesis (M) is β. l is the utility loss of treatment, which again is the utility loss of losing a healthy fetus. Hence, we set $l \equiv l'^M$. Under these specifications, the value of information derived from a combination of the triple test and the amniocentesis becomes

$$
VI_c^{TT}(p) = \begin{cases} p \cdot Se_{TT} \cdot g \\ -(1 - p)(1 - Sp_{TT})(l'^{TT} + \beta l'^M) & \text{for} \quad 0 \le p < p^{Rx}, \\[2ex] -p(1 - Se_{TT})g + (1 - p)l'^M \\ -(1 - p)(1 - Sp_{TT})(l'^{TT} + \beta l'^M) & \text{for} \quad p^{Rx} \le p \le 1. \end{cases}
\tag{8.16}
$$

For $0 \le p < p^{Rx}$, the reference situation without the triple test and amniocentesis is 'no treatment'. The first term on the right-hand side thus equals the expected gross utility from the sequential test. Subtract from this the expected costs, given by the product of the probability that the fetus is healthy, the false-positive rate (the probability that a healthy fetus is misinterpreted by the triple test) and the sum of two cost factors (the procedure-related increase in miscarriages and the intangible cost of a false-positive test).

For $p^{Rx} \le p < 1$, the reference situation without a test is a procedure-related abortion of the fetus. The first term on the right-hand side shows the utility loss of the false-negative cases of the sequential test. The second term reflects the utility gain from preventing the healthy fetus from undergoing the amniocentesis. From this gross utility one has to deduct the intangible costs of the false-positive cases as well as the procedure-related loss of healthy fetuses following false-positive outcomes in the triple test.

Calculating the total differential of the value of information function (8.16), we can derive the slope of the level curves:

$$
\frac{dSe_{TT}}{d(1 - Sp_{TT})} = \frac{\beta + l'^{TT}/l'^M}{\Omega(g/l'^M)} = \frac{\beta + i}{\Omega \cdot \hat{g}}.
\tag{8.17}
$$

Ω are the a priori odds that an unborn has a chromosomal anomaly; $\hat{g} = g/l'^M$ is the utility weight that is assigned to the detection of an affected fetus compared to the procedure-related loss of an unaffected fetus; and $i = l'^{TT}/l'^M$ are the intangible costs of a false-positive triple test, again in terms of the loss of an unaffected fetus. The slope Eq. (8.17) expresses the valuation of the trade-off between detecting an affected fetus and preventing the cost of a false-positive triple test, i.e., the miscarriage of an unaffected fetus and the intangible cost. The importance of detecting an affected fetus increases with the procedure-related abortion rate and the intangible cost of a false-positive triple test, but is inversely related to both $\hat{g}$ and the a priori odds. While the additional abortion rate and the odds are objective

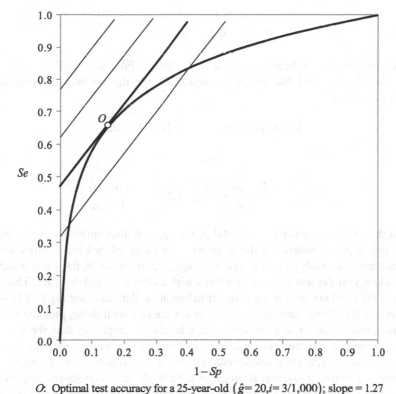

O: Optimal test accuracy for a 25-year-old $\left(\hat{g}= 20, i= 3/1,000\right)$; slope $= 1.27$

Fig. 8.5 Optimal discriminatory power of the triple test at maternal age of 25

measures known from the literature ($\beta = 1/62.5$; see Hook 1985, p. 495), $\hat{g}$ and i depend on the preferences of the women concerned and their spouses.

Figure 8.5 shows level curves for the value of information for a 25-year-old women with a priori odds of 1/1350 and values of $\hat{g} = 20$ and $i = 3/1000$, resulting in a slope of 1.27. This implies that this woman would be willing to trade 1.27 % points of test sensitivity for a 1 % point increase in specificity. The optimal choice is represented by the highest level curve (closest to the NW corner of the diagram) of the informational value the patient can achieve given the constraint of the ROC curve. Thus, the point with $Se^* = 0.65$, $Sp^* = 0.86$ and $LR^{+*} = 4.45$ represents the optimal discriminatory power of the triple test for the 25-year-old.

In the general case, we find the optimal values for Se and Sp by combining the equation of the ROC curve with the maximum condition (8.17). Inserting the first derivative of the ROC curve—$d(b\ln z)/dz = b/z$ holds true—in Eq. (8.17), we obtain

$$\frac{0.1827}{1 - Sp_{TT}^*} = \frac{\beta + i}{\Omega \cdot \hat{g}},$$

where the asterisk indicates the optimal choice. For $a = 0.1827$ and $z = \Omega \cdot \hat{g}/(\beta + i)$, we find the following equations for the optimal discriminatory power of the test:

$$1 - Sp_{TT}^* = az, \qquad Se_{TT}^* = 1 + a\ln(az)$$

and (8.18)

$$LR^{+*} = \frac{1 + a\ln(az)}{az}, \quad LR^{-*} = \frac{a\ln(az)}{1 - az}.$$

Given the constant parameters $\hat{g}$, i and β, the optimal discriminatory power of the triple test depends solely on the a priori probability of bearing a fetus with a chromosomal anomaly, i.e., on maternal age. An increase in the odds makes it more likely that the test can detect a fetus with a chromosomal disorder. Thus, the slope of the level curves for the value of information flattens—see Eq. (8.17)—and the optimal likelihood ratio of the triple test decreases with rising prevalence. The informational value of the sequential test increases, implying that the decision maker defines a positive test outcome earlier. At the same time, the relative attractiveness of applying amniocentesis directly increases, and at around age 35 there is a switch in the test strategy, and the triple test is no longer employed.

For the treatment threshold, which would determine the decision in a situation without prenatal diagnostics, we have

$$p^{Rx} = \frac{l^{t_M}}{g + l^{t_M}} = \frac{1}{\hat{g} + 1}. \tag{8.19}$$

For $\hat{g} = 20$, the treatment threshold is $p^{Rx} = 0.048$. This is roughly the a priori probability that a 46-year-old pregnant women bears a fetus with a chromosomal disorder. Her age is above 35, which marks the switching point from sequential testing to amniocentesis only.

8.4.3   Deciding on the Test Outcome

Given the outcome of the triple test, one value of each of the three markers, the question is then how to proceed. Unlike the test outcome with a single measurement variable, the observed values cannot be compared to optimal values, since optimal values cannot be determined simultaneously for the three markers. Instead, we have to compare probabilities. First, we use Eq. (8.16) to define the maximum expected utility that can be obtained if sensitivity and specificity are optimally chosen (note that we assume that the pregnant woman is younger than 46, so that $p < p^{Rx}$). This maximum value function, also called the envelope function, depends only on the exogenous variables g, β, p, $l^{t_{TT}}$ and l^{t_M} :

$$
\begin{aligned}
VI_c^{TT*}(p,g,\beta,l^{t_{TT}},l^{t_M}) &= p \cdot Se_{TT}^* \cdot g \\
&- (1-p)(1 - Sp_{TT}^*)(l^{t_{TT}} + \beta l^{t_M}),
\end{aligned}
\tag{8.20}
$$

with Se_{TT}^* and Sp_{TT}^* optimally chosen according to Eq. (8.17). $Se_{TT}(X,Y,Z)$ and $Sp_{TT}(X,Y,Z)$ can be computed for any given values of the three markers, i.e., for any observed realization of AFP, uE$_3$ and HCG (X,Y,Z); refer back to Eqs. (8.13) and (8.14).

The expected utility from declaring the triple test result positive, such that amniocentesis is indicated, is given by the value of information according to Eq. (8.16):

$$
VI_c^{TT} = p \cdot Se_{TT}(X,Y,Z)g - (1-p)(1 - Sp_{TT}(X,Y,Z))(l^{t_{TT}} + \beta l^{t_M}).
$$

We arrive at the following decision rule:

Test positive if $VI_c^{TT} \geq VI_c^{TT*}$, then proceed with amniocentesis.
Test negative if $VI_c^{TT} < VI_c^{TT*}$, then refrain from amniocentesis. $\qquad$ (8.21)

There is a simpler way to proceed than by calculating VI_c^{TT} and VI_c^{TT*} to derive the test outcome. The decision rule Eq. (8.21) is equivalent to

$$
\begin{aligned}
&\text{test positive if } \frac{Se_{TT}(X,Y,Z) - Se_{TT}^*}{Sp_{TT}^* - Sp_{TT}(X,Y,Z)} \geq \frac{\beta + i}{\Omega \cdot \hat{g}}, \\
&\text{test negative if } \frac{Se_{TT}(X,Y,Z) - Se_{TT}^*}{Sp_{TT}^* - Sp_{TT}(X,Y,Z)} < \frac{\beta + i}{\Omega \cdot \hat{g}}.
\end{aligned}
\tag{8.22}
$$

In other words, to interpret a test result, compare the ratio of the changes in sensitivity and specificity to the slope of the level curves of the value of information. This is similar to what we learned about the optimal choice for composite tests in Chap. 7. The reference point for this comparison is the tangential point on the ROC curve. Figure 8.6 gives a graphical representation of the test interpretation. Point A ($Se = 0.84$, $Sp = 0.54$) represents sensitivity and specificity for the values of the three markers ($X = 0.25$, $Y = 0$, $Z = -0.55$). We consider two optima, O_1 and O_2, connected by two different a priori odds, $\Omega_2 > \Omega_1$.

The left-hand side of Eq. (8.22) corresponds to the slope of the lines connecting the observational point A with the respective optimum, i.e., $\tan(\gamma_1)$ and $\tan(\gamma_2)$. If this slope exceeds (is flatter than) the slope of the tangents at the respective optima, i.e., $\tan(o_2)$ and $\tan(o_1)$, the test outcome is positive (negative). Note that this criterion also works for test observations on the ROC curve.

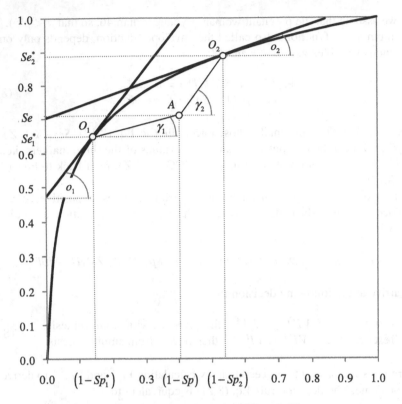

A : Test result (AFP = 0.25, uE3 = 0, HCG = −0.55)
O_1 : Optimum connected with a-priori odds Ω_1
O_2 : Optimum connected with a-priori odds Ω_2 ; $\Omega_2 > \Omega_1$

Fig. 8.6 Deciding on the test results

Box 8.3: Revealed Preferences and Practice Guidelines
It is possible to use decisions taken by patients and their physicians to derive
perceived utility gains and losses from tests and treatments. We want to illustrate this with the example of the triple test. Before biochemical testing was
available, professional institutions recommended employing amniocentesis
routinely beginning at a maternal age of 35, but not before. This recommendation reveals a particular valuation of detecting a fetus with a chromosomal
anomaly in relation to losing a healthy fetus due to the procedure. For the
value of information of amniocentesis, we find

(continued)

Box 8.3 (continued)

$$VI_M(p) = p \cdot g - (1 - p)\beta l^{t_M}.$$

The recommendation implies that the value of information is zero at age 35. With a prevalence rate of $1/385$ at age 35 and $\beta = 1/62.5$ we find $\hat{g} = g$ $/l^{t_M} = 6.14$. Hence, a decision board which recommended routine amniocentesis for women older than 35, before biochemical pretests became available, valued the detection of an abnormal fetus about six times higher than the procedurally induced loss of a healthy fetus.

Now that the triple test is available, the informational value of amniocentesis no longer has to equal zero at the age at which routine amniocentesis is recommended. Rather, the critical age is determined by the prevalence rate at which decision makers are indifferent between the expected utility of sequential testing and the expected utility of amniocentesis. Ignoring the intangible costs of the triple test ($l^{t_{TT}} = 0$), this difference amounts to

$$VI_c^{TT} - VI_M = -p(1 - Se_{TT})\hat{g} + (1 - p)Sp_{TT} \cdot \beta l^{t_M}.$$

This equation illustrates the trade-off involved in using the triple test. Healthy fetuses can be detected and are not subject to the risk of procedure-induced abortions, but fetuses with a chromosomal anomaly may remain undetected.

Suppose the decision board maintained the recommendation for routine amniocentesis at 35 even though biochemical testing is now available. Such a policy would reveal the relative valuation of the intangible costs of the false-positive cases in the triple test. With constant $\hat{g} = 6.14$, one calculates $i = 0.20$. In other words, the intangible costs of the false-positive cases would provide one fifth of the utility of protecting a healthy fetus from a procedure-related miscarriage. These rather high intangible costs are easy to explain. If a harmless pretest can be applied, routine amniocentesis at a higher age might be expected. Only if the intangible costs of false-positive test are considered to be substantial will the age of indication remain constant.

If the decision maker ignored the intangible costs, optimized the sequential test and switched to direct amniocentesis for women of 35 and above, one would obtain $\hat{g} = 29$. If the board had this in mind, the importance of detecting a fetus with a chromosomal anomaly would have increased by a factor of five, once the triple test became available.

Almost 40 years ago, Pauker and Pauker (1979) rationalized routine amniocentesis for women older than 35, because this is the age at which the probability of a procedure-related miscarriage is equal to the prevalence of Down's syndrome. This is equivalent to claiming that $\hat{g} = 1$, since with $\beta = \Omega$, the informational value of the amniocentesis is in fact zero.

(continued)

Box 8.3 (continued)

Kuppermann et al. (1998) study women's preferences regarding the triple test's trade-off. They report a $\hat{g} = 1.27$. If $\hat{g}$ is in fact close to one, the maternal age at which amniocentesis should be conducted without a pretest moves to above 45. We conclude that the recommendations given by professional bodies and current practice in prenatal diagnostics do not seem consistent with the average valuation of the trade-offs made by the patients concerned.

In the first case, the test result is considered negative (since $\tan\gamma_1 < \tan o_1$), in the second it is considered positive (since $\tan\gamma_2 > \tan o_2$). The second optimum corresponds to a higher a priori probability. The result is thus intuitively clear: As an increased prevalence rate lowers the hurdle for declaring the test outcome positive (i.e., the slope of the tangent), the test in our example jumps the hurdle.

The comparison of slopes to decide on test outcomes also works if more arguments, such as the monetary costs of testing, are included in the objective function. These arguments would affect the locus of the maximum on the ROC curve— i.e., the slope of the tangent at O—but not the criterion itself.

We illustrate the decision process using the example introduced above. To decide on the test outcome, the decision maker needs to know $\hat{g}$ and i. Assume that the patient reveals $\hat{g} = 20$. and $i = 3/1000$. If she is 25 years old, the optimal test is given by point O_1 in Fig. 8.6, and the slope of the tangent to the ROC curve equals 1.27. With $Se^* = 0.65$ and $Sp^* = 0.86$ at point O_1, we obtain $Se_{TT} - Se^*_{TT} = 0.19$ and $Sp^*_{TT} - Sp_{TT} = 0.32$. Since $0.19/0.32 = 0.59 < 1.27$, the test outcome is negative according to the criterion in Eq. (8.22). Only if the patient had a much higher $\hat{g}$ (the critical $\hat{g}$ is 25.7) or a substantially lower i (the critical i is negative) or if she were at least 38 years old would the test outcome be positive.

8.5   Notes

McNeil et al. (1975) and Metz (1978) provide a characterization of the optimal cutoff value on the ROC curve without making an explicit reference to the level curves for the value of information. Section 8.4 on the triple test borrows heavily from Felder et al. (2003).

Exercises

1. Assume a patient with an a priori probability of an illness of 20 %. If the patient is sick and gets treatment, he will gain 8 QALYs. If the patient is healthy but is treated he will lose 1 QALY. To detect the illness, the physician can use a

diagnostic test with endogenous test characteristics that are summarized in the following ROC curve: $Se = \sqrt[10]{1 - Sp}$.

(a) Calculate the sensitivity and specificity using the Manhattan norm and the weighted Manhattan norm (see Box 8.1).
(b) Show that the indifference curves of the Manhattan norm have a slope equal to one.
(c) Calculate the sensitivity and specificity using the concept of the optimal cutoff value.
(d) Draw the ROC curve for the diagnostic test and include the different optima.
(e) Compare the results of (b) and (c) and comment.

2. Diagnostic misclassification can be due not only to overlapping distributions of the marker values for the sick and the healthy, but also to measurement errors. Assume that the true measurement variable has only two values, one for the sick and one for the healthy, so that the observed distribution of the variables is due only to measurement errors. Let there be two tests that differ with respect to the variance of the distributions of the measurement error. Test 1 has a lower variance than test 2 for both $f_s(x)$ and $f_h(x)$.

(a) Draw ROC curves for the two tests and explain the difference.
(b) What can you say about the optimal cutoffs for a given prevalence rate p and utility gains and losses from treatment g and l?

3. Harris et al. (2001) discuss the implication of pregnant women's preferences for prenatal testing for chromosomal disorders. They argue that given $g = 1.27$, the maternal age for administering amniocentesis immediately should be lowered to about 30. Remember that for $g = 1$, Pauker and Pauker (1979) calculate an optimal age of around 35, which actually informed the official recommendations given in many countries.

(a) Restate the argument of Harris et al. (2001).
(b) Why were Pauker and Pauker possibly right in 1979? And why were Harris et al. maybe wrong in 2001? Discuss the role of biochemical testing in this context.

References

Anderson, J. L., Adams, C. D., Antman, E. M., Bridges, C. R., Califf, R. M., Casey, D. E., et al. (2011). The ACCF/AHA-focused update incorporated into the ACC/AHA 2007 guidelines for the management of patients' highly sensitive troponin and coronary computed tomography angiography in the evaluation of patients with unstable angina/non-ST-elevation myocardial infarction: A report of the American College of Cardiology Foundation/American Heart Association Task Force on Practice Guidelines. *Circulation, 123*, e426–e579.
Bandstein, N., Ljung, R., Johansson, M., & Holzmann, M. J. (2014). Undetectable high-sensitivity cardiac troponin T-level in the emergency department and risk of myocardial infarction. *Journal of the American College of Cardiology, 63*, 2569–2578.

Body, R., Carley, S., McDowell, G., Jaffe, A. S., France, M., Cruickshank, K., et al. (2011). Rapid exclusion of acute myocardial infarction in patients with undetectable troponin using a high-sensitivity assay. *Journal of the American College of Cardiology, 58*, 1332–1339.

Felder, S., & Mayrhofer, T. (2014). Risk preferences: Consequences for test and treatment thresholds and optimal cutoffs. *Medical Decision Making, 34*(1), 33–41.

Felder, S., Werblow, A., & Robra, B.-P. (2003). A-priori risk and optimal test accuracy in prenatal diagnostics. *Medical Decision Making, 23*(5), 406–413.

Ferencik, M., Liu, T., Mayrhofer, T., Puchner, S. B., Lu, M. T., Maurovich-Horvat, P., et al. (2015). Highly sensitive troponin I followed by advanced coronary artery disease assessment using computed tomography angiography improves acute coronary syndrome risk stratification accuracy and work-up in acute chest pain patients: Results from ROMICAT II trial. *JACC Cardiovascular Imaging, 8*, 1272–1281.

Harris, R. A., Washington, A. E., Feeny, D., & Kuppermann, M. (2001). Decision analysis of prenatal testing for chromosomal disorders: What do the preferences of pregnant women tell us? *Genetic Testing, 5*(1), 23–32.

Hook, E. B. (1985). Maternal age, paternal age and human chromosome abnormality: Nature, magnitude and mechanisms of effects. In V. L. Dellarco & P. E. Voytek (Eds.), *Aneuploidy, etiology and mechanisms* (pp. 117–132). New York: Plenum.

Januzzi, J. L., Sharma, U., Zakroysky, P., Truong, Q. A., Woodard, P. K., Pope, J. H., et al. (2015). Sensitive troponin assays in patients with suspected acute coronary syndrome: Results from the multicenter rule out myocardial infarction using computer assisted tomography II trial. *American Heart Journal, 169*, 572–578.

Kuppermann, M., Goldberg, J. D., Neese, R. F., & Washington, A. E. (1998). Who should be offered prenatal diagnosis? *American Journal of Public Health, 89*(2), 160–163.

Mansfield, C., Hopfer, S., & Marteau, T. M. (1999). Termination rates after prenatal diagnosis of Down Syndrome, Spina Bifida, anencephaly, and Turner and Klinefelter Syndromes: A systematic literature review. *Prenatal Diagnosis, 19*, 808–812.

McNeil, B. J., Keeler, M., & Adelstein, S. M. (1975). Primer on certain elements of medical decision making. *New England Journal of Medicine, 293*(5), 211–215.

Metz, C. E. (1978). Basic principles of ROC analysis. *Seminars in Nuclear Medicine, 8*(4), 283–298.

Niska, R., Bhuiya, F. & Xu, J. (2010). *National Hospital Ambulatory Medical Care Survey: 2007 Emergency Department Summary.* National Health Statistics Reports, Report No. 26, pp. 1–31.

Pauker, S. P., & Pauker, S. G. (1979). The amniocentesis decision: An explicit guide for parents. *Birth Defects, 15*(5C), 289–324.

Puchner, S. B., Liu, T., Mayrhofer, T., Truong, Q. A., Lee, H., Fleg, J. L., et al. (2014). High-risk plaque detected on coronary CT angiography predicts acute coronary syndromes independent of significant stenosis in acute chest pain: Results from the ROMICAT-II trial. *Journal of the American College of Cardiology, 64*, 684–692.

Roffi, M., Patrono, C., Collet, J-P., Mueller, C., Valgimigli, M., Andreotti, F., et al. (2016). 2015 ESC guidelines for the management of acute coronary syndromes in patients presenting without persistent ST-segment elevation: Task Force for the Management of Acute Coronary Syndromes in Patients Presenting without Persistent ST-Segment Elevation of the European Society of Cardiology (ESC). *European Heart Journal, 37*(3), 267–315.

Swap, C. J., & Nagurney, J. T. (2005). Value and limitations of chest pain history in the evaluation of patients with suspected acute coronary syndromes. *JAMA, 294*, 2623–2629.

Thygesen, K., Alpert, J. S., Jaffe, A. S., Simoons, M. L., Chaitman, B. R., White, H. D., et al. (2012). Third universal definition of myocardial infarction. *Journal of the American College of Cardiology, 60*, 1581–1598.

Youden, W. J. (1950). Index for rating diagnostic tests. *Cancer, 3*, 32–35.

Chapter 9
A Test's Total Value of Information

What would you do otherwise?

Howard Raiffa[1]

So far the objective of our analysis has been to guide the decision maker in selecting the optimal test strategy depending on each patient's probability of illness. Often, however, a decision maker needs an overall measure for a test. For instance, a physician who is considering buying a new diagnostic apparatus will be interested in its overall average performance. An aggregate measure is also helpful for government institutions when deciding on investments in public health. Think of screening programs for breast or cervical cancer which are only funded if they are cost-effective. We therefore extend our analysis to the aggregate level by integrating the entire value of information over the prevalence range and over individual patients.

We measure the value of a test in terms of utility. Sometimes, however, it is preferable to have a dimensionless index to characterize a test. This is a further subject that will be discussed in this chapter: We compare a given test with a perfect test to develop a performance index ranging in value from zero to one, where zero indicates a useless test and one a perfect test.

Section 9.1 introduces the concept of test performance when the test characteristics of sensitivity and specificity are given. It derives the index, characterizing aggregate test performance as a function of the a priori probability. On the aggregate level, we differentiate between two indices: one simply integrates the value of information over the prevalence interval, whereas the second does this while considering the number of patients concerned.

Section 9.2 analyzes the case of endogenous test characteristics using the ROC curve and the value of information function that maximizes the patient's expected utility.

Section 9.3 illustrates the different facets of this approach using prenatal diagnostics as an example.

---

[1]Raiffa, H.—*Decision Analysis: Introductory lectures on choices under uncertainty*—Addison-Wesley Publishing Company, Reading, MA—1968, p. 272.

© Springer-Verlag GmbH Germany 2017

S. Felder, T. Mayrhofer, *Medical Decision Making*,

DOI 10.1007/978-3-662-53432-8_9

9.1 Exogenous Test Characteristics

9.1.1 Performance as a Function of the Prevalence Rate

We measure test performance in relative terms, the benchmark being a perfect test defined by $Se = Sp = 1$. The information value of a perfect test, i.e., the value of perfect information, as a function of the prevalence rate is defined as

$$VI^p(p) = \begin{cases} p \cdot g & \text{for} \quad 0 \leq p < p^{Rx}, \\ (1-p)l & \text{for} \quad p^{Rx} \leq p \leq 1. \end{cases} \tag{5.4}$$

For an imperfect test, the value of information is

$$VI(p) = \begin{cases} p \cdot Se \cdot g - (1-p)(1-Sp)l & \text{for} \quad 0 \leq p < p^{Rx}, \\ -p \cdot g(1-Se) + (1-p)Sp \cdot l & \text{for} \quad p^{Rx} \leq p \leq 1. \end{cases} \tag{5.8}$$

The value of perfect information is strictly positive for any p, except for $p = 0$ and $p = 1$. By contrast, the value of imperfect information is negative for p below the test threshold p^t and above the test-treatment threshold p^{tRx} and is strictly positive for $p^t < p < p^{tRx}$.

The utility index $UI(p)$, which is the performance index as a function of the prevalence rate, is the ratio of the values of information of the imperfect and perfect tests:

$$UI(p) = \frac{VI(p)}{VI^p(p)}. \tag{9.1}$$

Let $k = g/l > 0$ denote the ratio of the respective utility gains and losses from treating the sick and the healthy. Inserting Eqs. (5.4) and (5.8) into (9.1), one obtains

$$UI(p) = \begin{cases} Se - (1-Sp) \cdot \dfrac{1}{\Omega \cdot k} & \text{for} \quad 0 \leq p < p^{Rx}, \\ Sp - (1-Se) \cdot \Omega \cdot k & \text{for} \quad p^{Rx} \leq p \leq 1, \end{cases} \tag{9.2}$$

where $\Omega = p/(1-p)$ are the odds of the prevalence p. In order to study the properties of this index, we first calculate the first derivative of the index with respect to Se and Sp, which yields

$$\frac{\partial UI(p)}{\partial Se} = \begin{cases} 1 & \text{for} \quad 0 \leq p < p^{Rx}, \\ k \cdot \Omega & \text{for} \quad p^{Rx} \leq p \leq 1 \end{cases} \tag{9.3}$$

and

$$\frac{\partial UI(p)}{\partial Sp} = \begin{cases} (k \cdot \Omega)^{-1} & \text{for} \quad 0 \leq p < p^{Rx}, \\ 1 & \text{for} \quad p^{Rx} \leq p \leq 1. \end{cases} \tag{9.4}$$

As expected, the utility index is increasing in the sensitivity and the specificity of a test. The index increases one-to-one with an increase in sensitivity (specificity) for prevalence rates below (above) the treatment threshold p^{Rx}. At low prevalence rates, specificity has a much higher weight, whereas at high prevalence rates sensitivity contributes more to the improvement of the test. Note that $UI(p)$ is bounded from above: for a perfect test, i.e., $Se = Sp = 1$, $UI(p) = 1$ over the total prevalence range.

With regard to the prevalence rate, the following results apply: the index is negative at prevalence rates below the test threshold p^t and above the test-treatment threshold p^{tRx}. This is due to the negative value of information in these intervals. Furthermore, we find

$$\frac{\partial UI(p)}{\partial p} = \begin{cases} (1 - Sp)\dfrac{1}{k \cdot p^2} > 0 & \text{for} \quad 0 \leq p < p^{Rx}, \\ -(1 - Se)\dfrac{k}{(1-p)^2} < 0 & \text{for} \quad p^{Rx} \leq p \leq 1. \end{cases} \tag{9.5}$$

This equation reflects the intuition that at low prevalence rates false-positive test results matter most, and at high prevalence rates, false-negative results matter most. The index is increasing in p for $0 \leq p < p^{Rx}$ and decreasing in p for $p^{Rx} \leq p \leq 1.$, producing a concave function which reaches a maximum at the treatment threshold p^{Rx}.

With regard to k, the respective relative utility gain and loss from treating a sick and a healthy individual, is formulated as

$$\frac{\partial UI(p)}{\partial k} = \begin{cases} \dfrac{1 - Sp}{\Omega \cdot k^2} > 0 & \text{for} \quad 0 \leq p < p^{Rx}, \\ -(1 - Se) \cdot \Omega < 0 & \text{for} \quad p^{Rx} \leq p \leq 1. \end{cases} \tag{9.6}$$

At low prevalence rates, $UI(p)$ is increasing in k. Remember that without testing there is no treatment in the low prevalence range. The test has a positive informational value only if the gains from treating the sick exceed the loss from treating the healthy. It is not surprising, then, that the performance index of the test is increasing in the relative advantage that a sick individual experiences from treatment. The opposite holds at high prevalence rates, where $UI(p)$ is decreasing in k. In the high-prevalence range, all individuals undergo treatment unless a test is available. The first function of the test is to spare healthy individuals unnecessary treatment. Consequently, the utility index must decrease if the relative advantage of treatment rises.

Equation (9.6) is helpful in characterizing the effects of risk aversion and prudence on the test's performance. We know, regarding the risk-aversion effect, that $k_A > k_N$, i.e., risk-averse individuals value the gains from treating the sick relative to the loss from treating the healthy more than risk-neutral individuals. The reason is the diminishing marginal utility of health, which puts more weight on increasing a sick patient's status than on preventing a healthy patient's loss.

With respect to prudent behavior, we derived $EG_P > g$. The gain from treating the sick is higher for a prudent decision maker, since he values the marginal value of health in the sick state higher in the presence of comorbidity risk than the risk-averse decision maker. This implies that $k_P > k_A$.

It follows, then, that risk aversion increases a test's utility index at low prevalence rates; and prudence increases the index even further. At high prevalence rates where the reference case is 'treatment', the diminishing marginal utility of health works in the opposite direction—hence the negative sign in Eq. (9.6).

$UI(p)$ is therefore a much more general measure than the common performance criteria of sensitivity and specificity, as it incorporates the respective utility gains and losses of subsequent treatment for the sick and the healthy. Moreover, it provides additional useful information by taking on negative values at prevalence rates where testing is more harmful than beneficial, and positive values where the informational value of the test is positive. Finally, $UI(p)$ is also dimensionless and equal to one if information is perfect.

9.1.2   Overall Performance

Eeckhoudt et al. (1984) propose a comprehensive overall performance measure for tests which integrates the value of information over the entire prevalence range:

$$TVI = \int_0^1 VI(p)dp. \tag{9.7}$$

Let us first establish the total value of perfect information. Inserting the two arms of Eqs. (5.4) into (9.7) and calculating the integrals yields

$$TVI^P = \int_0^{p^{Rx}} p \cdot g\,dp + \int_{p^{Rx}}^1 (1-p)l\,dp$$

$$= \left(\frac{(p^{Rx})^2}{2}\right)g + \left(\frac{1}{2} - p^{Rx} + \frac{(p^{Rx})^2}{2}\right)l$$

$$= \frac{(p^{Rx})^2}{2}(g+l) + \left(\frac{1}{2} - p^{Rx}\right)l. \tag{9.8}$$

Considering the equation for the treatment threshold $p^{Rx} = 1/(1 + g/l)$, we obtain

$$TVI^p = \frac{g}{2(1 + g/l)}.$$ (9.9)

The term in parentheses is the maximum value of perfect information, which is achieved at $p = p^{Rx}$. Now, remember that the value of perfect information as a function of the prevalence rate forms a triangle with a hypotenuse which has a length equal to one (see Fig. 5.2). The area of this triangle, i.e., the total value of perfect information, is thus one-half the length its base (the hypotenuse) times its height.

For the imperfect test, considering Eq. (5.8), we have

$$TVI = \int_0^{p^{Rx}} (p \cdot Se \cdot g - (1-p)(1-Sp)l)dp - \int_{p^{Rx}}^1 (p \cdot g(1 - Se) - (1-p)Sp \cdot l)dp$$

$$= \int_0^1 (p \cdot Se \cdot g + (1-p)Sp \cdot l)dp - l \cdot \int_0^{p^{Rx}} (1-p)dp - g \cdot \int_{p^{Rx}}^1 pdp$$

$$= \frac{1}{2}(Se \cdot g - Sp \cdot l) + Sp \cdot l - p^{Rx} \cdot l + \frac{(p^{Rx})^2}{2}(g + l) - \frac{g}{2}$$

$$= -\frac{1}{2}((1 - Se)g - Sp \cdot l) + p^{Rx}\left(\frac{p^{Rx}}{2}(g + l) - l\right).$$ (9.10)

Using $p^{Rx} = 1/(1 + g/l)$ again, we perform some transformations and arrive at

$$TVI = -\frac{1}{2}\left((1 - Se)g - Sp \cdot l + \frac{l^2}{g + l}\right).$$ (9.11)

Note that for $Se = Sp = 1$, TVI equals TVI^p: See Eqs. (9.9). Rewriting Eq. (9.11) leads to

$$TVI = -\frac{g \cdot l}{2(g + l)}\left(\frac{g(1 - Se)(g + l) - Sp \cdot l(g + l) + l^2}{g \cdot l}\right)$$

$$= \frac{l}{2}\left(Sp - \frac{1}{1 + g/l}\right) - \frac{g}{2}(1 - Se).$$ (9.12)

This expression can now easily be compared to the total value of perfect information to yield the overall performance PI of the test:

$$PI = \frac{TVI}{TVI^P}. \tag{9.13}$$

From Eqs. (9.12), (9.9) and $k = g/l > 0$, we obtain

$$PI = \frac{(1+k)(Sp - (1 - Se)k) - 1}{k}. \tag{9.14}$$

This index equals one if the test is perfect. It is increasing in both Se and Sp. It can be shown that $PI \leq 1$ is satisfied and that $PI \geq 0$ requires $LR^+ \leq k$. The direction of the effect of an increase in k depends on the relative sizes of Se and Sp and on k itself. This is not too surprising; after all, k has a positive effect on $UI(p)$ for $p < p^{Rx}$ and a negative effect for $p > p^{Rx}$: See (9.6).

One shortcoming of the performance index Eq. (9.13) is that it extends to prevalence rates outside the test range, where the informational value of the test is negative. Of course, a rational decision maker would not use the test if its expected utility is negative. These prevalence intervals should therefore be excluded from the calculation of the performance index.

We therefore define an alternative index which only considers prevalence rates at which the informational value of the test is positive. The integral is then bounded from below by the test threshold p^t and from above by the test-treatment threshold p^{tRx}.

Let us use the formula for calculating the area of the triangle with the hypotenuse $(p^{tRx} - p^t)$ and the height $VI(p^{Rx})$:

$$TVI' = \frac{1}{2}(p^{tRx} - p^t)VI(p^{Rx}). \tag{9.15}$$

From Eq. (5.6) and $p^{Rx} = 1/(1 + g/l)$, we derive

$$VI(p^{Rx}) = \frac{g}{1 + g/l}(Se + Sp - 1).$$

We also have

$$p^t = \frac{1 - Sp}{1 - Sp + Se \cdot k}$$

and

$$p^{tRx} = \frac{Sp}{Sp + (1 - Se)k}.$$

Inserting these expressions into Eq. (9.15) yields

$$TVI' = \frac{1}{2}\left(\frac{Sp}{Sp + (1 - Se)k} - \frac{1 - Sp}{1 - Sp + k}\right)\left(\frac{g(Se + Sp - 1)}{1 + g/l}\right)$$

$$= \frac{g(1 - Se - Sp)}{2(1 + g/l)}\left(\frac{(1 - Sp)(Sp + (1 - Se)k) - Sp(1 - Sp + Se \cdot g)}{(Sp + (1 - Se)g)(1 - Sp + Se \cdot k)}\right)$$

$$= \frac{g}{2(1 + g/l)}\left(\frac{(1 - Se - Sp)^2}{(Sp + (1 - Se)k)(1 - Sp + Se \cdot k)}\right).$$

$$(9.16)$$

For $Se = Sp = 1$, the expression in parenthesis equals $1/k$, so that Eq. (9.16) coincides with the equation for the total value of perfect information.

Again, we evaluate the performance of a test using perfect information as the yardstick:

$$PI' = \frac{TVI'}{TVI^p}. \tag{9.17}$$

This equation is then rewritten as

$$PI' = \frac{(1 - Se - Sp)^2}{(Sp/k + (1 - Se))((1 - Sp)/k + Se)}. \tag{9.18}$$

The value of this index also lies between zero and one: its value is zero for a test with no informational value, i.e., a useless test $Se + Sp = 1$, and is one for a perfect test, i.e., $Se = Sp = 1$. Accordingly, the index is increasing in both Se and Sp:

$$\frac{\partial PI'}{\partial Se} = \frac{2Se}{(Sp/k + (1 - Se))^2((1 - Sp)/k + Se)^2} > 0 \tag{9.19}$$

and

$$\frac{\partial PI'}{\partial Sp} = \frac{2Sp}{(Sp/k + (1 - Se))^2((1 - Sp)/k + Se)^2} > 0. \tag{9.20}$$

As before, the effect of k on test performance cannot be determined. Figure 9.1 provides an illustration, displaying PI' for a given ROC curve (which represents a set of different tests) and for different values of k. For $k = 1$, the maximum PI' is reached if $Se = 0.62$ and $Sp = 0.85$. For $k = 5$, the maximum is reached for $Se = 0.75$ and $Sp = 0.73$. For $k = 10$, we have $Se = 0.75$ and $Sp = 0.70$. In this example PI' is decreasing in k for $k \geq 1$. These tests are therefore particularly valuable in the prevalence range above the treatment threshold.

Instead of calculating the total performance of a test across the entire prevalence range, one could consider a smaller interval if the prevalence of a particular illness

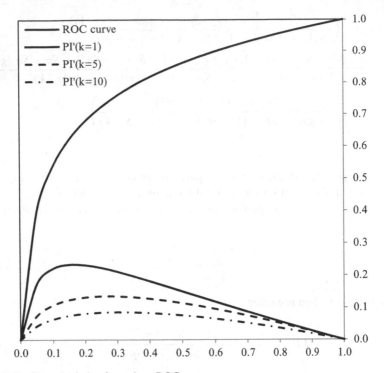

Fig. 9.1 Performance index for a given ROC curve

is known to lie mainly between two probabilities, p_0 and p_1. In this case, the performance index would be calculated for this confined interval.

Box 9.1: Needle Biopsy of the Kidney

This example is taken from Eeckhoudt et al. (1984), who themselves refer to Pauker and Kassirer (1980) for a full description of the medical problem.

A 55-year-old man has been suffering from severe hypertension for 5 years. He has no history to date of kidney disease. He is now suspected of developing renal vasculitis and has therefore been on corticosteroid therapy for the past 24 h. Let us assume the disease to be steroid-responsive vasculitis and the treatment to involve continuous corticosteroid therapy for 1 or 2 months. The parameters are as follows: The a priori probability of the disease is estimated to be 65 %, and the utility gain and loss from treatment is estimated to be 0.38 (if the disease is present) and 0.05 (if the patient does not suffer from renal vasculitis).

(continued)

Box 9.1 (continued)

The test that is available to support the therapeutic decision involves a needle biopsy of the kidney. The biopsy has a sensitivity of 90 % and a specificity of 95 %. The expected utility loss from severe complications due to the test procedure is 0.02.

With this knowledge, we can calculate the informational value of the test as a function of the prevalence rate. The following figure displays the value of information for the biopsy and compares it with a perfect test.

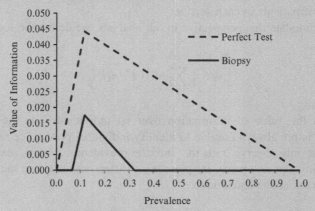

For the patient in our example, treatment should be pursued without a biopsy, since $UI' = 0$ at a prevalence of 0.65.

The positive likelihood ratio of the test is rather high:

$$LR^+ = \frac{Se}{1 - Sp} = 18.$$

The overall performance PI' of the biopsy is rather low:

$$PI' = \frac{TVI'}{TVI^p} = 0.10.$$

Eeckhoudt et al. (1984) point out the difference between a purely statistical and an economic approach: The needle biopsy has a fairly high likelihood ratio and seems very efficient from a statistical point of view. However, when economic parameters are considered its average performance relative to that of a perfect test drops considerably.

9.1.3 A Social Perspective

Integration over the entire prevalence range does not take account of the fact that patients are usually not uniformly distributed across this range. For instance, a physician might mainly diagnose and treat patients with a low a priori probability of illness and only rarely see high-risk patients. If he wants to evaluate the performance of a test for his purposes, he might consider weighting individual prevalence rates with the number of patients concerned. Along the same lines, a social planer would focus on the distribution of prevalence rates in the population and consider the number of patients in each section.

To accommodate this perspective in our analysis, we define the social value of information,

$$SVI = \sum_i p(i)VI^*(p(i)), \tag{9.21}$$

which sums the value of information over all individuals i in the population. However, it is not always feasible to identify individual prevalence rates directly; often we can only observe traits that indicate prevalence, such as sex or age. For instance, using age as a proxy for prevalence differences between individuals, we can redefine the above equation to

$$SVI = \sum_a p(a)B(a)VI^*(p(a)), \tag{9.22}$$

where $p(a)$ is the prevalence rate at age a, and $B(a)$ is the size of the population of age a. The social performance index then becomes

$$SPI = \frac{\sum_a p(a)B(a)VI^*(p(a))}{\sum_a p(a)B(a)VI^p(p(a))}. \tag{9.23}$$

It is evident that this index, like the other performance indices, spans the unit interval. The difference compared to PI' is that it represents a weighted average of a test's performance across the prevalence interval.

9.2 Endogenous Test Characteristics

In the last chapter, we discussed the optimal cutoff value in a test setting where the positivity criterion is not given, but has to be chosen by the decision maker. An application of this theory to the performance index of a test, both as a function of the prevalence rate and as a whole, is straightforward. Let us deal with the two performance measures in turn.

9.2.1 Performance as a Function of the Prevalence Rate

The optimal cutoff value x^* maximizes a test's informational value as a function of the exogenous variables p, g and l. We use this to derive the maximum informational value function

$$VI^*(p, g, l) = \begin{cases} p \cdot Se^* \cdot g - (1-p)(1 - Sp^*)l & \text{for} \quad 0 \leq p < p^{Rx}, \\ -p \cdot g(1 - Se^*) + (1-p)Sp^* \cdot l & \text{for} \quad p^{Rx} \leq p \leq 1, \end{cases}$$

(9.24)

where $Se^* \equiv Se(x^*) = Se(p, g, l)$ and $Sp^* \equiv Sp(x^*) = Sp(p, g, l)$ represent the optimal Se and Sp as functions of the exogenous variable. We can now write the prevalence-specific utility index as

$$UI^*(p) = \frac{VI^*(p)}{VI^p(p)} = \begin{cases} Se^* - (1 - Sp^*) \cdot \dfrac{l}{\Omega \cdot g} & \text{for} \quad 0 \leq p < p^{Rx}, \\ Sp^* - (1 - Se^*) \cdot \dfrac{\Omega \cdot g}{l} & \text{for} \quad p^{Rx} \leq p \leq 1. \end{cases}$$

(9.25)

Let $VI(p)$ denote the informational value of an arbitrarily chosen cutoff value. By definition $VI^*(p) \geq VI(p)$ must hold. It therefore follows that $UI^*(p) \geq UI(p)$. This result is straightforward and intuitively clear: The performance of a test is best if the cutoff value is optimally set.

9.2.2 Overall Performance

The property that performance is maximal if a test is optimally chosen must also hold with respect to a test's total performance. We refine the performance index Eq. (9.17) to include the maximum total value of information resulting from optimally chosen Se and Sp:

$$PI'^* = \frac{TVI'^*}{TVI^p},$$

(9.26)

with

$$TVI'^* = \int_0^{p^{Rx}} (p \cdot Se^* \cdot g - (1-p)(1-Sp^*)l)dp$$

$$\quad - \int_{p^{Rx}}^1 (p \cdot g(1-Se^*) - (1-p)Sp^* \cdot l)dp \tag{9.27}$$

and TVI^p according to Eq. (9.9). Note that the equation for the performance index Eq. (9.18) which we calculated as the area of a triangle, does not hold for optimally chosen Se and Sp, since $VI(p)$ is no longer linear in p.

TVI'^* can only be calculated if the ROC curve is known. Nevertheless, it is possible to derive a general property of the performance index Eq. (9.26). TVI^p remains constant, and since we know that $TVI'^* \geq TVI'$, we can conclude that $PI'^* \geq PI'$.

9.3   Application to Prenatal Diagnostics

Chapter 8 introduced the example of prenatal diagnostics. Let us repeat here the equations required to calculate the performance indices. The value of information of this sequential test, starting with the triple test and performing amniocentesis if the triple test is positive, amounts to

$$VI_c^{TT*}(p) = \begin{cases} p \cdot Se_{TT}^* \cdot g \\ -(1-p)\left(1-Sp_{TT}^*\right)(l^{t_{TT}} + \beta l^{t_M}) & \text{for} \quad 0 \leq p < p^{Rx}, \\[2mm] -p\left(1-Se_{TT}^*\right)g + (1-p)l^{t_M} \\ -(1-p)\left(1-Sp_{TT}^*\right)(l^{t_{TT}} + \beta l^{t_M}) & \text{for} \quad p^{Rx} \leq p \leq 1, \end{cases} \tag{9.28}$$

where g is the utility gain from detecting a fetus with a chromosomal disorder, $l^{t_{TT}}$ are the intangible costs of a false positive triple test result, l^{t_M} is the utility loss of losing a healthy fetus due to a procedure-related miscarriage, and β is the probability of this occurring. The asterisks indicate that Se and Sp are chosen to maximize the value of information, given the exogenous parameters such as the prevalence rate.

For a perfect triple test, the value of information reduces to

$$VI_c^{TTp}(p) = \begin{cases} p \cdot g & \text{for} \quad 0 \leq p < p^{Rx}, \\ (1-p)l^{t_M} & \text{for} \quad p^{Rx} \leq p < 1. \end{cases} \tag{9.29}$$

The following restrictions and parameter values shall apply to prenatal diagnostics: Feasible pairs of sensitivity and specificity of the triple test are given by the

ROC curve, $Se_{TT} = 1 + 0.1827\ln(1 - Sp_{TT})$. The probability of a pregnant woman bearing a fetus with a chromosomal anomaly is given by $p = 6.1E - 04 + exp(0.286a - 16.18)$, where a denotes maternal age. This probability increases exponentially with age. The procedure-related rate of miscarriage due to amniocentesis is $\beta = \frac{1}{62.5}$. The relative value of detecting an abnormal fetus compared to losing a healthy fetus is assumed to be $k = g/l^{t_M} = 20$. And the intangible cost of the triple test, again compared to the utility loss of losing a healthy fetus, is $i = l^{t_{TT}}/l^{t_M} = 3/1,000$. Under these parameters, it is optimal to switch to amniocentesis at age 35, as is often recommended in clinical guidelines.

9.3.1   Age-Specific Performance

The age-specific utility index compares the value of information of the triple test with that of a perfect test. The parameter values imply that the treatment threshold arises at the age of 46. The switch from performing the triple test first to direct amniocentesis occurs at an even younger age, as will we see below. Thus, we can restrict the calculation of the value of information of the triple test to the upper arms of Eqs. (9.28) and (9.29). We find

$$
\begin{aligned}
UI_c^{TT}(p(a)) &= \frac{VI_c^{TT*}}{VI_c^{TTp}} = \frac{p \cdot Se_{TT}^* \cdot g - (1-p)(1 - Sp_{TT}^*)(l^{t_{TT}} + \beta l^{t_M})}{p \cdot g} \\
&= Se_{TT}^* - \frac{(1-p)(1 - Sp_{TT}^*)l^{t_M}(l^{t_{TT}}/l^{t_M} + \beta)}{p \cdot g} \\
&= Se_{TT}^* - (1 - Sp_{TT}^*)\frac{(i + \beta)}{\Omega \cdot k},
\end{aligned}
\tag{9.30}
$$

where $k = g/l > 0$. We fix the test range for the triple test at the age interval [16, 35]. Figure 9.2 illustrates the test performance as a function of maternal age. The dark curve shows the performance of the sequential test. At younger ages the performance of the sequential test is nearly constant, as the prevalence rate for prenatal chromosomal anomaly does not change much. The figure is very different for ages above 25, where test performance rises with increasing age due to the rising prevalence rate.

The lowest curve represents the performance of amniocentesis. At age 35, the two curves intersect, implying that it is preferable, thenceforth, to perform the amniocentesis instead of the sequential test. The performance of amniocentesis is negative at maternal ages of 26 and below. Hence, without access to the triple test, amniocentesis would only be performed beyond the age of 26.

The third curve shows test performance when sensitivity and specificity are optimized for a 29-year-old woman ($Se = 0.70$, $Sp = 0.81$). This is also the age at which the optimized triple test reaches its maximum discriminatory power. Fixing sensitivity and specificity at these values does not change the performance of the

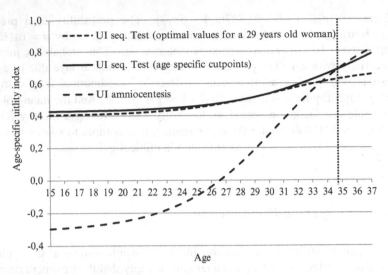

Fig. 9.2 Test performance as a function of maternal age

triple test for younger women. This, again, is due to the near-constant a priori risk of chromosomal anomalies at younger maternal ages. However, the performance loss is significant if the triple test is not readjusted for women beyond 30.

9.3.2 Overall Performance

To evaluate the overall performance of the composite test—triple test and amniocentesis—we first aggregate the maximal informational value function over the ROC curve and compare it to the informational value of the perfect test:

$$TVI_c^{TT*} = \sum_{a=16}^{35} p(a)Se_{TT}^* \cdot g - (1-p(a))(1-Sp_{TT}^*)(l^{t_{TT}} + \beta l^{t_M}), \qquad (9.31)$$

$$PI_c^{TT*} = \frac{\displaystyle\sum_{a=16}^{35} p(a)Se_{TT}^* da}{\displaystyle\sum_{a=16}^{35} p(a)} - \frac{(i+\beta)}{k} \frac{\displaystyle\sum_{a=16}^{35} (1-p(a))(1-Sp_{TT}^*)}{\displaystyle\sum_{a=16}^{35} p(a)}. \qquad (9.32)$$

The resulting value is $PI_c^{TT*} = 0.54$. The average performance of the composite test is 54 % of the level of a perfect test if the cutoff value is adjusted at every age so as to maximize expected utility. If the cutoff value is fixed at the value that is optimal for a 29 year old, performance decreases to 52 %.

Taking a societal perspective, we use maternal ages at birth in Germany in 2008 as a proxy for the age distribution of women seeking prenatal diagnostics:

$$SVI_c^{TT}* =$$

$$\sum_{a=16}^{35} p(a)B(a)Se_{TT}^* \cdot g - (1 - p(a))B(a)\left(1 - Sp_{TT}^*\right)\left(l^{t_{TT}} + \beta l^{t_M}\right) \tag{9.33}$$

and

$$SPI_c^{TT}* = \frac{\displaystyle\sum_{a=16}^{35} p(a)B(a)Se_{TT}^*}{\displaystyle\sum_{a=16}^{35} p(a)B(a)} - \frac{(i+\beta)}{k}\frac{\displaystyle\sum_{a=16}^{35}(1 - p(a))B(a)\left(1 - Sp_{TT}^*\right)}{\displaystyle\sum_{a=16}^{35} p(a)B(a)}, \tag{9.34}$$

where $B(a)$ is the number of births at maternal age a. As a result, the index rises to $SPI_c^{TT}* = 0.56$. This increase is due to the peak in women's fertility in their late twenties and early thirties where the performance of the triple test is higher than average.

Box 9.2: Alternative Overall Performance Indices
Sometimes the area under the ROC curve is taken as a proxy measurement for the overall performance of a test. As the perfect test corresponds to the area of the $(Se, 1 - Sp)$ square, which equals one, this approach is tantamount to a performance index with a maximum value of one. A useless test (i.e. $Se + Sp = 1$), however, would feature an index value of 0.5, the area under the diagonal. To overcome this, an alternative (common) approach is to calculate the area between the ROC curve and the diagonal (see Zhou et al. 2002, for an overview). The disadvantage of this method is that the maximum value is 0.5 and not one. To gain an index from zero to one, one could calculate the ratios of the areas between the ROC curve and the diagonal for imperfect and perfect tests.

This index, denoted by W, amounts to

$$W = 2\int_0^1 Se[1 - Sp]dSp - 1,$$

where $Se[1 - Sp]$ is the ROC function. This index incorporates only statistical information, abstracting from economic parameters such as utility and the cost of testing and treatment. The statistical approach implies that every point on the ROC curve has the same weight, while an economic approach

(continued)

Box 9.2 (continued)
considers that, depending on the prevalence rate and the g/l ratio, some parts
of the ROC curve are more valuable than others.

Compare, for example, the statistical and the economic approaches for our
prenatal diagnostics example. If the ROC curve can be represented by a semi-
logarithmic curve ($Se = 1 + aln(1 - Sp)$ with $0 < a < 1$), one finds that W
$= 1 - 2a$. In the example where $a = 0.18$, we calculate $W = 0.64$. This value
is much higher than the preference-based average performance of the test
($PI^* = 0.54$).

We can now finally compare the gross utility and the non-monetary costs of the
optimal test strategy. The corresponding cost-effectiveness ratio is

$$CER_c^{TT*} = \frac{(i + \beta)}{k} \frac{\sum\limits_{a=16}^{35} (1 - p(a))B(a)(1 - Sp_{TT}^*)}{\sum\limits_{a=16}^{35} p(a)B(a)Se_{TT}^*}. \tag{9.35}$$

This ratio amounts to 0.245 in our example. Hence, given the above parameters,
including the relative value of detecting an affected fetus and losing an unaffected
one, the average non-monetary cost of combining the triple test and amniocentesis
is approximately one quarter of the size of the benefits.

So far, we have not considered the monetary cost of diagnosis and treatment in
our analysis of test performance. A relative measure of performance for tests would
be hard to integrate in this setting. From a societal perspective, a decision between
tests would therefore be made based on assessing the respective expected monetized utilities and monetary costs (as a function of the prevalence rate as developed
in Sect. 5.5, and only for the range within which testing is indicated). This could be
realized as a variation of SVI (see Eq. (9.22)), extended to include the monetary cost
of testing and treating.

9.4 Notes

Diamond et al. (1981) follow a purely statistical approach. They also define a test's
value of information as a function of the prevalence rate, as well as an average
information content given by the area under the information curve. Eeckhoudt et al.
(1984) extend this approach to include the benefits and costs of testing and
treatment, similar to the argument we present here. They also hint at the possibility
of calculating the ratio of the total value of perfect information and the total value of

information of an imperfect test to obtain an indicator of efficiency. Felder and Robra (2006) propose an alternative performance measure and applied it to prenatal diagnostics.

Exercises

1. Overall performance of a test PI:

    (a) Show that $PI \geq 0$ is satisfied.
    (b) Show that $PI \leq 1$ requires $g \geq LR^+$. Explain why $PI \leq 1$ is not always satisfied.
    (c) Derive $\partial PI / \partial k$ and discuss its sign.

2. Patients with heart problems can be treated with digoxin. This might lead to digoxin poisoning, in which case treatment must be discontinued. Eraker and Sasse (1981) examine a serum test for digoxin poisoning. At serum digoxin concentrations above 2.0 ng/ml, the sensitivity and the specificity of the test are 0.47 and 0.96, respectively. The utility gain from discontinuing digoxin for intoxicated patients is stated as 0.99 and the utility loss from discontinuing digoxin for non-intoxicated patients as 0.1.

    (a) Calculate the treatment threshold as well as the test and test-treatment thresholds. Regard the discontinuation of digoxin therapy as the 'treatment' and the continuation of digoxin therapy as the 'no treatment' case.
    (b) Display the value of information of the serum digoxin test as a function of the prevalence rate and compare it to a perfect test.
    (c) Calculate the likelihood ratios of the digoxin test and interpret the results.
    (d) Calculate the overall performance PI' of the test and interpret the result in relation to (c).

3. Consider the example given in Box 5.1 in Chap. 5.

    (a) Calculate the total value of information for the imperfect and the perfect test TVI and TVI^P as well as the overall performance PI.
    (b) Now assume that the informational value of the test cannot fall below zero (otherwise the decision maker would not use it). How do the results of (a) change?
    (c) Compare PI and PI' and explain the difference.

References

Diamond, G. A., Hirsch, M., Forrester, J. S., Staniloff, H. M., Vasl, R., Halpern, S. W., et al. (1981). Application of information theory to clinical diagnostic testing. The electrocardiographic stress test. *Circulation, 63*(4), 915–921.

Eeckhoudt, L. R., Lebrun, T. C., & Sailly, J.-C. L. (1984). The informative content of diagnostic tests: An economic analysis. *Social Science & Medicine, 18*(10), 873–880.

Eraker, S. A., & Sasse, L. (1981). The serum digoxin test and digoxin toxicity: A Bayesian approach. *Circulation, 640*, 409–420.

Felder, S., & Robra, B.-P. (2006). A preference-based measure for test performance with an application to prenatal diagnostics. *Journal of Statistics in Medicine, 25*(21), 3696–3706.

Pauker, S. G., & Kassirer, J. P. (1980). The threshold approach to clinical decision making. *New England Journal of Medicine, 302*(20), 1109–1117.

Zhou, X.-H., Obuchowski, N. A., & McClish, D. K. (2002). *Statistical methods in diagnostic medicine* (2nd ed.). New York: Wiley.

Chapter 10
Valuing Health and Life

> Ob ich nun in Bayreuth noch 20 Gänse mehr esse
> oder 50 mal öfter in die Harmonie gehe,
> dies ist der Unterschied des längeren Lebens.
> Das Leben als Leben muss etwas wert sein, aber nicht als Zeit.
>
> Jean Paul[1]

In this book, we have distinguished between risk-neutral and risk-averse decision makers. Moreover, among the risk-averse types we identified the special case of prudent decision makers. We have shown that different risk preferences have an impact on test and treatment strategies. Risk-averse decision makers tend to test and treat at lower prevalence rates than risk-neutral ones, and prudent decision makers act even earlier.

In all settings, we have assumed that the effects of treatment on health are given; i.e., that the respective differences for sick and healthy patients, $h_s^+ - h_s^- > 0$ and $h_h^+ - h_h^- < 0$, are exogenous. In this chapter, we soften this assumption and endogenize the type or extent of treatment and thus the (potential) improvement in the patient's health. A natural way to proceed is to extend the decision maker's utility function to include, besides health, a composite consumer good and introduce a budget constraint. By doing so, a demand-side trade-off arises between the patient's enjoyment of health and his consumption of other goods. Here, the patient's solution to this trade-off, as decision maker, will tell us how he values his health.

We focus the analysis on the sick state. The objective is to determine the gain from treatment for the sick, $g = u(h_s^+) - u(h_s^-)$ if the patient's improvement in health $\hat{h}$, $\hat{h} = h_s^+ - h_s^-$, is endogenous. The demand for health then determines the

---

[1] If I enjoy eating 20 more geese or visiting the Harmonie 50 more times in Bayreuth, this is the difference of a longer life. Life as such must be evaluated in terms of something other than simply time. Inscription Town Hall of Bayreuth, Germany.

© Springer-Verlag GmbH Germany 2017
S. Felder, T. Mayrhofer, *Medical Decision Making*,
DOI 10.1007/978-3-662-53432-8_10

demand for medical services. Next, we introduce a health production function $\hat{h}$ $= f(m)$, where m is the input of medical services. We abstract from the utility loss, l, that a healthy patient suffers as a result of treatment, which could be made dependent on h as well, and also disregard the effect of the a priori rate of illness on the treatment decision. Instead, we introduce mortality as a further argument. Treatment is often directed towards preventing death and reducing the probability of dying. We will take this into account by modeling a survival production function where m is again the input. Furthermore, expected utility depends on the probability of survival.

We distinguish between health and health-survival models. In Sect. 10.1, we present the health model, which includes consumption and health as arguments in the utility function. We derive the demand for health as a function of the exogenous variables of income, the initial health level, and the price and the marginal product of medical inputs. In Sect. 10.2, we present the health-survival model. Here, we add the survival production function to the health model and derive the investment in health as a function of the exogenous variables in this health-survival model. Comparing the two models allows us to distinguish between quality and quantity aspects of health investments.

In Sect. 10.3, we define the values of health and life, which permits an alternative characterization of the optima with respect to medical demand in the two models. In the health model, the individual's optimum solution is where the value of health equals its marginal cost. In the health-survival model, the individual's optimum solution is where the value of life equals its marginal cost.

In Sect. 10.4, we use the health and health-survival models to characterize the allocation of a social planner faced with the problem of how to allocate consumption and health across individuals. We restrict our analysis to the utilitarian solution, which is a natural choice as issues of inequality are beyond the scope of our discussion and are ignored here. We show that in the health model the utilitarian planner equalizes the value of health across all individuals if they have equal preferences and production functions. In the health-survival model, he equalizes the values of health and life across all individuals only if they also earn the same income. We conclude the section by characterizing the allocation in the QALY model.

In Sect. 10.5, we draw implications from the results of this chapter for the test strategies and the test and test-treatment thresholds analyzed in the previous chapters.

10.1 Treatment and Health

We extend the patient's utility function, which so far only contained health as an argument, to include consumption as well. We keep the assumption that the physician's decisions follow the patient's preferences. The patient's new utility $u(c, h)$ is a strictly positive and strictly increasing function of his consumption c and health h, provided he stays alive, i.e., $u > 0$, $\partial u/\partial c = u_c > 0$, $\partial u/\partial h = u_h > 0$. Furthermore, we assume that the individual is risk-averse, so that $\partial^2 u/\partial c^2 = u_{cc} < 0$ and $\partial^2 u/\partial h^2 = u_{hh} < 0$, and that the mixed derivatives are zero, i.e., $\partial^2 u/\partial c \partial h = \partial^2 u/\partial h \partial c = 0$.

The individual faces a strictly positive probability of death. If the utility associated with the state of death were undefined or $-\infty$, we could not define a meaningful overall utility function. Still, individuals seem to handle choices involving risks to their lives quite rationally—for instance, climbing Swiss mountains rather than sitting at home and watching TV.

We proceed with the following set of assumptions:

$$u(c = 0, h > 0) > 0,$$
$$u(c, h = 0) = 0 \qquad \text{for all } c > 0. \tag{10.1}$$

The individual thus prefers to stay alive (avoid health state 0) even if this means that he can consume virtually nothing else and that no consumption level, however high (and transferrable to his heirs), can compensate for the loss of his own life.

To use the previous notation, we differentiate between health before and health after treatment in the following way: $h = h_s^- + \hat{h}$ where h_s^- is initial health and $\hat{h}$ is the health improvement resulting from treatment. Health can be produced with medical inputs m at a decreasing marginal product,

$$\hat{h} = f(m), \tag{10.2}$$

with $f'(m) = \partial f/\partial m > 0$ and $f''(m) = \partial^2 f/\partial m^2 < 0$.

With zero utility assigned to the state of death and π as the probability of survival, the individual's expected utility becomes

$$EU = \pi u(c, h). \tag{10.3}$$

The individual's budget is constrained by his income y, which can be spent on consumption c and medical inputs m. Let the price of consumption be equal to one and the price of medical inputs be p_m. The budget constraint then is

$$c + p_m m = y. \tag{10.4}$$

For the derivation of the optimal solution, we establish the Lagrangian function $L = \pi u\left(c, f(m) + h_s^-\right) + \lambda(y - c - p_m m)$, where $\hat{h}$ is replaced by $f(m)$ in the objective function. The first order conditions for a maximum are

$$\frac{\partial L}{\partial c} = \pi u_c - \lambda = 0, \tag{10.5}$$

$$\frac{\partial L}{\partial m} = \pi u_h f'(m) - \lambda p_m = 0, \tag{10.6}$$

$$\frac{\partial L}{\partial \lambda} = y - c - p_m m = 0, \tag{10.7}$$

where λ is the marginal utility of income and $f'(m)$ is the marginal product of medical inputs. From Eqs. (10.5) and (10.6), we obtain the combined first-order condition

$$\frac{u_h}{u_c} = \frac{p_m}{f'(m)}. \tag{10.8}$$

The ratio $p_m/f'(m)$ can be interpreted as the marginal cost of health investment. It is increasing in the price and decreasing in the marginal product of medical inputs. If we rewrite the first-order condition as $u_h f'(m)/p_m = u_c$ and take into account that the price of consumption is equal to one, we obtain an intuitive interpretation of Eq. (10.8): At the optimum, the last monetary unit spent yields the same marginal utility irrespective of whether it is spent on medical inputs or consumption.

Figure 10.1 illustrates the optimal choice of consumption and health on a graph with four quadrants. The NW quadrant shows the budget constraint for spending on consumption and medical inputs. The budget line has a slope equal to $-1/p_m$, which shows relative prices at which consumption is traded for medical inputs. The budget line intercepts the x and y axes at y/p_m and y, respectively, marking the extreme situations where the individual would spend all his income on one good.

The SE quadrant contains the health production function, starting at initial health h_s^-. Its shape is concave due to a decreasing marginal product: $\hat{h} = f(m)$ with $f(m) = 0$ for $m = 0$.

The NE quadrant displays the consumer's choice, featuring the consumption possibility curve and the indifference curve marking consumption-health bundles that produce the same expected utility level (i.e., $dEU = 0$). Up to $h = h_s^-$ the consumption possibility curve is horizontal. We can formulate the consumption possibility curve as

$$c(h) = c\left(h_s^- + f(m)\right). \tag{10.9}$$

Its derivative is

$$\frac{dc}{dm} = \frac{dc}{dh} f'(m). \tag{10.10}$$

The individual can trade consumption and medical inputs at a relative price equal to $1/p_m$; i.e., $dc/dm = -p_m$. This leads directly to the slope of the consumption possibility curve if $h = h_s^- + \hat{h} > h_s^-$:

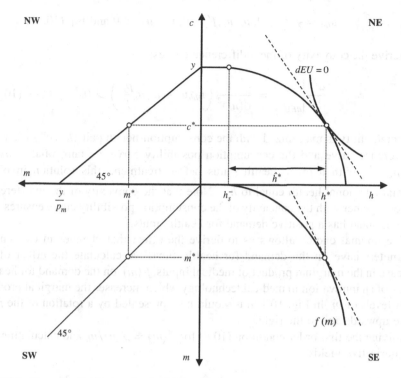

Fig. 10.1 The optimal consumption-health bundle

$$\frac{dc}{dh} = -\frac{p_m}{f'(m)}. \tag{10.11}$$

With $p_m < 1$, the consumption possibility curve is flatter than the health production curve in the quadrant, i.e., $-p_m/f' < -1/f'$.

The indifference curves each indicate loci of consumption-health bundles with the same utility. The marginal rate of substitution between consumption and medical inputs can be derived from the total differential $dEU = \pi(u_c \cdot dc + u_h \cdot dh) = 0$ to yield

$$\left.\frac{dc}{dh}\right|_{dEU=0} = -\frac{u_h}{u_c} < 0. \tag{10.12}$$

For the second derivative, we find

$$\left.\frac{d^2c}{dh^2}\right|_{dEU=0} = -\frac{1}{(u_c)^2}\left[\left(u_{hh} + u_{hc}\frac{dc}{dh}\right)u_c - \left(u_{ch} + u_{cc}\frac{dc}{dh}\right)u_h\right]. \tag{10.13}$$

Taking into account

$u_{ch} = \frac{\partial^2 u}{\partial c \partial h} = u_{hc} = \frac{\partial^2 u}{\partial h \partial c} = 0$, $u_c, u_h, f' > 0$, $u_{hh}, u_{cc} < 0$ and Eq. (10.11),

we derive the convexity of the indifference curves:

$$\left.\frac{d^2 c}{dh^2}\right|_{dEU=0} = -\frac{1}{(u_c)^2}\left(u_{hh}u_c + u_{cc}u_h\frac{p_m}{f'}\right) > 0. \tag{10.14}$$

Expected utility is maximized with the consumption-health pair (h^*, c^*) where an indifference curve and the consumption possibility curve are tangential: $-u_h/u_c = -p_m/f'$. With a given health status before treatment, this solution involves optimal additional health equal to $\hat{h}^*$. Note that the convexity of the indifference curves together with the concavity of the consumption possibility curve ensures that the individual has a positive demand for health inputs.

The optimal choice allows us to derive the effect that changes in exogenous parameters have on the demand for health. First, we calculate the effect of an increase in the marginal product of medical inputs, $f'(m)$, on the demand for health. Think of an innovation in medical technology which increases the marginal product at all levels of m. In Fig. 10.1, this would be represented by a rotation of the $f(m)$ curve upwards and to the right.

Solving the first order condition (10.8) for $f'(m) = p_m u_c/u_h$ and calculating the first derivative yields

$$\frac{\partial(f'(m))}{\partial m} = \frac{p_m(u_{ch}f'(m)u_h - u_{hh}f'(m)u_c)}{(u_h)^2} = -\frac{u_{hh}(f'(m))^2}{u_h}. \tag{10.15}$$

The inverse of this equation provides the desired result:

$$\frac{\partial m}{\partial(f'(m))} = -\frac{u_h}{u_{hh}(f')^2} > 0. \tag{10.16}$$

This is positive due to $u_h > 0$ and $u_{hh} < 0$. The change in demand for health follows directly from the change in demand for medical inputs:

$$\frac{\partial h}{\partial(f'(m))} = f'\frac{\partial m}{\partial(f'(m))} = -\frac{u_h}{u_{hh}f'} > 0. \tag{10.17}$$

Thus, the demands for health and for medical services are increasing in the marginal product of medical inputs. These results are intuitive: If the marginal cost of producing health decreases, ceteris paribus, the demand for health and thus for medical inputs rises.

A corresponding but negative effect can be expected from an increase in the price of medical inputs. Writing the first-order condition (10.8) as $p_m u_c = f'(m)u_h$, we derive

$$u_c + p_m u_{cc} \frac{\partial c}{\partial p_m} = f'' \frac{\partial m}{\partial p_m} u_h + u_{hh}(f')^2 \frac{\partial m}{\partial p_m}. \tag{10.18}$$

The budget constraint—see Eq. (10.4)—implies that

$$\frac{\partial c}{\partial p_m} = -m - p_m \frac{\partial m}{\partial p_m}. \tag{10.19}$$

Inserting this equation into Eq. (10.18) and rearranging the terms yields

$$u_c - p_m u_{cc} m = \frac{\partial m}{\partial p_m} \left(f'' u_h + u_{hh}(f')^2 + (p_m)^2 u_{cc} \right). \tag{10.20}$$

Then $u_{hh}, u_{cc}, f'' < 0$ and $u_c, u_h > 0$, so that $D = f'' u_h + u_{hh}(f')^2 + (p_m)^2 u_{cc} < 0$ and we find

$$\frac{\partial m}{\partial p_m} = \frac{u_c - p_m u_{cc} m}{D} < 0 \tag{10.21}$$

and

$$\frac{\partial h}{\partial p_m} = f' \frac{\partial m}{\partial p_m} = \frac{f'(u_c - p_m u_{cc} m)}{D} < 0. \tag{10.22}$$

In other words, the demands for medical inputs and health decrease if the price of medical inputs rises.

Regarding the effect of an increase in income, $p_m u_c = f'(m)u_h$ leads to

$$p_m u_{cc} \frac{\partial c}{\partial y} = f'' \frac{\partial m}{\partial y} u_h + u_{hh}(f')^2 \frac{\partial m}{\partial y}. \tag{10.23}$$

From the budget constraint Eq. (10.4), we have

$$\frac{\partial c}{\partial y} = 1 - p_m \frac{\partial m}{\partial y}. \tag{10.24}$$

We then obtain

$$\frac{\partial m}{\partial y} = \frac{p_m u_{cc}}{D} > 0 \tag{10.25}$$

and

$$\frac{\partial h}{\partial y} = f' \frac{\partial m}{\partial y} = \frac{f' p_m u_{cc}}{D} > 0. \tag{10.26}$$

As its demand increases as income rises, health is a normal good.

With respect to the health level before treatment, we return to the first-order condition and find

$$p_m u_{cc} \frac{\partial c}{\partial h_s^-} = f'' \frac{\partial m}{\partial h_s^-} u_h + u_{hh} f' \left(1 + f' \frac{\partial m}{\partial h_s^-}\right). \tag{10.27}$$

The budget constraint posits that

$$\frac{\partial c}{\partial h_s^-} = -p_m \frac{\partial m}{\partial h_s^-}. \tag{10.28}$$

We can perform some transformations to obtain

$$\frac{\partial m}{\partial h_s^-} = \frac{-u_{hh} f'}{D} < 0, \tag{10.29}$$

$$\frac{\partial h}{\partial h_s^-} = \frac{f'' u_h + (p_m)^2 u_{cc}}{D} > 0. \tag{10.30}$$

If initial health increases there is a positive endowment effect on the demand for health similar to that of an increase in income.

Finally, we can show that a change in the survival probability has no effect on the demand for consumption and health. From the budget constraint Eq. (10.4), we obtain

$$\frac{\partial c}{\partial \pi} + p_m \frac{\partial m}{\partial \pi} = 0. \tag{10.31}$$

In other words, a change in the probability of survival does not affect the budget constraint. Thus, it will have no effect on the decision maker's choice.

10.2 Treatment and Survival

In this section, we extend the model to include a second, likewise important criterion for medical treatment decisions: Medical inputs are directed towards reducing mortality. We assume that there is only one treatment m which has an impact on both the survival prospects and the health status of a patient.

Fig. 10.2 Medical
technology and survival

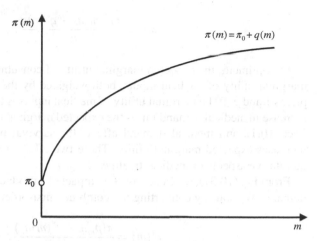

Alternatively, one could imagine different forms of treatments, each of which only influences either survival or the health, but not both.

In the simple case, the technology using medical input to improve a patient's survival outcome has the form

$$\pi(m) = \pi_0 + q(m), \tag{10.32}$$

where π_0 is the initial survival probability without medical treatment and $q(m)$ is the survival production function with the properties $q'(m) = \partial q/\partial m > 0$ and $q''(m) = \partial^2 q/\partial m^2 < 0$. Figure 10.2 illustrates the positive but decreasing marginal effect of medical technology on the survival probability.

The expected utility function changes slightly to

$$EU = \pi(m)u(c, h). \tag{10.33}$$

Maximizing this function subject to the unchanged budget constraint Eq. (10.4) yields the following first-order conditions for the corresponding Lagrangian function:

$$\frac{\partial L}{\partial c} = \pi u_c - \lambda = 0, \tag{10.34}$$

$$\frac{\partial L}{\partial m} = \pi u_h f'(m) + q'(m)u - \lambda p_m = 0, \tag{10.35}$$

$$\frac{\partial L}{\partial \lambda} = y - p_m m - c = 0. \tag{10.36}$$

We then have

$$\pi u_c = \frac{\pi f'(m)u_h + q'(m)u}{p_m}.$$ (10.37)

At the optimum, the expected marginal utility of consumption equals the expected marginal utility of medical inputs, both weighted by the inverse of the respective prices 1 and p_m. The marginal utility of medical inputs is the sum of two effects: An increase in medical demand raises the expected marginal utility of health (as seen in Sect. 10.1), and medical demand affects the survival probability, which in turn increases expected marginal utility. These two effects reflect the quantitative and qualitative aspects of medical treatment.

From Eq. (10.37), we can derive the impact of a productivity increase on medical demand. We start by converting the combined first-order condition to yield

$$q'(m) = \frac{\pi(p_m u_c - f'(m)u_h)}{u}.$$

From this we obtain

$$\frac{\partial q'(m)}{\partial m} = \frac{\left(q'(p_m u_c - f' u_h) - \pi\left(f'' u_h + u_{hh}(f')^2\right)\right)u - u_h f' \pi(p_m u_c - f' u_h)}{u^2}$$

$$= \frac{(p_m u_c - f' u_h)(q'u - u_h f'\pi) - \pi\left(f'' u_h + u_{hh}(f')^2\right)u}{u^2}.$$

Using Eq. (10.37), we then obtain

$$\frac{\partial q'(m)}{\partial m} = \frac{(q'u/\pi)(q'u - q'u + p_m u_c \pi) - \pi\left(f'' u_h + u_{hh}(f')^2\right)u}{u^2}$$

$$= \frac{q' p_m u_c - \pi\left(f'' u_h + u_{hh}(f')^2\right)}{u}.$$

The inverse of this equation finally gives the desired result:

$$\frac{\partial m}{\partial q'(m)} = \frac{u}{q' p_m u_c - \pi\left(f'' u_h + u_{hh}(f')^2\right)} > 0.$$ (10.38)

Medical demand thus increases with the marginal product of the survival function.

A corresponding effect can be expected from a change in the price of medical inputs. Writing the first-order condition (10.37) as $p_m \pi u_c = \pi f'(m)u_h + q'(m)u$, we derive

$$\pi u_c + \pi p_m u_{cc} \frac{\partial c}{\partial p_m} = \pi f'' \frac{\partial m}{\partial p_m} u_h + \pi u_{hh}(f')^2 \frac{\partial m}{\partial p_m}$$
$$+ q'' u \frac{\partial m}{\partial p_m} + q' u_c \frac{\partial c}{\partial p_m} + q' u_h f' \frac{\partial m}{\partial p_m}.$$

By inserting

$$\frac{\partial c}{\partial p_m} = -m - p_m \frac{\partial m}{\partial p_m} \tag{10.19}$$

and rearranging the terms, we obtain

$$u_c(\pi + q'm) - \pi p_m u_{cc} m = \frac{\partial m}{\partial p_m} \left(f'' u_h + (f')^2 u_{hh} + (p_m)^2 u_{cc} \right. \tag{10.39}$$
$$\left. + q'' u - q' u_c p_m + q' u_h f' \right).$$

From the first-order condition, we have $u_c p_m - u_h f' = q' u / \pi$. Inserting this into Eq. (10.39) and solving for $\partial m / \partial p_m$ yields

$$\frac{\partial m}{\partial p_m} = \frac{u_c(\pi + q'm) - \pi p_m u_{cc} m}{f'' u_h + (f')^2 u_{hh} + (p_m)^2 u_{cc} + q'' u - (q')^2 u / \pi} < 0 \tag{10.40}$$

and

$$\frac{\partial h}{\partial p_m} = f' \frac{\partial m}{\partial p_m} = \frac{f'(u_c(\pi + q'm) - \pi p_m u_{cc} m)}{f'' u_h + (f')^2 u_{hh} + (p_m)^2 u_{cc} + q'' u - (q')^2 u / \pi} < 0. \tag{10.41}$$

As in the health model, the demands for medical inputs and health decrease if the price of the medical inputs increases.

How does a change in the initial survival probability π_0 affect the demand for medical treatment? To answer this, we differentiate the first-order condition (10.37) with respect to π_0, taking into account that the mixed derivatives are zero ($u_{ch} = u_{hc} = 0$) :

$$p_m \left(1 + q' \frac{\partial m}{\partial \pi_0} \right) u_c + p_m \pi u_{cc} \frac{\partial c}{\partial \pi_0} = \left(1 + q' \frac{\partial m}{\partial \pi_0} \right) u_h f'$$
$$+ \pi u_{hh}(f')^2 \frac{\partial m}{\partial \pi_0} + \pi u_h f'' \frac{\partial m}{\partial \pi_0} + q'' u \frac{\partial m}{\partial \pi_0} + q' u_c \frac{\partial c}{\partial \pi_0} \tag{10.42}$$
$$+ q' u_h f' \frac{\partial m}{\partial \pi_0}.$$

Using

$$\frac{\partial c}{\partial \pi_0} = -p_m \frac{\partial m}{\partial \pi_0},$$ (10.31)

yields

$$\frac{\partial m}{\partial \pi_0} = \frac{p_m u_c - u_h f'}{\pi (p_m)^2 u_{cc} + \pi u_{hh} (f')^2 + \pi u_h f'' + q'' u - 2q' p_m u_c + 2q' f' u_h}.$$

By inserting a variant of the first-order condition (10.37),

$$p_m u_c - u_h f' = \frac{q'}{\pi} u,$$ (10.43)

in this equation and rearranging its terms, we obtain

$$\frac{\partial m}{\partial \pi_0} = \frac{q' u}{u\left(\pi q'' - 2(q')^2\right) + \pi^2 \left(u_{cc}(p_m)^2 + u_{hh}(f')^2 + u_h f''\right)} < 0.$$ (10.44)

Thus, if the initial survival probability decreases, demand for medical treatment increases.

Figure 10.3 illustrates the effect of an increase in the initial survival probability on medical demand. Point A marks the initial equilibrium depicted in Fig. 10.2, where the corresponding indifference curve and the consumption possibility curve are tangential.

Setting the total differential of the expected utility equal to zero, $dEU = \pi u_c \cdot dc + (q' u + u_h) \cdot dh/f' = 0$, we obtain the slope of the indifference curve

$$\frac{dc}{dh} = -\frac{q' u + \pi f' u_h}{f' \pi u_c}.$$ (10.45)

For the slope of the consumption possibility curve, we still have

$$\frac{dc}{dh} = -\frac{p_m}{f'(m)}.$$ (10.11)

Combining the two equations leads to an explicit formulation of the tangential point representing the optimum:

$$\frac{dc}{dh} = -\frac{q' u + \pi f' u_h}{f' \pi u_c} = -\frac{p_m}{f'}.$$

If the initial survival probability increases, $\pi_B > \pi_A$, the consumption possibility curve remains unchanged while the indifference curve becomes flatter. To see this, we rewrite the slope of the indifference curve as

Fig. 10.3 Initial survival probability ($\pi_B > \pi_A$) and demand for medical treatment

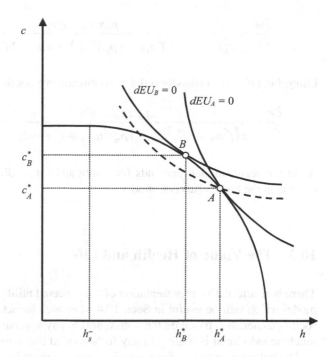

$$-\frac{q'u}{f'\pi u_c} - \frac{u_h}{u_c}.$$

The first ratio is decreasing in the argument π, whereas the second ratio remains constant. Hence, the (negative) slope of the indifference curve is lower for π_B than for π_A.

Point B represents the new optimum where consumption is higher and medical demand is lower. Point B lies on a higher expected utility level, as the new indifference curve through B lies above the indifference curve through A.

Finally, we derive the effect of an increase in income on the demand for medical inputs:

$$p_m q' \frac{\partial m}{\partial y} u_c + \pi p_m u_{cc} \frac{\partial c}{\partial y} = q' \frac{\partial m}{\partial y} f' u_h + \pi f'' \frac{\partial m}{\partial y} u_h$$
$$+ \pi u_{hh}(f')^2 \frac{\partial m}{\partial y} + q'' u \frac{\partial m}{\partial y} + q' u_c \frac{\partial c}{\partial y} + q' u_{hf'} \frac{\partial m}{\partial y}.$$

Using Eq. (10.24), we obtain

$$\frac{\partial m}{\partial y} = \frac{p_m \pi u_{cc} - q' u_c}{\pi \left(f'' u_h + (f')^2 u_{hh} + (p_m)^2 u_{cc} \right) + q'' u - 2q' (p_m u_c - u_h f')}.$$

Using Eq. (10.43) to transform the denominator, we obtain

$$\frac{\partial m}{\partial y} = \frac{p_m \pi u_{cc} - q' u_c}{\pi \left(f'' u_h + (f')^2 u_{hh} + (p_m)^2 u_{cc} \right) + q'' u - 2(q')^2 u / \pi} > 0. \qquad (10.46)$$

As in the health model, demands for health and for medical inputs increase with income in the health-survival model.

10.3   The Value of Health and Life

There is an alternative representation of the expected utility maximum in the health model which will be useful in Sect. 10.4 when we characterize the allocation of a social planner. It is based on the willingness to pay approach, which measures how much an individual is willing to pay for a good at the margin.

The willingness to pay for a marginal improvement in health is defined as

$$v \cong \frac{-dy}{dh}\bigg|_{dEU=0} = \frac{\partial EU / \partial h}{\partial EU / \partial y}, \qquad (10.47)$$

where v stands for the value of health. Using the target function of the individual's expected utility Eq. (10.3)

$$\frac{\partial EU}{\partial h} = \pi u_h. \qquad (10.48)$$

The denominator of Eq. (10.47) can be calculated from the first-order conditions— see (10.5)–(10.7)—or directly, using the envelope theorem to obtain

$$\frac{\partial EU}{\partial y} = \lambda. \qquad (10.49)$$

Inserting the last two equations into Eq. (10.47) and taking into account Eq. (10.5), $\lambda = \pi u_c$, yields

$$v = \frac{\pi u_h}{\lambda} = \frac{u_h}{u_c}. \qquad (10.50)$$

Note that v equals the absolute value of the slope of the indifference curve at the optimal point (see NE quadrant in Fig. 10.1). From the first-order condition of the individual's expected utility maximum Eq. (10.8), we obtain

$$v = \frac{p_m}{f'(m)}. \tag{10.51}$$

We already characterized the right-hand side of Eq. (10.51) as representing the marginal cost of medical investments. Thus, we might say that for the individual's optimum decision, the marginal value of health equals its marginal cost.

We can use Eq. (10.50) to analyze how the value of health changes with an increase in initial health:

$$\frac{\partial v}{\partial h_s^-} = \frac{u_{hh} \partial h / \partial h_s^-}{u_c} < 0, \tag{10.52}$$

given that $\partial h / \partial h_s^- > 0$ (see Eq. (10.30)). Thus, the lower the health level is, the higher is the willingness to pay for an improvement in health. This result is due to the convexity of the indifference curve, implying that the individual prefers more 'balanced' consumption bundles to less balanced ones. The more the individual has of one good, the more willing he is to give some of it up in exchange for the other good. Note that this echoes the results on the effect of risk aversion in our previous chapters. The lower an individual's initial health level is, the keener he is to get tested and to receive treatment.

For a change of the price of medical inputs, we obtain

$$\frac{\partial v}{\partial p_m} = \frac{1}{(u_c)^2} \left(u_{hh} f'(m) \frac{\partial m}{\partial p_m} u_c - u_{cc} \frac{\partial c}{\partial p_m} u_h \right).$$

Invoking the definition of the value of health yields

$$\frac{\partial v}{\partial p_m} = v \left(\frac{u_{hh}}{u_h} f'(m) \frac{\partial m}{\partial p_m} - \frac{u_{cc}}{u_c} \frac{\partial c}{\partial p_m} \right).$$

Given that $\partial m / \partial p_m < 0, \partial c / \partial p_m > 0$ is sufficient but not necessary for the value of health to decrease with an increase in the price of medical inputs. In the Appendix, we derive the conditions under which consumption and medical inputs are gross substitutes; i.e., under which the demand for consumption increases with an increase in the price of medical inputs. If these conditions are met, the value of health is negatively correlated with the price of health services.

With respect to the effect of a change in income on the value of health Eqs. (10.50), and (10.24), i.e., $\partial c / \partial y = 1 - p_m \partial m / \partial y$, lead to

$$\frac{\partial v}{\partial y} = \frac{u_{hh}f'(m)\dfrac{\partial m}{\partial y}u_c - u_{cc}\dfrac{\partial c}{\partial y}u_h}{(u_c)^2}$$

$$= v\left(\frac{u_{hh}}{u_h}f'(m)\frac{\partial m}{\partial y} - \frac{u_{cc}}{u_c}\frac{\partial c}{\partial y}\right).$$

(10.53)

The sign of this derivative cannot be established, as two countervailing effects are at play. On the one hand, the demand for medical inputs increases, which tends to decrease the value of health due to diminishing marginal utility. On the other hand, more wealth also increases consumption demand, which leads to an increase in the value of health.

Finally, we derive the impact of survival on the value of health:

$$\frac{\partial v}{\partial \pi} = 0.$$

(10.54)

The survival probability does not affect the marginal rate of substitution between consumption and health. This is not too surprising, given that both consumption and health are conditioned on survival.

In the health-survival model, the optimal solution for an individual's investment in his health can also be characterized using the willingness to pay approach. The marginal willingness to pay dy for a small increase in survival probability $d\pi$ equals the marginal rate of substitution between survival and income:

$$l = -\left.\frac{dy}{d\pi}\right|_{dEU=0} = \frac{\partial EU/\partial \pi}{\partial EU/\partial y}.$$

(10.55)

This equation represents the value of life l or, more accurately, the value of a statistical life, since the survival change is infinitesimal and the integral value of life is not necessarily bounded from above.

From Eq. (10.33), we obtain

$$\frac{\partial EU}{\partial \pi} = u.$$

(10.56)

Considering Eqs. (10.49), (10.56) and the first-order conditions (10.34), (10.35) and (10.36), we obtain

$$l = \frac{u}{\lambda} = \frac{u}{\pi u_c}.$$

(10.57)

As this equation shows, the value of life is given by the ratio of total utility to expected marginal utility of consumption.

Solving the first-order condition (10.37) for

$$u = \frac{p_m \pi u_c - \pi f' u_h}{q'} \tag{10.58}$$

and inserting this into Eq. (10.57) yields

$$l = \frac{p_m - f' u_h / u_c}{q'} = \frac{p_m - f'v}{q'}, \tag{10.59}$$

where the right-hand side represents the marginal cost of life. The marginal cost would equal p_m/q' if medical inputs only increase the probability of survival. However, the cost of spending one monetary unit on medical inputs is reduced by $f'v$, as it improves the individual's health. At his decision optimum, the individual will demand medical inputs such that the value of life equals its marginal cost.

We can transform the maximum condition (10.59) to obtain:

$$q' \cdot l + f' \cdot v = p_m. \tag{10.60}$$

This formulation states that the individual will extend his demand for medical inputs up to the point where marginal value equals price.

For the comparative statics results of the value of life with respect to income and the initial survival rate, see Box 10.1.

Box 10.1: Life as a Luxury Good and the Dead-Anyway Effect
The expected utility foundation of the value of a statistical life is based on seminal contributions by Jones-Lee (1974), Arthur (1981) and Rosen (1988). To see why the marginal willingness to pay for a reduction in mortality risk measures the value of a statistical life, consider an individual who pays $500 extra in order to have an airbag in his car. Assume that this investment in safety reduces the mortality risk by $\Delta \pi = -1/100,000$. With this information, we can easily calculate a lower bound for the individual's valuation of his life:

$$l = -\Delta y / \Delta \pi = \$500/(1/100,000) = \$5 \text{ million.}$$

The empirical literature on the value of a statistical life encompasses a wide range of values, from a low $2 million (see Ashenfelter and Greenstone 2004) to $9 million and more (see the literature survey by Viscusi and Aldy 2003).

A key question in this literature is how the value of a statistical life is influenced by the characteristics of the individual under consideration, in particular by his income and the initial value of the mortality risk. From the health model, we learn the following for the derivative with respect to income:

(continued)

Box 10.1 (continued)

$$\frac{\partial l}{\partial y} = \frac{1}{\pi}\left(1 - \frac{u_{cc}u}{(u_c)^2}\frac{\partial c}{\partial y}\right) > 0.$$

Studies suggest that the value of a statistical life is a luxury good, i.e., it is not just increasing in income, but rises faster than income. Costa and Kahn (2004) and Clemente et al. (2004) indeed found that the income elasticity of the value of life was greater than unity.

For the effect of an increase in survival on the value of life, Eq. (10.57) leads us to

$$\frac{\partial l}{\partial \pi_0} = -\frac{u}{\pi^2 u_c} < 0.$$

The value of life is thus higher, the lower the initial survival rate is. Pratt and Zeckhauser (1996) coined this phenomenon as 'the dead-anyway effect', due to the assumption that utilities and marginal utilities are larger during life than in death. Breyer and Felder (2005) revisited the dead-anyway effect and identified cases where it does not hold. Empirical results on the dead-anyway effect are mixed (see Bellavance et al. 2009).

The dead-anyway effect opens up an approach to dealing with emergency medical procedures. For situations such as natural catastrophes or war, guidelines inform physicians on how to prioritize treatment among the casualties. Severely wounded individuals with positive probabilities of survival will receive preferred treatment vis-a-vis individuals with less serious injuries and thus higher survival probabilities.

10.4 Optimal Allocation of Health Across Individuals

Except for Chap. 9, we have been concerned mainly with test and treatment decisions at the individual level. In this section, we extend the analysis to include scarcity at an aggregate level. Consider the example of a hospital with a limited bed capacity which has to decide which patients to treat and which patients to defer or even decline; or the classic problem in social health insurance of deciding which medical services to include and which to exclude from public financing. We present the allocation problem within both the health and the health-survival models and draw implications for the QALY model.

10.4.1 The Health Model

We consider a social planner who maximizes the total welfare of a population. This planner is assumed to be a utilitarian, as he is interested only in 'the greatest good of the greatest number'. Furthermore, we assume that the social planner can freely reallocate income across individuals. The utilitarian program can then be written as follows:

$$\max W = \sum_i \pi_i u_i \left(c_i, h_{s,i}^- + f_i(m_i) \right)$$
$$\text{subject to } \sum_i \pi_i(c_i + p_m m_i) = \sum_i \pi_i y_i, \tag{10.61}$$

where $f_i(m_i)$ is substituted for $\hat{h}_i$ in the utility function. The target function sums expected utilities over individuals i, taking into account, among other things, different individual survival probabilities. The constraint also considers the fact that not all individuals will survive. All quantities are thus multiplied by the survival probabilities at the individual level. Maximizing a corresponding Lagrangian function leads to the following first-order conditions:

$$\frac{\partial L}{\partial c_i} = \pi_i u_{i,c_i} - \lambda \pi_i = 0, \tag{10.62}$$

$$\frac{\partial L}{\partial m_i} = \pi_i u_{i,h_i} f_i'(m_i) - \lambda \pi_i p_m = 0, \tag{10.63}$$

$$\frac{\partial L}{\partial \lambda} = \sum_i \pi_i(y_i - c_i - p_m m_i) = 0. \tag{10.64}$$

The combined first-order condition for the social optimum is

$$\frac{u_{i,h_i}}{u_{i,c_i}} = \frac{p_m}{f_i'(m_i)}, \text{ or } v_i = \frac{p_m}{f_i'(m_i)} \tag{10.65}$$

This is the same equation that we derived at the individual level. The expected utility maximum is reached where the value of health equals its marginal cost. Since the budget constraints differ, an individual's decision on consumption and health will not generally coincide with that of the social planner. Under a utilitarian regime, richer individuals will consume less and enjoy a state of health that is below their optimum level, while the reverse will hold for poorer individuals. Consequently, due to $f_i''(m_i) < 0$, the value of health is higher for a rich person and lower for a poor person when individuals make choices than when a utilitarian regime makes choices on their behalf.

Assume that $u_i = u_j, f_i = f_j$ and $h_{s,i}^- = h_{s,j}^-$ for all $i \neq j$. Considering Eq. (10.50), we obtain from Eq. (10.65)

Fig. 10.4 The utilitarian allocation

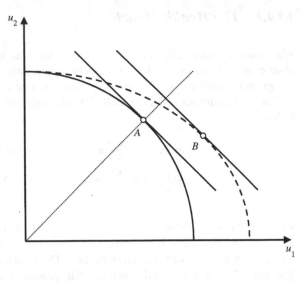

$$v_i = v_j \; \text{for all} \; i \neq j. \tag{10.66}$$

Figure 10.4 illustrates the utilitarian allocation solution. The utility possibility curve is symmetric across of the 45° line. The social indifference curves are downward slanted lines with slopes of -1. The utilitarian planner is blind to inequality in the distribution of utility: He is willing to give up one unit of individual 1's utility in order to gain one unit for individual 2's utility. If preferences and production technologies do not differ between individuals, the utilitarian solution is a perfect egalitarian allocation: All individuals have the same utility level, consume the same level and enjoy the same health level. Given that initial income is unequally distributed, the utilitarian allocation then implies a reallocation of incomes among individuals.

Now, assume the following asymmetry in the health production function between two individuals: $f'_1(m) > f'_2(m)$ for all m. In other words, at any level of medical input its marginal product is higher for individual 1 than for individual 2. The utility frontier curve in Fig. 10.4 is no longer symmetric across the 45° line; it is broader on the side of individual 1's utility. Under these circumstances the utilitarian allocator will increase the utility level of individual 1 at the expense of individual 2 (point B).[2] Of course, the allocation will also be non-egalitarian if the individuals' utility functions differ.

To gain a more realistic restriction function for the social planner, we reformulate the maximization problem as follows:

---

[2]If the social welfare function exhibits inequality aversion, the social indifference curves are convex. In this case, the allocation will tend to be more equitable than under the utilitarian regime.

$$\max W = \sum_i \pi_i u_i \left(c_i, h_{s,i}^- + f_i(m_i) \right)$$

$$\text{subject to } c_i = (1 - t)y_i \text{ and} \qquad (10.67)$$

$$p_m \sum_i \pi_i m_i = t \sum_i \pi_i y_i.$$

This reflects a social health insurance system financed by an exogenous income tax rate t. $t \sum_i \pi_i y_i$, then, is the social planner's budget. His Lagrangian function is

$$L = \sum_i \pi_i u_i \left(c_i, h_{s,i}^- + \hat{h}_i \right) + \sum_i \mu_i ((1 - t)y_i - c_i) + \lambda \left(t \sum_i \pi_i y_i - p_m \sum_i \pi_i m_i \right),$$

where λ and μ_i are multipliers for the aggregate health budget and the individual income budgets, respectively. The first-order conditions for the social optimum are

$$\frac{\partial L}{\partial c_i} = \pi_i u_{i,c_i} - \mu_i = 0, \qquad (10.68)$$

$$\frac{\partial L}{\partial m_i} = \pi_i u_{i,h_i} f_i'(m_i) - \pi_i \lambda p_m = 0, \qquad (10.69)$$

$$\frac{\partial L}{\partial \mu_i} = (1 - t)y_i - c_i = 0, \qquad (10.70)$$

$$\frac{\partial L}{\partial \lambda} = t \sum_i \pi_i y_i - p_m \sum_i \pi_i m_i = 0. \qquad (10.71)$$

According to the second equation, social welfare maximization requires that medical inputs be allocated in such a way that their marginal social value is equal for each individual i.

Since we exclude the possibility of reallocating income across individuals, the social planner cannot influence the expected marginal utility of income at the individual level. The individual consumption level is determined by the after-tax income $(1 - t)y_i$. Combining Eqs. (10.68) and (10.69) yields the value of health of individual i:

$$v_i = \frac{u_{i,h_i}}{u_{i,c_i}} = \pi_i \frac{\lambda}{\mu_i} \frac{p_m}{f_i'(m_i)}. \qquad (10.72)$$

Since the shadow values of the budgets differ between the aggregate and the individual levels, the planner's allocation differs with regard to individual choices: The planner allocates too many medical resources to individuals with a high survival probability and too few to rich individuals (μ_i is decreasing in income).

If everyone is in the same position along all dimensions other than before-tax income, i.e., $u_i = u_j, f_i = f_j h_{s,i}^- = h_{s,j}^-$ and $y_i \neq y_j$ for all $i \neq j$, then the utilitarian solution does not imply an equalization of the values of health across individuals. The reason is that the linear tax schedule does not allow the social planner to equalize after-tax income across individuals.

10.4.2 The Health-Survival Model

In the health-survival model, medical inputs affect both the quality and the quantity of life. The optimization problem for the social planner then reads as

$$\max W = \sum_i \pi_i(m_i)u_i\big(c_i, h_{s,i}^- + f_i(m_i)\big)$$
$$\text{subject to } \sum_i \pi_i(m_i)(c_i + p_m m_i) = \sum_i \pi_i(m_i)y_i, \tag{10.73}$$

which results in the following first-order conditions:

$$\frac{\partial L}{\partial c_i} = \pi_i u_{i,c_i} - \lambda \pi_i = 0, \tag{10.74}$$

$$\frac{\partial L}{\partial m_i} = q_i'(m_i)u_i + \pi_i u_{i,h_i} f_i'(m_i)$$
$$+ \lambda\big(q_i'(m_i)(y_i - c_i - p_m m_i) - \pi_i\big) = 0, \tag{10.75}$$

$$\frac{\partial L}{\partial \lambda} = \sum_i \pi_i(y_i - c_i - p_m m_i) = 0. \tag{10.76}$$

In the health-survival model, medical inputs also affect the aggregate budget constraint: If more individuals survive due to increased medical investments, aggregate income and consumption rise. The first two equations give the combined first-order condition

$$\pi_i u_{i,c_i} = \pi_i u_{i,h_i} f_i'(m_i) + q_i'(m_i)u_i + u_{i,c_i}\Delta_i, \tag{10.77}$$

where $\Delta_i = q_i'(m_i)(y_i - c_i - p_m m_i)$. Except for the term Δ_i, this is the equation we derived at the individual level—see Eq. (10.37). Δ_i is the social marginal net revenue gained from increasing individual i's probability of survival by $q_i'(m_i)$ at the optimal level of demand for consumption and medical inputs, which can be positive or negative according to

$$\Delta_i \gtrless 0 \text{ if } y_i \gtrless c_i + p_m m_i. \tag{10.78}$$

Hence, individuals with above-average income gain additional social utility from investing in their survival. A utilitarian planner thus allocates more health to wealthy individuals. Note that this resembles the practice of considering the indirect cost of treatment in the evaluation of medical intervention, as patients whose treatment restores their ability to work generate an economic benefit to society. In our framework, the change in productivity is reflected by $q_i'(m_i)y_i$. Taking into account Δ_i, on the other hand, goes one step further and incorporates the additional cost of an increase in the survival rate in terms of consumption and medical cost.[3]

By using the first equation of Eq. (10.73) and rearranging Eqs. (10.74)–(10.76), we find the expression for the value of a statistical life:

$$l_i = \frac{u_i}{\lambda} = \frac{\pi_i(p_m - f_i'v_i) - \Delta_i}{q_i'}. \tag{10.79}$$

The social optimum is characterized by the property that the value of life equals its marginal cost for each individual. Equation (10.79) differs from the value of life we derived for the individual decision—see Eq. (10.57)—in two respects. First, the shadow value of the constraints is different in the two optimizations: it is $\lambda_i = \pi u_{i,c}$ in the individual and $\lambda = u_{i,c_i}$ in the aggregate choice. Second, in the social optimization Δ_i is not zero as it is in the individual choice where the budget constraint applies at the individual level. The marginal cost of life decreases if $\Delta_i > 0$, resulting in higher health investments. An egalitarian allocation ($v_i = v_j$ and $l_i = l_j$) will only result if $u_i = u_j, f_i = f_j, \pi_i = \pi_j, h_{s,i}^- = h_{s,j}^-$ and $y_i = y_j$ for all $i \neq j$.

Hence, as long as earnings differ between individuals, the value of life and the value of health will not be equalized, even if utility and production functions were the same for everyone.

If we decouple the decision on the allocation of medical resources from the one on individual consumption and let the social planner decide on the medical allocation only, his maximization problem is

$$\max W = \sum_i \pi_i(m_i)u_i\left(c_i, h_{s,i}^- + f_i(m_i)\right)$$

$$\text{subject to} \quad c_i = (1-t)y_i \text{ and} \tag{10.80}$$
$$p_m\sum_i \pi_i(m_i)m_i = t\sum_i \pi_i(m_i)y_i.$$

The first-order conditions for the optimal allocation of the medical resources among individuals are:

$$\frac{\partial L}{\partial m_i} = q_i'(m_i)u_i + \pi_i u_{i,h_i}f_i'(m_i) + \lambda\left(q_i'(m_i)(ty_i - p_m m_i) - \pi_i\right) = 0. \tag{10.81}$$

---

[3]For a complete analysis along these lines see Meltzer (1997).

With differing incomes, the values of life and health will generally not be equal across individuals.

An allocation according to the health-survival model would maximize social welfare and abstract from equity issues. This model appears to provide accurate guidance in deciding which medical services should be financed by public money, as it not only considers the marginal utility of health investments, but also the associated marginal costs in terms of foregone consumption.

10.4.3 The QALY Model

The QALY model is the primary guideline for allocating health care resources in many countries, in particular within the U.K. National Health Service. In Chap. 3, we presented the QALY model as an application of expected utility theory. It combines the utility of possible health states with their probabilities of occurrence and their expected durations. Considering one period only, we can restate the QALY model as follows:

$$QALY = \sum_i \pi_i(m_i)u_i(f_i(m_i)). \tag{10.82}$$

The QALY model can be regarded as a 'half-baked' health-survival model. These two models both take the survival production function into account, but the QALY model's utility function does not take consumption into account. In this sense, the QALY model represents an 'extra-welfarism' position.

A social planner applying the QALY function and endowed with a health budget faces the following optimization problem:

$$\begin{aligned} \max QALY &= \sum_i \pi_i(m_i)u_i\big(h^-_{s,i} + f_i(m_i)\big) \\ \text{subject to } p_m\sum_i \pi_i(m_i)m_i &= t\sum_i \pi_i(m_i)y_i. \end{aligned} \tag{10.83}$$

The first-order conditions with respect to medical demands are

$$\frac{\partial L}{\partial m_i} = q'_i(m_i)u_i + \pi_i u_{i,h_i}f'_i(m_i) + \lambda\big(q'_i(m_i)(ty_i - p_m m_i) - \pi_i\big) = 0. \tag{10.84}$$

This is analogous to Eq. (10.81), except for the difference in the utility functions, as the QALY model disregards the utility of consumption. It considers the budget impact of an increase in survival in terms of additional revenue and additional health care expenditure, but not the cost of additional consumption.

The equivalent to the value of life in the QALY model amounts to

$$l_i = \frac{u_i(h_i)}{\lambda} = \frac{\pi_i\left(p_m - f_i'v_i\right) - \tau_i}{q_i'}, \tag{10.85}$$

where $\tau_i = q_i'(m_i)(ty_i - p_m m_i)$. $\tau_i > 0$ if an individual has below-average medical demand or above-average income, so that his health budget is enlarged by an increase in his probability of survival. Accordingly, the marginal cost of life decreases. If $\tau_i < 0$ (i.e., if $ty_i < p_m m_i$), the marginal cost of life increases. Again, the value of life equals its marginal cost at the optimum. The optimum condition includes an evaluation of both the utility and the marginal utility of health. In this respect, the QALY model is an improvement over the health model, but falls short of the health-survival model.

Box 10.2: NICE's End of Life Premium

In November 2008, Professor Richards, the UK Director of National Cancer, published the report 'Improving Access to Medicines for NHS Patients', commissioned by the Secretary of State for Health, in which he recommended that the Department of Health and NICE 'assess urgently what affordable measures could be taken to make available drugs used near the end of life that do not meet the cost-effectiveness criteria currently applied to all drugs' (recommendation 5).

In January 2009, NICE subsequently issued supplementary advice to the Appraisal Committees, instructing them to evaluate drugs designed to treat patients with rare terminal diseases with greater flexibility (NICE 2009). Contrary to press reports, no specific limit was set in this document for cost per QALY beyond the usual £20,000—£30,000 range. However, treatments admitted under the new guideline as of July 2009 were assessed at up to £102,000 per QALY.

The QALY approach per se does not differentiate between situations with low and high survival probabilities. If QALYs are weighted ex post, as in the case of increased consideration of end-of-life QALYs by NICE, it is usually due to concerns of equity or access.

In contrast to this, the willingness to pay approach which we developed in the health-survival model accommodates differences in the initial survival rate. We demonstrated in Box 10.1 that the value of a statistical life decreases with the initial survival. In fact, the dead-anyway effect offers a rationale for NICE's end-of-life premium that does not depend on equity issues.

Despite what its name suggests, the QALY model does not consider quality of life comprehensively, since it values only health and disregards the utility individuals draw from consumption. Hence, in contrast to a welfare-maximizing individual, a QALY-type planner does not compare the marginal utilities of both the quantity and the quality of health with the marginal utility of consumption when deciding on health investments. In particular, he does not take into account differences in marginal utility attributable to differing incomes at the individual level. In other words, an allocation according to the QALY model cannot adequately represent individual preferences.

10.5   Conclusion

It is important to note first that the willingness to pay for the quality and the quantity of life, as derived in this chapter, can be used to assign a value to medical interventions which affect both the health status and the survival prospects of patients. The QALY approach, for instance, requires information on the willingness to pay for a QALY in order to reach a conclusive decision. The health-survival model provides an analytical basis for the conceptualization of the willingness to pay for a QALY. More specifically, if this willingness is elicited and the QALY of a diagnosis as a function of the a priori probability of illness determined, one can additionally calculate a monetized additional utility function which also permits a derivation of the test and test-treatment thresholds as presented in Chap. 5.

We want to discuss the implication of differing values of health and life between individuals for the threshold analysis presented in the previous chapters. Let us start by summarizing the comparative statics results that we derived for the health and health-survival models. We focus on the effects of changes in the exogenous variables in the demand function for medical inputs (see Table 10.1).

An increase in income increases demand for treatment in both models. An increase in the marginal product of medical inputs in the production of health also increases demand, while an increase in the price of medical inputs decreases demand. An improvement in the initial status of health has a negative effect on medical demand in the health model, while this effect is undetermined in the health-survival model. The latter effect, however, has no implication for the value of health before treatment. As derived by us in Sect. 10.3, the value of health before treatment increases if the initial health status deteriorates.

The two models differ with regard to the impact of a change in the initial survival probability. In the health model, the survival probability has no effect on health demand. Income and consumption are conditioned on being alive, and positive utility is also conditioned on survival. This is different in the health-survival model, where medical inputs are also productive for survival. If the initial survival probability increases, the demand for medical inputs decreases, and vice versa.

It is quite obvious what effects these changes in exogenous parameters have on the test and test-treatment thresholds. If medical demand increases, the thresholds decrease; i.e., decision makers test and treat at lower prevalence rates. Thus, if income or the productivities of the production functions increase or the initial survival productivity decreases, the thresholds decrease.

Another interesting aspect is that income might affect the threshold in that it influences an individual's degree of risk aversion. Assuming decreasing absolute risk aversion, individuals become less risk-averse with increasing income. If this

Table 10.1 The change in demand for medical treatment

Exogenous parameter changes	Health model	Health-survival model
Income y	+	+
Marginal product of medical inputs $f'(m)$	+	+[a]
Price of medical inputs p_m	−	−[a]
Initial health h_s^-	−	*/−[a]
Initial survival probability π_0	0	−
Productivity of survival production $q'(m)$		+

[a]Not formally shown

holds true, it is not possible to identify an income effect on the thresholds. If the degree of risk aversion decreases as income increases, the thresholds shift upwards. On the other hand, an increase in income raises health demand and thus lowers the thresholds, leaving the sign of the total effect unclear.

10.6 Notes

There is a broad field of literature on the value of health and life. For literature on the value of life, see Box 10.1. Schelling (1968) provides a fundamental treatise on the topic. Johannson's (1996) 'Evaluating Health Risks' is an advanced text in welfare economics and its application to health economics. For the QALY approach and its shortcomings, see the textbook by Zweifel et al. (2009).

Appendix

Here, we derive the conditions for the demand for consumption to increase with the price of medical inputs in the case of the health model. Starting with the first-order condition $p_m u_c = f'(m)u_h$, we derive

$$u_c + p_m u_{cc}\frac{\partial c}{\partial p_m} = f''\frac{\partial m}{\partial p_m}u_h + u_{hh}(f')^2\frac{\partial m}{\partial p_m}. \tag{10.18}$$

Inserting

$$\frac{\partial m}{\partial p_m} = -\frac{1}{p_m}\left(\frac{\partial c}{\partial p_m}+m\right) \tag{10.19}$$

into Eq. (10.18) and transforming and multiplying both sides with p_m yields

$$p_m u_c + m\left(f'' u_h + u_{hh}(f')^2\right) = -\frac{\partial c}{\partial p_m}\left((p_m)^2 u_{cc} + f'' u_h + u_{hh}(f')^2\right). \quad (10.86)$$

Further transformations produce

$$
\begin{aligned}
\frac{\partial c}{\partial p_m} &= -\frac{p_m u_c + m\left(f'' u_h + u_{hh}(f')^2\right)}{f'' u_h + u_{hh}(f')^2 + (p_m)^2 u_{cc}} \\
&= -\frac{f' u_h + m\left(f'' u_h + u_{hh}(f')^2\right)}{f'' u_h + u_{hh}(f')^2 + (p_m)^2 u_{cc}} \\
&= -\frac{f' u_h(1 + \varepsilon(f') + (m/h)\varepsilon(u_h))}{f'' u_h + u_{hh}(f')^2 + (p_m)^2 u_{cc}}.
\end{aligned}
\quad (10.87)
$$

$\varepsilon(f') = m f''/f' < 0$ and $\varepsilon(u_h) = h u_{hh}/u_h < 0$ are the elasticity of the marginal product of medical inputs and the elasticity of the marginal utility of health, respectively. Thus, to ensure $\partial c/\partial p_m > 0$, the marginal product of medical inputs should be elastic, i.e., $(\varepsilon(f') < -1)$, and at the same time the marginal utility of health should not be too elastic. This is tantamount to a price-inelastic demand for medical inputs,[4] as derived from the budget constraint:

$$\frac{\partial c}{\partial p_m} = -m - p_m \frac{\partial m}{\partial p_m} = -m(1 + \varepsilon(p_m)). \quad (10.88)$$

Exercises

1. Assume the following utility function with health (h) and consumption (c): $u = \alpha \ln c + (1 - \alpha)\ln h$. The health production function takes the form $h = m^\beta$ with $0 < \beta < 1$. The budget constraint is $p \cdot m + c = y$, where m is the demand for medical services and p is its price.

   (a) Determine the optimal demand for health and consumption.
   (b) Calculate changes in health and consumption from a marginal increase in income.
   (c) What is the value of health?
   (d) Determine the effect that a marginal increase in β has on the demand for health and medical services. What is the impact of this on the value of health?

---

[4]That is: $-1 < \varepsilon(p_m) = (\partial m/m)/(\partial p_m/p_m) < 0$.

2. Let π be the joint probability that an individual experiences income Y, consumption c and health h. The utility function for health and consumption and the health production function are identical to those in Exercise 10.1.

(a) Define and calculate the value of life.
(b) Now assume that $\pi = \pi_0 + m^\gamma$ with $0 < \gamma < 1$. Determine the effect of a change in income and in the initial survival rate on the value of life and explain the difference to (a).

3. Derive $\partial l / \partial y$ and $\partial l / \partial \pi$ in the health and the health-survival models. Interpret the differences between the two models.

References

Arthur, W. B. (1981). The economics of risks to life. *American Economic Review, 71*(1), 54–64.

Ashenfelter, O., & Greenstone, M. (2004). Using mandatory speed limits to measure the value of a statistical life. *Journal of Political Economy, 112*(2), 227–267.

Bellavance, F., Dionne, G., & Lebeau, M. (2009). The value of a statistical life: A meta-analysis with a mixed effects regression model. *Journal of Health Economics, 28*(2), 444–464.

Breyer, F., & Felder, S. (2005). Mortality risk and the value of a statistical life: The dead-anyway effect revis(it)ed. *Geneva Papers on Risk and Insurance Theory, 30*(1), 41–55.

Clemente, J., Marcuello, C., Montañés, A., & Pueyo, F. (2004). On the international stability of health care expenditure functions: Are government and private functions similar? *Journal of Health Economics, 23*(3), 589–613.

Costa, D. L., & Kahn, M. E. (2004). Changes in the value of life, 1940–1980. *Journal of Risk and Uncertainty, 29*(2), 159–180.

Johannson, P. O. (1996). *Evaluating health risk: An economic approach.* New York: Cambridge University Press.

Jones-Lee, M. (1974). The value of changes in the probability of death or injury. *Journal of Political Economy, 82*(4), 835–849.

Meltzer, D. (1997). Accounting for future costs in medical cost-effectiveness analysis. *Journal of Health Economics, 16*(1), 33–64.

NICE. (2009). *Appraising life-extending, end of life treatments.* https://www.nice.org.uk/guid ance/gid-tag387/resources/appraising-life-extending-end-of-life-treatments-paper2

Pratt, J. W., & Zeckhauser, R. J. (1996). Willingness to pay and the distribution of risk and wealth. *Journal of Political Economy, 104*(4), 747–763.

Richards, M. (2008). *Improving access to medicines for NHS patients.* Commissioned by the Secretary of State for Health. http://www.dh.gov.uk/prod_consum_dh/groups/dh_digitalassets/ @dh/@en/documents/digitalasset/dh_089952.pdf. Accessed 24 Oct 2010.

Rosen, S. (1988). The value of changes in life expectancy. *Journal of Risk and Uncertainty, 1*(3), 285–304.

Schelling, T. C. (1968). The life you save may be your own. In S. B. Chase Jr. (Ed.), *Problems in public expenditure analysis* (pp. 127–162). Washington, DC: The Brookings Institution.

Viscusi, W. K., & Aldy, J. E. (2003). The value of a statistical life: A critical review of market estimates throughout the world. *Journal of Risk and Uncertainty, 27*(1), 5–76.

Zweifel, P., Breyer, F., & Kifmann, M. (2009). *Health Economics* (2nd ed.). Heidelberg: Springer.

Chapter 11
Imperfect Agency and Non-Expected Utility Models

I hate to change my mind,
but I hate worse to hold wrong views
Paul Samuelson[1]

Expected utility theory (EUT) by von Neumann and Morgenstern is the fundamental approach used in this textbook for analyzing physicians' test and treatment decisions. Factual observations and experimental evidence, however, indicate that physicians' actual behavior contradicts the predictions of EUT. Various alternatives to EUT have been proposed. In this chapter, we present some of them and analyze their relevance and scope.

In the first part, we still remain within the EUT framework, but attenuate the strong assumption that physicians are perfect agents of their patients. In fact, this is an unrealistic assumption: after all, we cannot expect physicians to behave differently from the average person. Rather, it seems to be more appropriate to assume that physicians also follow their own interest when practicing medicine.

In the second and third part of this chapter, we leave the EUT framework and introduce non-EUT models under risk and uncertainty that might be more in line with actual behavior but which lack the normative character of expected utility theory. We urge the reader to differentiate between these alternative models that might better explain observed behavior and expected utility theory that informs the physician about the optimal decision he should make. However, we think that it is important to present alternative models of medical decision making to our readers, so that they can compare various approaches and assess the value of normative principles drawn from expected utility theory.

---

[1]In a letter to Milton Friedman, dated August 25, 1950, Paul Samuelson, an originally severe critic, wrote that he accepted the expected utility theory after Leonard Savage persuaded him of the normative force of the Independence Axiom (quoted after Moscati 2016).

© Springer-Verlag GmbH Germany 2017
S. Felder, T. Mayrhofer, *Medical Decision Making*,
DOI 10.1007/978-3-662-53432-8_11

11.1   Imperfect Physician Agency

Let us assume that the physician internalizes a share α of the patient's utility only. Sometimes α is called the altruistic parameter in the physician's utility function. Furthermore, assume that the physician will also take into account the effect that his decision will have on his monetary payoff. To keep the model simple, we assume that the physician's profit equals a share β of the cost of testing and treatment. The parameter β is an indication of the strength of the physician's profit motive.

First, we address the treatment threshold in this extended model. The physician's expected net benefit from treatment as a function of the a priori probability of illness can be written as follows:

$$ENB^{\alpha}(p) = \alpha\left(p \cdot \lambda \cdot q_g - (1-p)\lambda \cdot q_l\right) - (1-\beta)c^{Rx}. \qquad (11.1)$$

This equation reveals that imperfect agency causes opposite effects on the expected net benefit of treatment (for a detailed explanation of the notations, see Chap. 5). The expected net benefit decreases if the full effect of the physician's decision on the patient's utility is not considered (i.e., $\alpha < 1$). On the other hand, the profit motive implies that the physician does not fully internalize the cost of his actions (i.e., $0 < \beta \leq 1$), which in turn increases the expected net benefit.[2] From Eq. (11.1), we see that we obtain the original model presented in Chap. 5 if $\alpha = 1$ and $\beta = 0$.

Setting $ENB^{\alpha}(p)$ equal to zero and solving for p yields the treatment threshold at which the physician is indifferent between treatment and no treatment

$$p_{\alpha}^{Rx} = \frac{1 + (1-\beta)c^{Rx}/(\alpha \cdot \lambda \cdot q_l)}{1 + q_g/q_l}. \qquad (11.2)$$

Taking the derivatives of interest, we obtain

$$\frac{\partial p_{\alpha}^{Rx}}{\partial \alpha} = -\frac{1 + (1-\beta)c^{Rx}}{\left(1 + q_g/q_l\right)\lambda \cdot q_l \cdot \alpha^2} < 0 \qquad (11.3)$$

and

$$\frac{\partial p_{\alpha}^{Rx}}{\partial \beta} = -\frac{c^{Rx}}{\left(1 + q_g/q_l\right)\alpha \cdot \lambda \cdot q_l} < 0. \qquad (11.4)$$

---

[2]Note that the parameter β can also capture potential moral hazard in the case of the patient whose medical costs are covered by health insurance coverage. Instead of paying the full price, this patient only pays a fraction $1 - \beta$ of the treatment cost.

The inequality Eq. (11.3) reveals that a decrease in α increases the treatment threshold. In other words, if a physician only partly considers patient's expected utility, he tends to treat less often. By comparison, according to the inequality Eq. (11.4), the treatment threshold decreases if β increases. Thus, the physician's profit motive leads him to provide treatment too often. Both predictions appear to be accurate from an intuitive point of view.

A comparison with the threshold in the model with perfect agency shows

$$p_\alpha^{Rx} > p_m^{Rx} = \frac{1 + c^{Rx}/(\lambda \cdot q_l)}{1 + q_g/q_l} \quad \text{if} \quad \frac{\alpha}{1 - \beta} < 1. \tag{11.5}$$

Hence, depending on the relative strength of these opposite effects, the treatment threshold either increases or decreases compared to the normatively accurate model.

Using the treatment threshold, we can derive the incremental expected net benefit of the test, compared to the situation without the test, as follows:

$$INB^\alpha(p) = \begin{cases} -(1-\beta)c^t + p \cdot Se\left(\alpha \cdot \lambda \cdot q_g - (1-\beta)c^{Rx}\right) \\ -(1-p)(1-Sp)(\alpha \cdot \lambda \cdot q_l + (1-\beta)c^{Rx}) \quad \text{for} \quad 0 \leq p < p_m^{Rx}, \\ \\ -(1-\beta)c^t - p(1-Se)\left(\alpha \cdot \lambda \cdot q_g - (1-\beta)c^{Rx}\right) \\ +(1-p)Sp(\alpha \cdot \lambda \cdot q_l + (1-\beta)c^{Rx}) \quad \text{for} \quad p_m^{Rx} \leq p \leq 1. \end{cases} \tag{11.6}$$

Setting the incremental net benefit to zero in the lower range of the a priori probability of illness, after rearranging the terms, yields the test threshold

$$p_\alpha^t = \frac{1 + \dfrac{c^t/(1 - Sp)}{\dfrac{\alpha}{1-\beta}\lambda \cdot q_l + c^{Rx}}}{1 + LR^+ \dfrac{\frac{\alpha}{1-\beta}\lambda \cdot q_g - c^{Rx}}{\frac{\alpha}{1-\beta}\lambda \cdot q_l + c^{Rx}}}. \tag{11.7}$$

Here, comparative statics analysis will show that the test threshold increases when the altruistic parameter α decreases. Furthermore, the test threshold decreases with an increase in the parameter β. Thus, an increase in the profit motive leads the physician to test at a lower a priori probability of illness. As with the treatment threshold before, we find that the two parameters indicating imperfect agency have opposite effects on the test threshold.

Compared to the test threshold with perfect agency, we obtain

$$p_\alpha^t > p_m^t = \frac{1 + c^t/(1-Sp)(\lambda \cdot q_l + c^{Rx})}{1 + LR^+\left(\lambda \cdot q_g - c^{Rx}\right)/(\lambda \cdot q_l + c^{Rx})} \quad \text{if} \quad \frac{\alpha}{1-\beta} < 1. \quad (11.8)$$

Again, the outcome depends on the relative strength of the two parameters α and β; i.e., whether the test threshold increases or decreases compared to a situation with perfect agency.

In the upper range of the a priori probabilities of illness, the test-treatment threshold becomes

$$p_\alpha^{tRx} = \frac{1 - \dfrac{c^t/Sp}{\dfrac{\alpha}{1-\beta}\lambda \cdot q_l + c^{Rx}}}{1 + LR^-\dfrac{\dfrac{\alpha}{1-\beta}\lambda \cdot q_g - c^{Rx}}{\dfrac{\alpha}{1-\beta}\lambda \cdot q_l + c^{Rx}}}. \quad (11.9)$$

It can be shown that the signs of the derivatives in Eqs. (11.3) and (11.4) also apply for p_α^{tRx}, provided that $(1-Se)c^{Rx} > c^t$ and $Sp \cdot c^{Rx} > c^t$ hold.[3] A physician will treat his patient later, i.e., at a higher a priori probability if he is less altruistically motivated, while a stronger profit motive will induce him to treat his patient earlier, i.e., at a lower a priori probability.

Compared to the test-treatment threshold in the model with perfect agency, we obtain

$$p_\alpha^{tRx} > p_m^{tRx} = \frac{Sp(\lambda \cdot q_l + c^{Rx}) - c^t}{Sp(\lambda \cdot q_l + c^{Rx}) + (1-Se)\left(\lambda \cdot q_g - c^{Rx}\right)} \quad \text{if} \quad \frac{\alpha}{1-\beta} < 1. \quad (11.10)$$

Hence, again the relative strengths of the two parameters which indicate the degree of the physician's imperfect agency determine whether the test-treatment threshold increases or decreases relative to the model with perfect agency.

We can conclude that imperfect agency has an effect on physicians' test and treatment decisions. If physicians do not fully comply with the Hippocrates oath, they tend to test and to treat less often. The profit motive, on the contrary, leads them to test and treat too often. Since under a regular incentive regime a physician's profit increases with his level of activity, he will tend to test and treat more, the stronger his profit motive is. Thus, the overall effect of imperfect agency cannot be signed, but depends on the relative strengths of the opposite forces.

What can be done to ensure that physicians make accurate decisions? One can expect that the intrinsic motivation of physicians will induce them to act in the right direction. Moreover, the negligence rule in liability law forces physicians to comply

---

[3]Note that these conditions were also required in Chap. 5 for the effect of an increase in the willingness to pay for a QALY on the test-treatment threshold being positive.

with medical standards at least to some extent. If they fail to do so, they will have to compensate the patient for the adverse effects of rendering their service in a negligent manner and will also run the risk of a loss of reputation, which in turn will lead physician's to internalize patient utility.

Moral hazard on the part of the patients can be controlled by coinsurance. If patients are subject to insurance schemes where they pay a portion of the medical bills, the diagnostic and therapeutic costs will naturally be considered in the test and treatment decisions.

Box 11.1: Is Defensive Medicine Defensible?

DeKay and Asch (1998) analyzed the effect of physician liability on test and test-treatment thresholds. To this end, they assume that testing reduces the physician's expected liability. This results in an increase in the informational value of a test, which in turn increases the range in patient eligibility for testing: The test threshold decreases and the test-treatment threshold increases. They further show that the mere risk of liability increases the testing range. In their comment, Pauker and Pauker (1998) welcome the contribution by DeKay and Asch (1998) to the threshold literature. They stress the need for educating physicians not to practice defensive medicine, as they would not be acting in their patients' best interest.

This literature does not explicitly discuss the role of liability in regulating physicians' discretionary behavior. The real source of the adverse outcome is, in fact, not the tort law, but cases where physicians do not act in the best interest of their patients. Furthermore, the profit motive leads physicians to test and to treat too often. It is true that court decisions in malpractice cases can be erroneous owing to a lack of information. This can induce defensive medicine. Nevertheless, the baseline holds that if physicians comply with medical standards, they will not be held liable.

11.2 Non-Expected Utility Theories Under Risk

Alternative non-expected utility theories have been suggested as being more in line with actual behavior under risk. For instance, in practice, decision makers tend to over-weight low probabilities and under-weight high probabilities. This leads to an inverse S-shaped probability transformation that has been confirmed in empirical studies (see Abdellaoui 2000 and Bleichrodt and Pinto 2000).

Eeckhoudt (2002) studied medical decision making under risk within the framework of Yaari's (1987) dual theory under risk, which belongs to the class of rank-dependent choice models (see Chap. 3 for a short presentation). In this section, we will follow Eeckhoudt (2002) and give a brief overview regarding the treatment threshold when using the dual theory of choice under risk.

Under expected utility theory (EUT), a utility function $u(h)$ is used to measure the preferences of an individual for all the possible consequences that tests and treatments might have, i.e., the resulting health states. Moreover, utilities are then weighted by their corresponding probabilities, thereby yielding the expected utilities of a decision maker's actions. The elementary utility function $u(h)$ is linear for a risk-neutral decision maker, while it is concave for a risk-averse one. Hence, in EUT risk preferences, such as risk aversion, are reflected by the curvature of the elementary utility functions regarding health states. This is not the case, however, in Yaari's dual theory under risk, where the outcomes are accepted as they are, but instead probabilities are transformed. This transformation is performed in a well-ordered manner.[4]

Under the dual theory, the evaluation of a lottery requires that the decision maker ranks its possible outcomes in an increasing order. Afterwards, the decision maker will weight the corresponding probabilities. Risk aversion is reflected by overweighting the probabilities of inferior outcomes and underweighting the probabilities of superior outcomes. If the decision maker would not weight either outcomes or probabilities, he would value lotteries according to their expected values and thus act in a risk-neutral manner. Let $w(p)$ denote the transformation function of p (which is the probability of being in a sick state and thus the worse outcome in a binary model).

Figure 11.1 shows a transformation function for a risk-averse decision maker. The 45° line mirrors the same values of p for the values of the ordinate. Thus, this would represent risk-neutral behavior. The sick state h_s (with corresponding probability p) is considered to be worse than the healthy state h_h (with corresponding probability $(1-p)$). Accordingly, we have $w(p) > p$ and $(1-w(p)) < (1-p)$. Moreover, Fig. 11.1 shows that the weights sum up to unity: $w(p) + (1-w(p)) = 1$, as it is the case for probabilities.

Then, the value attached to the decision (former expected utility) to provide treatment changes to

$$V^+(p) = w(p)h_s^+ + (1-w(p))h_h^+, \qquad (11.11)$$

and the value referring to the decision to withhold treatment changes to

$$V^-(p) = w(p)h_s^- + (1-w(p))h_h^-. \qquad (11.12)$$

To find the indifference threshold between treatment and no treatment, we start with

$$V^+(p) = V^-(p) \Leftrightarrow$$
$$w(p)h_s^+ + (1-w(p))h_h^+ = w(p)h_s^- + (1-w(p))h_h^-. \qquad (11.13)$$

---

[4]This explains the classification as rank-dependent choice model.

Fig. 11.1 Transformation function of p

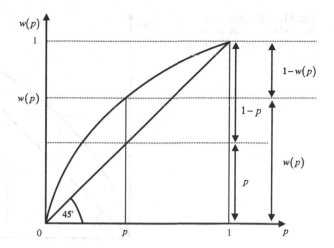

Solving for $w(p)$, we obtain the weight attached to the treatment threshold under the dual theory p_d^{Rx}:

$$w\left(p_d^{Rx}\right) = \frac{1}{1 + g_N/l_N}. \tag{11.14}$$

Applying the concept of an inverse function to Eq. (11.14) yields the treatment threshold under the dual theory of risk:

$$p_d^{Rx} = w^{-1}\left(\frac{1}{1 + g_N/l_N}\right). \tag{11.15}$$

Note, that in EUT g and l reflect utility differences, while here we use the respective difference between outcomes. However, this is equivalent to assuming a risk-neutral decision maker who has, by definition, a linear utility function. Since a risk-neutral decision maker will neither weight outcomes nor probabilities, the treatment threshold will be the same under EUT and dual theory. This, however, no longer holds for a risk-averse decision maker, because he values a lottery less than its mathematical expectation.

Figure 11.2 shows the treatment threshold for a risk-averse decision maker under the dual theory. Since $w(p) > p$, it follows that $p_{dA}^{Rx} < p_N^{Rx}$, where p_{dA}^{Rx} stands for the treatment threshold for a risk-averse decision maker under dual theory.[5]

In the case of diagnostic risk, treatment is the risk-reducing strategy, since it reduces the spread between the health outcomes. This is the case independent of the underlying model, whether it be EUT or the dual theory. Assuming the following

---

[5]Note the similarity between the threshold analysis under the dual theory and the analysis of the certainty equivalent under EUT.

Fig. 11.2 The treatment threshold for a risk-averse decision maker under the dual theory

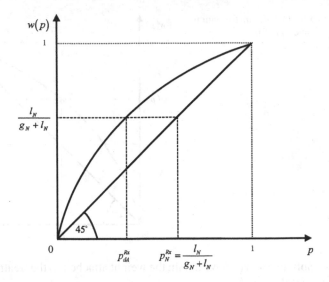

Fig. 11.3 The respective treatment threshold for a risk-averse and a risk-neutral decision maker under the dual theory

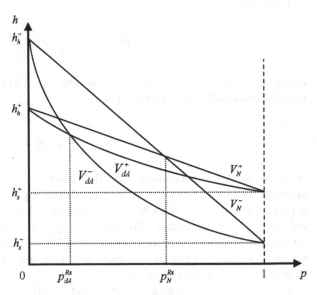

order of health outcomes, $h_h^- > h_h^+ > h_s^+ > h_s^-$, we show the values attached to the decision (treatment or no treatment) as a function of p in Fig. 11.3.

Figure 11.3 illustrates the difference between a risk-neutral and a risk-averse decision maker regarding p under the dual theory. In contrast to EUT, outcomes are shown on the ordinate and not expected utilities. Moreover, the value function of a risk-averse decision maker is no longer linear, but convex in p. The intersection of V_{dA}^+ and V_{dA}^- gives the treatment threshold for a risk-averse decision maker which is below that of the risk-neutral one: $p_{dA}^{Rx} < p_N^{Rx}$. Therefore, the effects of diagnostic risk on the treatment threshold for risk-averse decision makers are qualitatively the same in both worlds, i.e., p^{Rx} will decrease under EUT as well as under Yaari's dual theory. However, depending on the shape of the weighting function, the decision to treat or not to treat can differ strongly.

Box 11.2: Non-Expected Utility Threshold Models in Medical Decision Making

Besides the dual theory of choice under risk, there are many more non-EUT models that can be applied to the threshold model. Alternatives are the regret-based model, the hybrid model and, most recently, the dual-processing model (for an extensive discussion, see Djulbegovic et al. (2015)).

Regret theory was proposed by Loomes and Sugden (1982) as an alternative to prospect theory. Hozo and Djulbegovic (2008) extended this approach by introducing acceptable regret and applied it to the threshold model. This concept allows for individual differences regarding the tolerance towards accepting potential decision errors (it thus follows the same direction as EUT when taking individual risk preferences into account). The threshold model based on the acceptable regret approach can therefore explain actual variation in test and treatment decisions for patients who have the same a priori probability of illness.

Van den Ende and colleagues advocate the use of a hybrid model (Basinga et al. 2007) that introduces a multiplicative judgement factor that weights health outcomes differently between patients with disease and those without disease. They found that treatment thresholds based on their method were higher than treatment thresholds based on literature data, but lower than intuitive treatment thresholds based on interviews.

Recently, Djulbegovic et al. (2012) applied a dual-model of decision making to the threshold approach. The dual process theory takes both type 1 and type 2 cognitive systems into account. While type 1 relates to intuitive, automatic, affective processes (and thus distorts probabilities), type 2 relates to analytical processes (and thus calibrates probabilities without distortion and in line with EUT). They find that when benefits from treatment are smaller (greater) than the harm it causes, the treatment threshold is always higher (lower) than thresholds based on EUT.

The problem with all these models is that they make threshold comparisons with the risk-neutral EUT model. It thus remains to be seen whether new models explain actual variations in test and treatment decisions better than the EUT model once risk preferences and costs are taken into account. Above all, however, they lack the normative character of EUT thresholds and are thus not informative regarding the question: "What should the physician do?"

The dual theory also allows us to derive the test and test-treatment threshold when a diagnostic test is available. Applying the concept of the informational value of a test introduced in Chap. 5, we can derive the test and the test-treatment thresholds under the dual theory by setting the informational value equal to zero. We obtain:

$$w\left(p_d^t\right) = \frac{1}{1 + LR^+ g_N/l_N} \quad \Rightarrow \quad p_d^t = w^{-1}\left(\frac{1}{1 + LR^+ g_N/l_N}\right), \qquad (11.16)$$

$$w\left(p_d^{tRx}\right) = \frac{1}{1 + LR^- g_N/l_N} \quad \Rightarrow \quad p_d^{tRx} = w^{-1}\left(\frac{1}{1 + LR^- g_N/l_N}\right). \qquad (11.17)$$

The expressions in the parentheses on the right-hand side of these equations equal the well-known thresholds under EUT. If $w(p)$ is monotonically increasing in p, the rank order of the thresholds, given the characteristics of the likelihood ratios $(LR^+ > 1$ and $LR^- < 1)$, is as follows:

$$p_d^t < p_d^{Rx} < p_d^{tRx}. \qquad (11.18)$$

So far, we have assumed that physicians do not weight the conditional probabilities regarding the test characteristics, sensitivity and specificity. But this might not be the case. If so, we could no longer characterize the likelihood ratios of the test, and nothing could be predicted regarding the values of the test and test-treatment thresholds.

Even more troubling is the fact that qualitative results could differ when we compare test and test-treatment thresholds between the EUT the and non-EUT models. An imperfect diagnostic test implies the addition of sequential (compound) lotteries to the decision problem. Under dual theory, probabilities are weighted and are thus "non-linear". This is relevant for the presentation of a decision problem. Results differ depending on whether lotteries are presented in compound or in reduced format (for the difference, see Raiffa 1968). Moreover, Eeckhoudt (2002) demonstrated that the value of perfect information[6] can become negative under the dual theory of choice under risk, which he regards as a weakness.

From a normative point of view, there is no justification for weighting probabilities. Probabilities are what they are: objective values gained from the available information. Moreover, recent studies challenge the validity of rank-dependent models. List (2004), among others, showed that individuals with intense experience behave largely in accordance with rational expected utility theory. As Wakker (2008) pointed out: "Behavior will move toward the rational expected utility model if subjects can think deeply about their decisions and have the chance to learn" (p. 697). Physicians have to decide routinely on test and treatment strategies. Therefore, we should expect them to make unbiased estimations of probabilities, such as the a priori probability of an illness.

---

[6]In the framework of non-EUT models, the value of information relates to differences in outcomes rather than differences in EUT.

Box 11.3: The Mystery of the Stolen Life Years—Compound vs. Reduced Lotteries

One of the problems of non-EUT models is that they are prone to framing. More specifically, it matters whether the decision problem is presented in an extensive form (compound lotteries) or in a normal form (reduced lottery).

The following illustrative example is adapted from Eeckhoudt (2002, Chap. 9). Let's assume a patient with a 0.1 a priori probability of illness. A test is available that has a sensitivity and specificity of 0.9. Outcomes are measured in life years as follows: $h_h^- = 32$, $h_h^+ = 30$, $h_s^+ = 14$ and $h_s^- = 10$.

There are two physicians: one visited a lecture in medical decision making and acts according to EUT, the other behaves according to Yaari's dual theory under risk. While the first physician weights outcomes according to $u(h) = \sqrt{h}$, the second weights probabilities using $w(p) = \sqrt{p}$.

The decision tree can then be presented in the extensive (left-hand side in the figure below) and normal forms (right-hand side). Note that we ranked the outcomes from lowest to highest in both presentations.

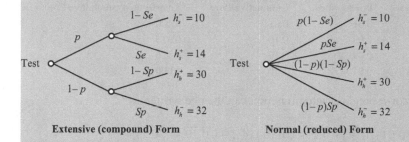

Extensive (compound) Form   **Normal (reduced) Form**

While the extensive form comprises compound lotteries, the normal form uses a reduced presentation. The question now is whether the presentation of the decision problems matters for the decision makers.

Let us start with the first physician who acts according to EUT. In the case where the patient is sick, $EU(s) = 0.1\sqrt{10} + 0.9\sqrt{14} = 3.684$ and the corresponding certainty equivalent in life years is 13.57. In the case where the patient is healthy, $EU(h) = 0.1\sqrt{30} + 0.9\sqrt{32} = 5.639$ and the corresponding certainty equivalent in life years is 31.80. Folding back the decision tree leads to an overall expected utility of $EU = 0.1\sqrt{13.57} + 0.9\sqrt{31.80} = 5.443$ and the corresponding certainty equivalent amounts to $(5.433)^2 = 29.63$. Using the normal form $EU = 0.01\sqrt{10} + 0.09\sqrt{14} + 0.09\sqrt{30} + 0.81\sqrt{32} = 5.443$ and thus the same expected utility as in the case of compound lotteries (the same is true for the life years).

(continued)

Box 11.3 (continued)

Under Yaari's dual theory, the decision maker will first rank the outcomes of a lottery in an increasing order and then weight the corresponding probabilities.

We start with the compound lottery case. If the patient is sick, the value attached to the decision (in life years) amounts to $V(s) = \sqrt{0.1} \cdot 10 + (1 - \sqrt{0.1}) 14 = 12.735$, while for the case of a healthy patient $V(h) = \sqrt{0.1} \cdot 30 + (1 - \sqrt{0.1}) 32 = 31.368$. The total value then becomes $V = \sqrt{0.1} \cdot 12.735 + (1 - \sqrt{0.1}) 31.368 = 25.475$.

What happens if the decision problem is presented in the normal (reduced) form? Unfortunately, we <u>cannot</u> simply write $V = w(p_1)h_1 + w(p_2)h_2 + w(p_3)h_3 \ldots$ since the weights would not sum up to unity. To calculate weighted probabilities in the case of more than two outcomes, it helps to display a table for the (ranked) outcomes and corresponding probabilities (for a detailed explanation, see Eeckhoudt (2002, Chap. 8)).

Outcomes	Probabilities	Cumulative Prob.	Transformed cumulative Prob.
10	0.01	0.01	0.100
14	0.09	0.10	0.316
30	0.09	0.19	0.436
32	0.81	1.00	1.000

The corresponding value function can then be written as:

$$V = (\sqrt{0.01}) 10 + (\sqrt{0.1} - \sqrt{0.01}) 14 + (\sqrt{0.19} - \sqrt{0.1}) 30$$
$$+ (\sqrt{1.00} - \sqrt{0.19}) 32 = 25.669.$$

While the presentation of the decision problem in an extensive form leads to an outcome of 25.475 life years, a presentation in the reduced form leads to 25.669 life years, and thus, unlike under the EUT model, to a different result. "The mystery of the stolen life years" is thus a major drawback of non-EUT models.

11.3   Non-Expected Utility Theories Under Uncertainty

Another explanation for the discrepancy between predicted and actual behavior is uncertainty (ambiguity) regarding probabilities. In this book, we have analyzed decisions under the notion of diagnostic and therapeutic risk and, thus, assumed that probabilities are known. In real-life situations, however, this is not always the case. Often probabilities are unknown or uncertain, and available information based on statistical data is given with different degrees of precision. For instance, prevalence rates are based on recorded numbers from the past and calculated for a population of a country which does not necessarily reflect the patient population of the decision maker's region.

The term ambiguity refers to the case where the probability distribution of outcomes is unknown, while the notion of risk refers to the case when probabilities are known. An ambiguity-averse individual would rather choose an alternative with known probabilities than an alternative with unknown probabilities.

In the case of an ambiguity-neutral decision maker, assume that the probability of illness can take two values, p_1 and p_2 with $p_1 < p_2$. Furthermore, let us assume that μ denotes the subjective probability of the decision maker that p_1 is the true probability of illness. Correspondingly, $1 - \mu$ denotes the subjective probability with which the decision maker believes that p_2 is the true a priori probability of illness.[7]

Instead of comparing a single probability to the treatment threshold, the decision maker now faces two possible probabilities. If $p_1 < p_2 < p^{Rx}$, the simple solution is no treatment, while for $p^{Rx} < p_1 < p_2$ treatment is indicated. However, for $p_1 < p^{Rx} < p_2$ we cannot rely on the original threshold model. In this case, we have to rewrite our original equations and take the uncertainty about p into account. Then, the expected utility of treatment changes to

$$EU^+(\mu,p) = \mu\left(p_1 u\left(h_s^+\right) + (1 - p_1)u\left(h_h^+\right)\right)$$
$$+(1 - \mu)\left(p_2 u\left(h_s^+\right) + (1 - p_2)u\left(h_h^+\right)\right) \tag{11.19}$$

and the utility of no treatment changes to

$$EU^-(\mu,p) = \mu\left(p_1 u\left(h_s^-\right) + (1 - p_1)u\left(h_h^-\right)\right)$$
$$+(1 - \mu)\left(p_2 u\left(h_s^-\right) + (1 - p_2)u\left(h_h^-\right)\right). \tag{11.20}$$

Accordingly, the treatment threshold where $EU^+ = EU^-$ can be rewritten as

$$p^{Rx} = \mu p_1 + (1 - \mu)p_2 = \frac{1}{1 + g/l}. \tag{11.21}$$

Since the decision maker is ambiguity-neutral, the threshold does not change compared to the situation without diagnostic ambiguity. However, instead of comparing a certain single a priori probability with the treatment threshold, the decision maker now uses the weighted expected a priori probability $\bar{p} = \mu p_1 + (1 - \mu)p_2$. Therefore, if the weighted expected a priori probability is lower (higher) than the treatment threshold p^{Rx}, the ambiguity-neutral decision maker should opt for no treatment (treatment). An example is given in Fig. 11.4

---

[7]Another interpretation is that these are weighting factors for the size of a trial in a meta-analysis of prevalence estimates.

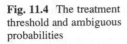

Fig. 11.4 The treatment threshold and ambiguous probabilities

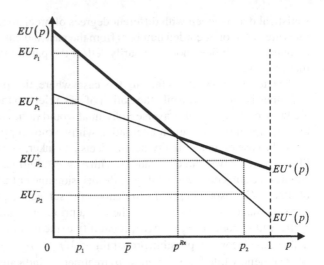

where $p_1 < p^{Rx} < p_2$, but the weighted expected a priori probability $\bar{p} = \mu p_1 + (1 - \mu)p_2$ lies below the treatment threshold p^{Rx}.

Thus, nothing changes for an ambiguous-neutral decision maker compared to his action under EUT, except that he uses an average of a priori probabilities.

Box 11.4: The Ellsberg Paradox

In 1961, Daniel Ellsberg presented some examples showing that many individuals have non-neutral preferences towards ambiguity and thus violate the assumptions made by the subjective expected utility model (Ellsberg 1961). Ellsberg's contribution was so important that his examples are now known as the Ellsberg Paradox (besides his contributions to decision theory, Ellsberg is also known for leaking the Pentagon papers in 1971—a top-secret study that showed that the United States was not only involved in Vietnam, but also in bombings in surrounding countries).

In his hypothetical experiment, he presented two urns, each containing a mixture of a 100 red and black balls. The participants are informed that while the first urn contains red and black balls in an unknown ratio, the second urn contains exactly 50 red and 50 black balls. Subjects now have to choose from which urn they want to draw and bet on the color of the ball that will be drawn. They receive US$ 100 if their color is drawn, and US$ 0 otherwise. Subjects are then shown the following pairs of gambles and asked about their preferences:

1. A red draw from urn 1, or a black draw from urn 1
2. A red draw from urn 2, or a black draw from urn 2
3. A red draw from urn 1, or a red draw from urn 2

(continued)

Box 11.4 (continued)
4. A black draw from urn 1, or a black draw from urn 2

Most individuals are indifferent regarding the first and second sets of alternative choices. This is not the case for the third and fourth sets of alternative choices. Here, the majority prefer urn 2—the one with the known ratio—in both cases. This, however, violates the so-called Savage's normative axioms of subjective expected utility (which allows subjective probabilities to be drawn from a subject's preferences) (Savage 1954). Preferring urn 2 in the third case implies that one implicitly assumes that there are more black balls than red balls in urn 1. This, however, would mean that one should prefer urn 1 in the fourth case—something that is not observed in actual behavior.

In conclusion, Ellsberg found that the majority of individuals are ambiguity-averse: they prefer known to unknown probabilities. Although this behavior is judged as irrational, even Ellsberg asked: "Are they clearly mistaken?" (Ellsberg 1961, p. 669).

This is no longer the case for an ambiguous-averse decision maker. Let us assume that the ordering of health states is the following: $h_h^- > h_h^+ > h_s^+ > h_s^-$ and that—as in Berger et al. (2013)—the decision maker behaves according to the smooth ambiguity model, as introduced by Klibanoff et al. (2005). Then, the value attached to the decision to opt for treatment changes to

$$V^+(\mu, p) = \mu\varphi\big(p_1 u\big(h_s^+\big) + (1 - p_1)u\big(h_h^+\big)\big)$$
$$+(1 - \mu)\varphi\big(p_2 u\big(h_s^+\big) + (1 - p_2)u\big(h_h^+\big)\big) \tag{11.22}$$

and the value referring to the decision to opt for no treatment changes to

$$V^-(\mu, p) = \mu\varphi\big(p_1 u\big(h_s^-\big) + (1 - p_1)u\big(h_h^-\big)\big)$$
$$+(1 - \mu)\varphi\big(p_2 u\big(h_s^-\big) + (1 - p_2)u\big(h_h^-\big)\big), \tag{11.23}$$

where φ denotes a function that measures the ambiguity aversion of the decision maker. Similar to the elementary utility function u and its relationship to risk aversion, the decision maker is ambiguity-averse (ambiguity seeking) if φ is concave (convex), while for an ambiguity-neutral decision maker φ is a linear function.

One feature of the smooth ambiguity model is that it separates the degree of ambiguity, measured through μ and $1 - \mu$, from ambiguity aversion, measured through φ. Moreover, the smooth ambiguity model can be interpreted as a two-stage model. In the first stage, the decision maker uses φ reflecting his ambiguity aversion to weight the expected utilities that are determined in the second stage. In the second stage, he determines expected utilities using u to weight different health states which reflects his risk aversion. The second stage follows our previous analysis for decisions under diagnostic risk. Although the decision maker uses a weighting function that can be seen as an expected utility evaluation in each stage, the weighting functions differ between each stage: φ in the first stage, whereas u in the second stage.

The 'expected utility' evaluation in the first stage is equivalent to its evaluation in the second stage. Figure 11.5 shows the effects of ambiguity aversion under diagnostic ambiguity. Similar to the case of risk aversion, an ambiguity-averse decision maker exhibits a concave utility function. However, while in the case of risk aversion the utility function u reflects the weighted health states, the value function of the first stage weights the expected utilities that are determined in the second stage. From Fig. 11.4, we know that $EU_{p_1}^- - EU_{p_2}^- > EU_{p_1}^+ - EU_{p_2}^+$, i.e., the spread between expected utilities regarding no treatment is higher than that for expected utilities regarding treatment. This is similar to the case of our original analysis where the spread between health states without treatment was larger than the spread between health states with treatment: $h_h^- - h_s^- > h_h^+ - h_s^+$. While a risk-neutral individual is indifferent regarding the spread, a risk-averse individual prefers less risk and thus a smaller spread. Similarly, an ambiguity-neutral individual is indifferent regarding the spreads between the expected utilities. Therefore, an ambiguity-neutral individual will have a linear weighting function. By comparison, an ambiguity-averse individual will dislike the spread and will give the inner EU states a higher weighting than the ambiguity-neutral individual would. Therefore, the ambiguity-averse decision maker will have a concave weighting function φ with

$$\varphi\left(EU_{p_1}^+\right) > EU_{p_1}^+ \text{ and } \varphi\left(EU_{p_2}^+\right) > EU_{p_2}^+.$$

Figure 11.6 illustrates the treatment threshold for an ambiguity-averse decision maker. Diagnostic ambiguity makes the treatment option more attractive to an

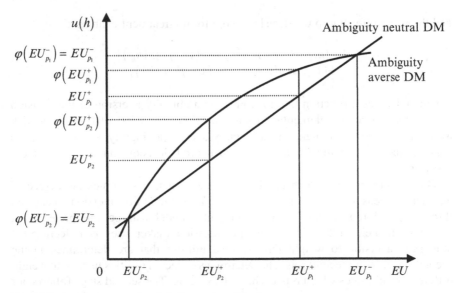

Fig. 11.5 Ambiguity aversion and diagnostic ambiguity

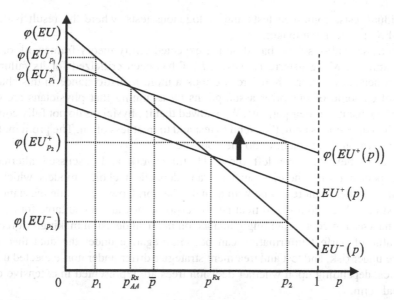

Fig. 11.6 The treatment threshold under ambiguity aversion

ambiguity-averse decision maker. Therefore, the line of the expected utility of treatment will shift upwards leading to a lower treatment threshold $p_{AA}^{Rx} < p^{Rx}$. Hence, an ambiguity-averse decision maker will treat his patient earlier than an ambiguity-neutral decision maker would.

It has been argued that ambiguity aversion is not rational (Raiffa 1961; Wakker 2010). However, many experiments have confirmed that people display ambiguity-averse behavior and, thus, act inconsistently when probabilities are uncertain. While some might conclude that expected utility theory is not sufficient, we want to reply with Raiffa's (1961) remark that observed non-rational behavior "clearly demonstrates how important it is to have a theory which can be used to aid in the making of decisions under uncertainty. If most people behaved in a manner roughly consistent with Savage's theory, then the theory would gain stature as a descriptive theory but would lose a good deal of its normative importance. We do not have to teach people what comes naturally" (pp. 690–691).

11.4 Conclusion

In this textbook, we combined informative test theory with the expected utility hypothesis to offer a comprehensive theory of medical decision making under risk. We demonstrated how the parameters of Bayes' theorem can be combined with a value function of health states to arrive at informed test and treatment decisions. We distinguished between risk-neutral, risk-averse and prudent decision makers and demonstrated the effects of risk preferences on physicians' decisions. We analyzed individual tests, combined tests and endogenous tests, where the result is determined by the decision maker.

All these analyses were based on the expected utility theory framework of von Neumann and Morgenstern. However, EUT has been criticized for its failure to predict actual behavior. Therefore, we took a more realistic stance in this chapter and soften some of our prior assumptions by assuming that physicians are only imperfect agents of their patients. We showed that if physicians do not fully comply with the Hippocrates oath, they tend to test and to treat less often. The profit motive, by comparison, leads them to do the opposite.

In a further step, we left the EUT framework and discussed alternative non-expected utility theories such as rank-dependent choice models which are appraised as being more in line with actual behavior. However, while these models can explain observed test and treatment decisions, they are not suitable for normative analyses aimed at providing guidance on medical decision making. Moreover, the value of perfect information can become negative under the dual theory of choice under risk, and test and treatment strategies differ under non-expected utility theories, depending upon whether decision trees are represented in extensive or in normal form.

Recent studies challenge the validity of rank-dependent theory. List (2004), among others, showed that individuals with intense experience behave largely in accordance with rational expected utility theory. Physicians have to decide routinely on test and treatment strategies. We should expect them to make unbiased estimations of probabilities, such as the a priori probability of an illness, and form coherent decisions.

The use of expected utility theory is also warranted in the prescriptive realm of optimal decision making. If an optimal policy has to be chosen or recommended, 'expected utility is the best theory to determine which decisions to take' (Wakker 2008, p. 697).

11.5 Notes

Ellis and McGuire (1986) introduced the now classical economic model for physician behavior. For an overview of physician agency see McGuire (2000). Danzon (2000) provides for a comprehensive analysis of liability for medical malpractice. For an overview of non-EUT models including probability weighting functions with an application to medical decision analysis, see Abdellaoui (2000), Bleichrodt and Pinto (2000), as well as Eeckhoudt (2002). A comprehensive analysis of non-EUT models for treatment decisions under ambiguity is given in Berger et al. (2013).

Exercises

1. Consider a lottery with the following outcomes: $h_1 = 10; h_2 = 16; h_3 = 25$ and the corresponding probabilities $p_1 = 0.1, p_2 = 0.5, p_3 = 0.4$. The utility function is $u(h) = h$ the probability weighting function is $w(p) = \sqrt{p}$. What is the value of the lottery under EUT and under the dual theory framework, resp.?

2. Assume the following utility function $u(h) = \sqrt{h}$ and the following probability weighting function $w(p) = \sqrt{p}$. Moreover, let's assume a patient with an a priori probability of illness equal to $p = 0.2$ and a diagnostic test with characteristics $Se = Sp = 0.8$. Outcomes (measured in life years) are as follows: $h_s^- = 9; h_s^+ = 16; h_h^+ = 25; h_h^- = 36$.

   (a) Draw the decision tree in extensive and normal forms (note that the outcomes should be ranked from lowest to highest)

   (b) What is the certainty equivalent, i.e., value attached to the decision (in life years) using the extensive form under

   (1) EUT
   (2) Yaari's dual theory

   (c) What is the certainty equivalent (in life years) using the normal form under

   (1) EUT
   (2) Yaari's dual theory

   (d) Compare the results of (b) and (c) and discuss.

3. Let's assume two physicians, one is ambiguity neutral and acts according to EUT with $u(h) = \sqrt{h}$ and one is ambiguity averse with the same (elementary) utility function but also $\varphi(EU) = \sqrt{EU}$. Moreover, both physicians see the same patient. Health outcomes are as follows $h_s^- = 4; h_s^+ = 16; h_h^+ = 25; h_h^- = 36$.

   (a) Assume that the a priori probability of illness for that patient is 30%.

   (1) Calculate EU^+ and EU^- for the first physician. What will he do?
   (2) Calculate V^+ and V^- for the second physician. What will he do?

   (b) Assume now that the a priori probability of illness is uncertain and can take two values, p_1 and p_2 with $p_1 = 10\%$ and $p_2 = 50\%$. Furthermore, $\mu = 50\%$ denotes the subjective probability of both physicians that p_1 is the true probability of illness and $1 - \mu = 50\%$ denotes the subjective probability with which both physicians believe that p_2 is the true a priori probability of illness (note that the weighted expected a priori probability of illness is the same as before: $\bar{p} = \mu p_1 + (1 - \mu)p_2 = 30\%$).

   (1) Calculate EU^+ and EU^- for the first physician. What will he do?
   (2) Calculate V^+ and V^- for the second physician. What will he do?
   (3) Compare the results of (a) and (b) and discuss observed behavior vs. "what should a physician do"?

References

Abdellaoui, M. (2000). Parameter-free elicitation of utility and probability weighting functions. *Management Sciences, 46*(11), 1497–1512.

Basinga, P., Moreira, J., Bisoffi, Z., Bisig, B., & Van den Ende, J. (2007). Why are clinicians reluctant to treat smear-negative tuberculosis? An inquiry about treatment thresholds in Rwanda. *Medical Decision Making, 27*, 53–60.

Berger, L., Bleichrodt, H., & Eeckhoudt, L. (2013). Treatment decisions under ambiguity. *Journal of Health Economics, 32*, 559–569.

Bleichrodt, H., & Pinto, J. L. (2000). A parameter-free elicitation of the probability weighting function in medical decision analysis. *Management Sciences, 46*(11), 1485–1496.

Danzon, P. M. (2000). Liability for medical malpractice. In A. J. Culyer & J. P. Newhouse, J. (Eds.), *Handbook of health economics* (1st ed., pp. 1339–1404). New York: Elsevier Science, North-Holland.

DeKay, M. L., & Asch, D. A. (1998). Is the defensive use of diagnostic tests good for patients, or bad? *Medical Decision Making, 18*, 19–28.

Djulbegovic, B., Hozo, I., Beckstead, J., Tsalatsanis, A., & Pauker, S. G. (2012). Dual processing model of medical decision-making. *BMC Medical Informatics and Decision Making, 12*, 94.

Djulbegovic, B., van den Ende, J., Hamm, R. M., Mayrhofer, T., Hozo, I., & Pauker, S. (2015). When is rational to order a diagnostic test, or prescribe treatment: The threshold model as an explanation of practice variation. *European Journal of Clinical Investigation, 45*(5), 485–493.

Eeckhoudt, L. (2002). *Risk and medical decision making*. Boston: Kluwer.

Ellis, R. P., & McGuire, T. G. (1986). Provider behavior under prospective reimbursement. *Journal of Health Economics, 5*, 129–151.

Ellsberg, D. (1961). Risk, ambiguity, and the savage axioms. *Quarterly Journal of Economics, 75* (4), 643–669.

Hozo, I., & Djulbegovic, B. (2008). When is diagnostic testing inappropriate or irrational? Acceptable regret approach. *Medical Decision Making, 28*, 540–553.

Klibanoff, P., Marinacci, M., & Muerkji, S. (2005). A smooth model of decision making under ambiguity. *Econometrica, 73*(6), 1849–1892.

List, J. (2004). Neoclassical theory versus prospect theory: Evidence from the market place. *Econometrica, 72*(2), 615–625.

Loomes, G., & Sugden, R. (1982). Regret theory: An alternative theory of rational choice. *Economic Journal, 92*, 805–824.

McGuire, T. G. (2000). Physician agency. In: A. J. Culyer & J. P. Newhouse, J. (Eds.), *Handbook of health economics* (1st ed., pp. 461–536). New York: Elsevier Science, North-Holland.

Moscati, I. (2016). How economists came to accept expected utility theory: The case of Samuelson and Savage. *The Journal of Economic Perspectives, 30*(2), 219–236.

Pauker, S. G., & Pauker, S. P. (1998). Expected utility perspectives on defensive testing: Torts, tradeoffs, and thresholds—Is defensive medicine defensible? *Medical Decision Making, 18*, 29–31.

Raiffa, H. (1968). *Decision analysis: Introductory lectures on choices under uncertainty*. Reading, MA: Addison-Wesley.

Raiffa, H. (1961). Risk, uncertainty and the savage axioms: Comment. *Quarterly Journal of Economics, 75*, 690–694.

Savage, L. J. (1954). *The foundations of statistics*. New York: Wiley.

Wakker, P. P. (2008). Lessons learned by (from?) an economist working in medical decision making. *Medical Decision Making, 28*(5), 690–698.

Wakker, P. P. (2010). *Prospect theory: For risk and ambiguity*. Cambridge: Cambridge University Press.

Yaari, Y. (1987). The dual theory of choice under risk. *Econometrica, 55*(1), 95–115.

References

Abdellaoui, M. (2000). Parameter-free elicitation of utility and probability weighting functions. *Management Sciences, 46*(11), 1497–1512.

Allais, M. (1987). *The general theory of random choices in relation to invariant cardinal utility function and the specific probability function: The (U, Θ) Model—a general overview*. Paris: Centre National de la Recherche Scientific.

Ament, A., & Hasman, A. (1993). Optimal test strategy in the case of two tests and one disease. *International Journal of Bio-Medical Computing, 33*(3–4), 179–197.

Anderson, J. L., Adams, C. D., Antman, E. M., Bridges, C. R., Califf, R. M., Casey, D. E., et al. (2011). The ACCF/AHA-focused update incorporated into the ACC/AHA 2007 guidelines for the management of patients' highly sensitive troponin and coronary computed tomography angiography in the evaluation of patients with unstable angina/non-ST-elevation myocardial infarction: A report of the American College of Cardiology Foundation/American Heart Association Task Force on practice guidelines. *Circulation, 123*, e426–e579.

Arrow, K. J. (1971). *Essays in the theory of risk-bearing*. London: North-Holland.

Arthur, W. B. (1981). The economics of risks to life. *American Economic Review, 71*(1), 54–64.

Ashenfelter, O., & Greenstone, M. (2004). Using mandatory speed limits to measure the value of a statistical life. *Journal of Political Economy, 112*(2), 227–267.

AWMF (Arbeitsgemeinschaft der Wissenschaftlichen Medizinischen Fach-gesellschaften). (2002). *PSA-Bestimmung in der Prostatakarzinom-diagnostik*. Leitlinie-Nr. 043/036.

Bandstein, N., Ljung, R., Johansson, M., & Holzmann, M. J. (2014). Undetectable high-sensitivity cardiac troponin T-level in the emergency department and risk of myocardial infarction. *Journal of the American College of Cardiology, 63*, 2569–2578.

Basinga, P., Moreira, J., Bisoffi, Z., Bisig, B., & Van den Ende, J. (2007). Why are clinicians reluctant to treat smear-negative tuberculosis? An inquiry about treatment thresholds in Rwanda. *Medical Decision Making, 27*, 53–60.

Bellavance, F., Dionne, G., & Lebeau, M. (2009). The value of a statistical life: A meta-analysis with a mixed effects regression model. *Journal of Health Economics, 28*(2), 444–464.

Berger, L., Bleichrodt, H., & Eeckhoudt, L. (2013). Treatment decisions under ambiguity. *Journal of Health Economics, 32*, 559–569.

Bernoulli, D. (1738). Specimen Theoriae Novae de Mensura Sortis. Commentarii Academiae Scientiarum Imperialis Petropolitanae, Translated from Latin into English by L. Sommer (1954). Exposition of a new theory on the measurement of risk. *Econometrica, 22*, 23–36.

Bleichrodt, H., & Johannesson, M. (1997). Standard gamble, time trade-off and rating scale: Experimental results on the ranking properties of QALYs. *Journal of Health Economics, 16*(2), 155–175.

© Springer-Verlag GmbH Germany 2017
S. Felder, T. Mayrhofer, *Medical Decision Making*,
DOI 10.1007/978-3-662-53432-8

Bleichrodt, H., & Pinto, J. L. (2000). A parameter-free elicitation of the probability weighting function in medical decision analysis. *Management Sciences, 46*(11), 1485–1496.

Body, R., Carley, S., McDowell, G., Jaffe, A. S., France, M., Cruickshank, K., et al. (2011). Rapid exclusion of acute myocardial infarction in patients with undetectable troponin using a high-sensitivity assay. *Journal of the American College of Cardiology, 58*, 1332–1339.

Bramoullé, Y., & Treich, N. (2009). Can uncertainty alleviate the commons problem? *Journal of the European Economic Association, 7*(5), 1042–1067.

Breyer, F., & Felder, S. (2005). Mortality risk and the value of a statistical life: The dead-anyway effect revis(it)ed. *Geneva Papers on Risk and Insurance Theory, 30*(1), 41–55.

Brocket, P. L., & Golden, L. L. (1987). A class of utility functions containing all the common utility functions. *Management Science, 33*(8), 955–964.

Caballé, J., & Pomansky, A. (1996). Mixed risk aversion. *Journal of Economic Theory, 71*(2), 485–513.

Clemente, J., Marcuello, C., Montañés, A., & Pueyo, F. (2004). On the international stability of health care expenditure functions: Are government and private functions similar? *Journal of Health Economics, 23*(3), 589–613.

Costa, D. L., & Kahn, M. E. (2004). Changes in the value of life, 1940–1980. *Journal of Risk and Uncertainty, 29*(2), 159–180.

Courbage, C., & Rey, B. (2006). Prudence and optimal prevention for health risks. *Health Economics, 15*(12), 1323–1327.

Crainich, D., Eeckhoudt, L., & Trannoy, A. (2013). Even (Mixed) risk-lovers are prudent. *American Economic Review, 103*(4), 1529–1535.

Culyer, A. J. (1989). The normative economics of health care finance and provision. *Oxford Review of Economic Policy, 5*(1), 34–58.

Danzon, P. M. (2000). Liability for medical malpractice. In A. J. Culyer & J. P. Newhouse (Eds.), *Handbook of health economics* (1st ed., pp. 1339–1404). New York: Elsevier Science, North-Holland.

Deck, C., & Schlesinger, H. (2010). Exploring higher order risk effects. *Review of Economic Studies, 77*(4), 1403–1420.

Deck, C., & Schlesinger, H. (2014). Consistency of higher order risk preferences. *Econometrica, 82*(5), 1913–1943.

DeKay, M. L., & Asch, D. A. (1998). Is the defensive use of diagnostic tests good for patients, or bad? *Medical Decision Making, 18*, 19–28.

Diamond, G. A., Hirsch, M., Forrester, J. S., Staniloff, H. M., Vasl, R., Halpern, S. W., et al. (1981). Application of information theory to clinical diagnostic testing. The electrocardiographic stress test. *Circulation, 63*(4), 915–921.

Djulbegovic, B., Hozo, I., Beckstead, J., Tsalatsanis, A., & Pauker, S. G. (2012). Dual processing model of medical decision-making. *BMC Medical Informatics and Decision Making, 12*, 94.

Djulbegovic, B., van den Ende, J., Hamm, R. M., Mayrhofer, T., Hozo, I., & Pauker, S. (2015). When is rational to order a diagnostic test, or prescribe treatment: The threshold model as an explanation of practice variation. *European Journal of Clinical Investigation, 45*(5), 485–493.

Drummond, M. F., O'Brien, B., Stoddart, G. L., & Torrance, G. W. (1987). *Methods for the economic evaluation of health care programmes*. Oxford: Oxford University Press.

Ebert, S., & Wiesen, D. (2011). Testing for prudence and skewness seeking. *Management Science, 57*(7), 1334–1349.

Ebert, S., & Wiesen, D. (2014). Joint measurement of risk aversion, prudence, and temperance. *Journal of Risk and Uncertainty, 48*(3), 231–252.

Eddy, D. M. (1982). Probabilistic reasoning in clinical medicine: Problems and opportunities. In D. Kahneman, P. Slovic, & A. Tversky (Eds.), *Judgment under uncertainty: Heuristics and biases* (pp. 249–267). Cambridge: Cambridge University Press.

Eeckhoudt, L. (2002). *Risk and medical decision making*. Boston: Kluwer.

Eeckhoudt, L., & Gollier, C. (2005). The impact of prudence on optimal prevention. *Economic Theory, 26*(4), 989–994.

Eeckhoudt, L., Gollier, C., & Treich, N. (2005). Optimal consumption and the timing of the resolution of uncertainty. *European Economic Review, 49*(3), 761–773.

Eeckhoudt, L., & Kimball, M. (1992). Background risk, prudence and the demand for insurance. In G. Dionne (Ed.), *Contributions to insurance economics* (pp. 239–254). Boston: Kluwer.

Eeckhoudt, L. R., Lebrun, T. C., & Sailly, J.-C. L. (1984). The informative content of diagnostic tests: An economic analysis. *Social Science & Medicine, 18*(10), 873–880.

Ellis, R. P., & McGuire, T. G. (1986). Provider behavior under prospective reimbursement. *Journal of Health Economics, 5*, 129–151.

Ellsberg, D. (1961). Risk, ambiguity, and the savage axioms. *Quarterly Journal of Economics, 75* (4), 643–669.

Eraker, S. A., & Sasse, L. (1981). The serum digoxin test and digoxin toxicity: A Bayesian approach. *Circulation, 640*, 409–420.

Esö, P., & White, L. (2004). Precautionary bidding in auctions. *Econometrica, 72*(1), 77–92.

Fechner, G. G. (1860). *Elemente der Psychophysik*. Leipzig: Breitkopf and Härtel.

Fei, W., & Schlesinger, H. (2008). Precautionary insurance demand with state-dependent background risk. *Journal of Risk and Insurance, 75*(1), 1–16.

Felder, S., & Mayrhofer, T. (2014). Risk preferences: Consequences for test and treatment thresholds and optimal cutoffs. *Medical Decision Making, 34*(1), 33–41.

Felder, S., & Robra, B.-P. (2006). A preference-based measure for test performance with an application to prenatal diagnostics. *Journal of Statistics in Medicine, 25*(21), 3696–3706.

Felder, S., Werblow, A., & Robra, B.-P. (2003). A-priori risk and optimal test accuracy in prenatal diagnostics. *Medical Decision Making, 23*(5), 406–413.

Ferencik, M., Liu, T., Mayrhofer, T., Puchner, S. B., Lu, M. T., Maurovich-Horvat, P., et al. (2015). Highly sensitive troponin I followed by advanced coronary artery disease assessment using computed tomography angiography improves acute coronary syndrome risk stratification accuracy and work-up in acute chest pain patients: Results from ROMICAT II trial. *JACC Cardiovascular Imaging, 8*, 1272–1281.

Fletcher, R. H., Fletcher, S. W., & Wagner, E. H. (1996). *Clinical epidemiology: The essentials*. Baltimore, MD: Williams & Wilkins.

Friedman, M., & Savage, L. J. (1948). The utility analysis of choices involving risk. *Journal of Political Economy, 56*(4), 279–304.

Gigerenzer, G., & Hoffrage, U. (1995). How to improve Bayesian reasoning without instruction: Frequency formats. *Psychological Review, 102*(4), 684–704.

Gollier, C. (1996). Decreasing absolute prudence: Characterization and applications to second-best risk sharing. *European Economic Review, 40*(9), 1799–1815.

Gollier, C., & Pratt, J. W. (1996). Risk vulnerability and the tempering effect of background risk. *Econometrica, 64*(5), 1109–1123.

Gomes, F., & Michaelides, A. (2005). Optimal life-cycle asset allocation: Under-standing the empirical evidence. *Journal of Finance, 60*(2), 869–904.

Gould, J. P. (1974). Risk, stochastic preference, and the value of information. *Journal of Economic Theory, 8*(1), 64–84.

Harris, R. A., Washington, A. E., Feeny, D., & Kuppermann, M. (2001). Decision analysis of prenatal testing for chromosomal disorders: What do the preferences of pregnant women tell us? *Genetic Testing, 5*(1), 23–32.

Heinrich, T., & Mayrhofer, T. (2014). *Higher-order risk preferences in social settings*. Ruhr Economic Paper No. 508.

Hershey, J. C., Cebul, R. D., & Williams, S. V. (1986). Clinical guidelines for using two dichotomous tests. *Medical Decision Making, 6*(2), 68–78.

Hirshleifer, J., & Riley, J. G. (1992). *The analytics of uncertainty and information*. Cambridge: Cambridge University Press.

Hoffman, R. M., Gilliland, F. D., Adams-Cameron, M., Hunt, W. C., & Key, C. R. (2002). Prostate-specific antigen testing accuracy in community practice. *BMC Family Practice, 3* (19), 1–8.

Hook, E. B. (1985). Maternal age, paternal age and human chromosome abnormality: Nature, magnitude and mechanisms of effects. In V. L. Dellarco & P. E. Voytek (Eds.), *Aneuploidy, etiology and mechanisms* (pp. 117–132). New York: Plenum.

Hozo, I., & Djulbegovic, B. (2008). When is diagnostic testing inappropriate or irrational? Acceptable regret approach. *Medical Decision Making, 28*, 540–553.

Hull, R., Hirsh, J., Sackett, D. L., & Stoddart, G. L. (1981). Cost-effectiveness of clinical diagnosis, venography and non-invasive testing in patients with symptomatic deep-vein thrombosis. *New England Journal of Medicine, 304*, 1561–1567.

Hunink, M., Glasziou, P., Siegel, J., Weeks, J., Pliskin, J., Elstein, A., et al. (2004). *Decision making in health and medicine*. Cambridge: Cambridge University Press.

Januzzi, J. L., Sharma, U., Zakroysky, P., Truong, Q. A., Woodard, P. K., Pope, J. H., et al. (2015). Sensitive troponin assays in patients with suspected acute coronary syndrome: Results from the multicenter rule out myocardial infarction using computer assisted tomography II trial. *American Heart Journal, 169*, 572–578.

Johannson, P. O. (1996). *Evaluating health risk: An economic approach*. New York: Cambridge University Press.

Jones-Lee, M. (1974). The value of changes in the probability of death or injury. *Journal of Political Economy, 82*(4), 835–849.

Kahneman, D., & Tversky, A. (1979). Prospect theory: An analysis of decision under risk. *Econometrica, 47*, 263–291.

Kimball, M. S. (1990). Precautionary saving in the small and in the large. *Econometrica, 58*(1), 53–73.

Klarman, H., Francis, J., & Rosenthal, G. (1968). Cost-effectiveness analysis applied to the treatment of chronic renal disease. *Medical Care, 6*(1), 48–56.

Klibanoff, P., Marinacci, M., & Muerkji, S. (2005). A smooth model of decision making under ambiguity. *Econometrica, 73*(6), 1849–1892.

Kling, A. (2010). *I thought you might be interested in doctors' statistical ignorance*. EconLog. Library of Economics and Liberty. http://econlog.econlib.org/archives/2007/10/doctors_stat ist.html. Accessed 31 Aug 2010.

Krahn, M. D., Mahoney, J. E., Eckman, M. H., Trachtenberg, J., Pauker, S. G., & Detsky, A. S. (1994). Screening for prostate cancer: A decision analytic view. *JAMA, 272*(10), 773–780.

Krieger, M., & Mayrhofer, T. (2012). *Patient preferences and treatment thresholds under diagnostic risk—an economic laboratory experiment*. Ruhr Economic Papers No. 321.

Krieger, M., & Mayrhofer, T. (2016). Prudence and prevention: An economic laboratory experiment. *Applied Economics Letters*. doi:10.1080/13504851.2016.1158909.

Kuppermann, M., Goldberg, J. D., Neese, R. F., & Washington, A. E. (1998). Who should be offered prenatal diagnosis? *American Journal of Public Health, 89*(2), 160–163.

Leland, H. E. (1968). Saving and uncertainty: The precautionary demand for saving. *Quarterly Journal of Economics, 82*(3), 465–473.

List, J. (2004). Neoclassical theory versus prospect theory: Evidence from the market place. *Econometrica, 72*(2), 615–625.

Loomes, G., & Sugden, R. (1982). Regret theory: An alternative theory of rational choice. *Economic Journal, 92*, 805–824.

Machina, M. J. (1982). 'Expected Utility' analysis without the independence axiom. *Econometrica, 50*(2), 277–323.

Machina, M. J. (1987). Choices under uncertainty: Problems solved and unsolved. *Journal of Economic Perspectives, 1*(1), 112–152.

Maier, J., & Rüger, M. (2012). *Experimental evidence on higher-order risk preferences with real monetary losses*. Working Paper.

Mansfield, C., Hopfer, S., & Marteau, T. M. (1999). Termination rates after prenatal diagnosis of Down Syndrome, Spina Bifida, anencephaly, and Turner and Klinefelter Syndromes: A systematic literature review. *Prenatal Diagnosis, 19*, 808–812.

McGuire, T. G. (2000). Physician agency. In A. J. Culyer & J. P. Newhouse (Eds.), *Handbook of health economics* (1st ed., pp. 461–536). New York: Elsevier Science, North-Holland.

McNeil, B. J., Keeler, M., & Adelstein, S. M. (1975). Primer on certain elements of medical decision making. *New England Journal of Medicine, 293*(5), 211–215.

Meltzer, D. (1997). Accounting for future costs in medical cost-effectiveness analysis. *Journal of Health Economics, 16*(1), 33–64.

Menger, K. (1934). Das Unsicherheitsmoment in der Wertlehre—Betrachtungen im Anschluß an das sogenannte Petersburger Spiel. *Zeitschrift für Nationalökonomie (Journal of Economics), 5* (4), 459–485.

Metz, C. E. (1978). Basic principles of ROC analysis. *Seminars in Nuclear Medicine, 8*(4), 283–298.

Miyamato, J. M. (1999). Quality-adjusted Life Years (QALY) utility models under expected utility and rank-dependent utility assumptions. *Journal of Mathematical Psychology, 43*(2), 201–237.

Moscati, I. (2016). How economists came to accept expected utility theory: The case of Samuelson and savage. *The Journal of Economic Perspectives, 30*(2), 219–236.

NICE. (2009). *Appraising life-extending, end of life treatments.* https://www.nice.org.uk/guid ance/gid-tag387/resources/appraising-life-extending-end-of-life-treatments-paper2

Niska, R., Bhuiya, F., & Xu, J. (2010). *National Hospital ambulatory medical care survey: 2007 Emergency Department summary.* National Health Statistics Reports, Report No. 26, pp 1–31.

Noussair, C. N., Trautmann, S. T., & van de Kuilen, G. (2014). Higher order risk attitudes, demographics, and financial decisions. *Review of Economic Studies, 81*(1), 325–355.

Pauker, S. G., & Kassirer, J. P. (1975). Therapeutic decision making: A cost benefit analysis. *New England Journal of Medicine, 293*(5), 229–234.

Pauker, S. G., & Kassirer, J. P. (1980). The threshold approach to clinical decision making. *The New England Journal of Medicine, 302*(20), 1109–1117.

Pauker, S. P., & Pauker, S. G. (1979). The amniocentesis decision: An explicit guide for parents. *Birth Defects, 15*(5C), 289–324.

Pauker, S. G., & Pauker, S. P. (1998). Expected utility perspectives on defensive testing: Torts, tradeoffs, and thresholds—Is defensive medicine defensible? *Medical Decision Making, 18*, 29–31.

Perone, N., Bounameaux, H., & Perrier, A. (2001). Comparison of four strategies for diagnosing deep vein thrombosis: A cost-effectiveness analysis. *The American Journal of Medicine, 110* (1), 33–40.

Pratt, J. W. (1964). Risk aversion in the small and in the large. *Econometrica, 32*(1–2), 122–136.

Pratt, J. W., & Zeckhauser, R. J. (1996). Willingness to pay and the distribution of risk and wealth. *Journal of Political Economy, 104*(4), 747–763.

Puchner, S. B., Liu, T., Mayrhofer, T., Truong, Q. A., Lee, H., Fleg, J. L., et al. (2014). High-risk plaque detected on coronary CT angiography predicts acute coronary syndromes independent of significant stenosis in acute chest pain: Results from the ROMICAT-II trial. *Journal of the American College of Cardiology, 64*, 684–692.

Quiggin, J. (1982). A theory of anticipated utility. *Journal of Economic Behavior and Organization, 3*, 323–343.

Raiffa, H. (1961). Risk, uncertainty and the savage axioms: Comment. *Quarterly Journal of Economics, 75*, 690–694.

Raiffa, H. (1968). *Decision analysis: Introductory lectures on choices under uncertainty.* Reading, MA: Addison-Wesley.

Read, J. L., Quinn, R. J., Berwick, D. M., Fineberg, H. V., & Weinstein, M. C. (1984). Preference for health outcomes: Comparison of assessment methods. *Medical Decision Making, 4*(3), 315–329.

Richards, M. (2008). *Improving access to medicines for NHS patients.* Commissioned by the Secretary of State for Health. http://www.dh.gov.uk/prod_consum_dh/groups/dh_digitalassets/ @dh/@en/documents/digitalasset/dh_089952.pdf. Accessed 24 Oct 2010.

Robert Koch Institut. (2010). *Verbreitung von Krebserkrankungen in Deutschland. Entwicklung der Prävalenzen zwischen 1990 und 2010. Beiträge zur Gesundheitsberichterstattung des Bundes.* Berlin: RKI.

Roffi, M., Patrono, C., Collet, J-P., Mueller, C., Valgimigli, M., Andreotti, F., et al. (2016). 2015 ESC guidelines for the management of acute coronary syndromes in patients presenting without persistent ST-segment elevation: Task Force for the Management of Acute Coronary Syndromes in patients presenting without persistent ST-segment elevation of the European Society of Cardiology (ESC). *European Heart Journal, 37*(3), 267–315.

Rosen, S. (1988). The value of changes in life expectancy. *Journal of Risk and Uncertainty, 1*(3), 285–304.

Sackett, D. L., Guyatt, G. H., Haynes, R. B., & Tugwell, P. (1991). *Clinical epidemiology: A basic science for clinical medicine.* Philadelphia: Lippincott Williams & Wilkins.

Sackett, D. L., & Torrance, G. W. (1978). The utility of different health states as perceived by the general public. *Journal of Chronic Disease, 31*(11), 697–704.

Sandmo, A. (1970). The effect of uncertainty on saving decisions. *Review of Economic Studies, 37* (3), 353–360.

Savage, L. J. (1954). *The foundations of statistics.* New York: Wiley.

Schelling, T. C. (1968). The life you save may be your own. In S. B. Chase Jr. (Ed.), *Problems in public expenditure analysis* (pp. 127–162). Washington, DC: The Brookings Institution.

Sinn, H. W. (1985). Psychophysical laws in risk theory. *Journal of Economic Psychology, 6*, 185–206.

Sox, H. S., Blatt, M. A., Higgins, M. C., & Marton, K. I. (2007). *Medical Decision Making.* Philadelphia/Boston: American College of Physicians/Butterworth-Heinemann. Reprint, originally published: 1988.

Swap, C. J., & Nagurney, J. T. (2005). Value and limitations of chest pain history in the evaluation of patients with suspected acute coronary syndromes. *JAMA, 294*, 2623–2629.

Tarazona-Gómez, M. (2004). *Are individuals prudent? An experimental approach using lottery choices.* Working Paper. Laboratoire d'Economie des Ressources Naturelles (LERNA).

Thygesen, K., Alpert, J. S., Jaffe, A. S., Simoons, M. L., Chaitman, B. R., White, H. D., et al. (2012). Third universal definition of myocardial infarction. *Journal of the American College of Cardiology, 60*, 1581–1598.

Torrance, G. W. (1976). Social preferences for health states—An empirical evaluation of three measurement techniques. *Socio-Economic Planning Sciences, 10*(3), 129–136.

Torrance, G. W., Thomas, W. H., & Sackett, D. L. (1972). A utility maximization model for evaluation of health care programs. *Health Services Research, 7*(2), 118–133.

Van Gossum, A., Munoz-Navas, M., Fernandez-Urien, I., et al. (2009). Capsule endoscopy versus colonoscopy for the detection of polyps and cancer. *The New England Journal of Medicine, 361*(3), 264–270.

Varian, H. R. (1992). *Microeconomic analysis* (3rd ed.). New York: Norton.

Viscusi, W. K., & Aldy, J. E. (2003). The value of a statistical life: A critical review of market estimates throughout the world. *Journal of Risk and Uncertainty, 27*(1), 5–76.

Von Neumann, J., & Morgenstern, O. (1947). *Theory of games and economic behavior* (2nd ed.). Princeton, NJ: Princeton University Press.

Wakker, P. P. (2008). Lessons learned by (from?) an economist working in medical decision making. *Medical Decision Making, 28*(5), 690–698.

Wakker, P. P. (2010). *Prospect theory: For risk and ambiguity.* Cambridge, UK: Cambridge University Press.

Weber, E. W. (1846). *Die Lehre vom Tastsinne und Gemeingefühle auf Versuche gegründet.* Braunschweig: Vieweg & Sohn.

Weinstein, M. C., Fineberg, H. V., Elstein, A. S., Frazier, H. S., Neuhauser, D., Neutra, R. R., et al. (1980). *Clinical decision analysis.* Philadelphia: W.B. Saunders.

Weinstein, M. C., & Stason, W. B. (1977). Foundations of cost-effectiveness analysis for health and medicine practice. *New England Journal of Medicine, 296*, 716–721.

White, L. (2008). Prudence in bargaining: The effect of uncertainty on bargaining outcomes. *Games and Economic Behavior, 62*(1), 211–231.

Yaari, Y. (1987). The dual theory of choice under risk. *Econometrica, 55*(1), 95–115.

Youden, W. J. (1950). Index for rating diagnostic tests. *Cancer, 3*, 32–35.

Zhou, X.-H., Obuchowski, N. A., & McClish, D. K. (2002). *Statistical methods in diagnostic medicine* (2nd ed.). New York: Wiley.

Zweifel, P., Breyer, F., & Kifmann, M. (2009). *Health economics* (2nd ed.). Heidelberg: Springer.

Index

A

Acute coronary syndrome, 156, 159
Altruistic behavior, 222
Ambiguity aversion, 232
Amniocentesis, triple test, 161
    decision rule, 167, 168, 170
    envelope function, 167
    fetal chromosomal disorders, 161
    level curve and sensitivity and
        specificity, 167
    multiple markers, 161
    non-invasive triple test, 161
    optimal discriminatory power, 165, 166
    positivity criterion, 163
    preferences and practice guidelines, 168
    ROC curve, 161
    treatment threshold, 166
    value of information, 163, 164, 167, 168
A priori probability of illness, 8
    optimal cutoff value, 156
    test threshold, 82, 91, 116, 131
    test-treatment threshold, 82, 91, 116, 131
    treatment threshold, 54, 60, 106
Arrow-Pratt coefficient, 40

B

Bayes' Theorem, 9, 10, 12

C

Colorectal polyps testing, 13
Comorbidity risk, 106–109, 111, 112, 115–117
    imperfect test
        decision tree, 115

        prudent decision maker, 115
        risk aversion, 116
        test threshold, 116
        test-treatment threshold, 117
        value of information, 116, 117
    perfect test, expected utility, 111
    therapeutic risk, 118
    treatment threshold
        decision tree, 106
        expected utilities, 107, 109
        expected utility gain, 107
        prudent decision maker, 108
        risk-averse decision maker, 108
        risk-neutral decision maker, 108
        Taylor expansion, 107
        uncontrollable and controllable risks, 108
        utility loss and gain, 106
    value of information, 112
Composite test, 124
    conjunctive and disjunctive, 128
    discriminatory power, 129
    vs. individual tests, 129
    level curves, 130
    likelihood ratio, 129, 130
    sensitivity and specificity, 129, 130
    tan, 130
    test and test-treatment thresholds,
        131, 135, 136
Constant absolute risk aversion (CARA)
        utility function, 44
Constant relative risk aversion (CRRA)
        utility function, 44
Cost of risk, 39, 40
Cost of testing, 99, 157
Cost of treatment, 65, 71, 99, 157

Printed in the United States
By Bookmasters